Dynamic HTML

Illustrated Introductory

SIBYL

Sasha Vodnik

COURSE
TECHNOLOGY

ONE MAIN STREET, CAMBRIDGE, MA 02142

an International Thomson Publishing company I(T)P®

Cambridge • Albany • Bonn • Boston • Cincinnati • London • Madrid • Melbourne • Mexico City
New York • Paris • San Francisco • Singapore • Tokyo • Toronto • Washington

Dynamic HTML—Illustrated Introductory is published by Course Technology

Associate Publisher:	Carolyn Henderson
Senior Product Manager:	Jeanne Herring
Contributing Author:	Donald I. Barker
Development Editor:	Pam Conrad
Production Editor:	Melissa Panagos
Composition House:	GEX, Inc.
QA Manuscript Reviewer:	Brian McCooey
Text Designer:	Joseph Lee
Cover Designer:	Joseph Lee

© 1999 by Course Technology—I(T)P®

For more information contact:

Course Technology
One Main Street
Cambridge, MA 02142

ITP Europe
Berkshire House 168-173
High Holborn
London WCIV 7AA
England

Nelson ITP/Australia
102 Dodds Street
South Melbourne, 3205
Victoria, Australia

ITP Nelson Canada
1120 Birchmount Road
Scarborough, Ontario
Canada M1K 5G4

International Thomson Editores
Seneca 53
Colonia Polanco
11560 Mexico D.F. Mexico

ITP GmbH
Königswinterer Strasse 418
53227 Bonn
Germany

ITP Asia
60 Albert Street, #15-01
Albert Complex
Singapore 189969

ITP Japan
Hirakawacho Kyowa Building, 3F
2-2-1 Hirakawacho
Chiyoda-ku, Tokyo 102
Japan

Trademarks

Course Technology and the Open Book logo are registered trademarks of Course Technology.

Illustrated Projects and the Illustrated Series are trademarks of Course Technology.

I(T)P® The ITP logo is a registered trademark of International Thomson Publishing Inc.

Some of the product names and company names used in this book have been used for identification purposes only and may be trademarks or registered trademarks of their respective manufacturers and sellers.

Disclaimer

Course Technology reserves the right to revise this publication and make changes from time to time in its content without notice.

ISBN 0-7600-6079-7

Printed in the United States of America

2 3 4 5 6 7 8 9 BM 02 01 00

Exciting New Illustrated Products

The Illustrated Projects™ Series: The Quick, Visual Way to Apply Computer Skills

Looking for an inexpensive, easy way to supplement almost any application text and give your students the practice and tools they'll need to compete in today's competitive marketplace? Each text includes more than 50 real-world, useful projects—like creating a resume and setting up a loan worksheet—that let students hone their computer skills. These two-color texts have the same great two-page layout as the Illustrated Series.

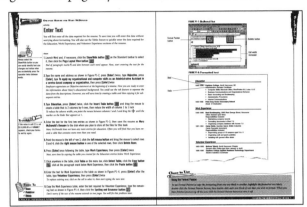

Illustrated Projects titles are available for the following:

- ▶ Microsoft Access
- ▶ Microsoft Excel
- ▶ Microsoft Office Professional
- ▶ Microsoft Publisher
- ▶ Microsoft Word

- ▶ Creating Web Sites
- ▶ World Wide Web
- ▶ Adobe PageMaker
- ▶ Corel WordPerfect

Illustrated Interactive® Series: The Safe, Simulated Way to Learn Computer Skills

The Illustrated Interactive Series uses multimedia technology to teach computer concepts and application skills. Students learn via a CD-ROM that simulates the actual software and provides a controlled learning environment in which every keystroke is monitored. Plus, all products in this series feature the same step-by-step instructions as the Illustrated Series. An accompanying workbook reinforces the skills that students learn on the CD.

Illustrated Interactive titles are available for the following applications:*

- ▶ Microsoft Office 97
- ▶ Microsoft Word 97
- ▶ Microsoft Excel 97

- ▶ Microsoft Access 97
- ▶ Microsoft PowerPoint 97
- ▶ Computer Concepts

Standalone & networked versions available. Runs on Windows 3.1, 95, and NT. CD-only version available for Computer Concepts and Office 97.

CourseKits™: Offering You the Freedom to Choose

Balance your course curriculum with Course Technology's mix-and-match approach to selecting texts. CourseKits provide you with the freedom to make choices from more than one series. When you choose any two or more Course Technology products for one course, we'll discount the price and package them together so your students pick up one convenient bundle at the bookstore.

Contact your sales representative to find out more about these Illustrated products.

Preface

Welcome to *Dynamic HTML – Illustrated Introductory*! This highly visual book offers a hands-on introduction to the creation of dynamic Web pages and also serves as an excellent reference for future use.

▶ Organization and Coverage

This text contains seven units: six units that cover the use of HTML, scripting, and Cascading Style Sheet skills to create dynamic Web pages; and a concluding unit that introduces students to the basics of XML. In these units students learn how to add dynamic text and images to a Web page, control positioning, bind data to a Web page, and implement advanced dynamic HTML features such as filters and transitions. An appendix at the end of the book contains JavaScript, Cascading Style Sheet, and Filters and Transitions reference tables.

▶ About this Approach

What makes the Illustrated approach so effective at teaching software skills? It's quite simple. Each skill is presented on two facing pages, with the step-by-step instructions on the left page, and large screen illustrations on the right. Students can focus on a single skill without having to turn the page. This unique design makes information extremely accessible and easy to absorb, and provides a great reference for after the course is over. This hands-on approach also makes it ideal for both self-paced or instructor-led classes.

Each lesson, or "information display," contains the following elements:

Each 2-page spread focuses on a single skill.

Clear step-by-step directions explain how to complete the specific task, with what students are to type in red. When students follow the numbered steps, they quickly learn how each procedure is performed and what the results will be.

Concise text that introduces the basic principles discussed in the lesson. Procedures are easier to learn when concepts fit into a framework.

C HTML

Creating an Image Map

Pixel coordinates are stored in a separate document that identifies which Web site the reader will jump to when the image is clicked. In an online Web session, clicking an image map connects you to the site identified in the image map document. When not online, clicking an image map results in the pointer changing to an hourglass while your computer searches for the site. You can also create an e-mail link so readers can send mail directly to the page administrator. ➤ Grace creates the image map document that contains the pixel coordinates to other Web sites that she will insert later.

Steps

1. Click the text editor program button on the taskbar
   The image map document is created in a new document in the editor.

   Trouble?
   If you are using a text editor other than WordPad, open a new document.

2. Click File on the menu bar, click New, then click OK
   You determined a single point in each image that links to Web sites that you insert later. In addition to the pixel coordinates, you can include comment lines to identify the sites by name. Each comment line begins with the pound sign (#). You type placeholders for the real Web sites.

3. Type the comment lines and coordinates shown in Figure C-11
   You have typed the coordinates for each image.

   Trouble?
   Verify that this file has been saved with the .map extension, not .txt.

4. Save the file as a text document with the filename Nomad image.map
   The image map document is complete, so when you view the original document, Nomad Home Page.htm, it can refer to the image map.

5. Click the browser program button on the taskbar, then view the changes to Nomad Home Page.htm by refreshing your screen
   The image is updated, as shown in Figure C-12. You can return to the image map document later and insert the Web site locations that the reader will jump to when each image is clicked.

6. Print the browser document

TABLE C-1: Common graphic file formats

format	extension	support provided
Graphics Interchange Format	GIF	Native
Joint Photographic Experts Group	JPEG, JPG	Native
PC Paintbrush	PCX	External
Tagged Image File Format	TIFF	External
Windows Bitmap	BMP	External

▶ HTML C-12 **ADDING GRAPHICS AND MULTIMEDIA**

Tips as well as trouble-shooting advice right where you need it – next to the step itself.

Quickly accessible summaries of key terms, toolbar buttons, or keyboard alternatives connected with the lesson material. Students can refer easily to this information when working on their own projects at a later time.

Every lesson features large-size, full-color representations of what the students' screen should look like after completing the numbered steps.

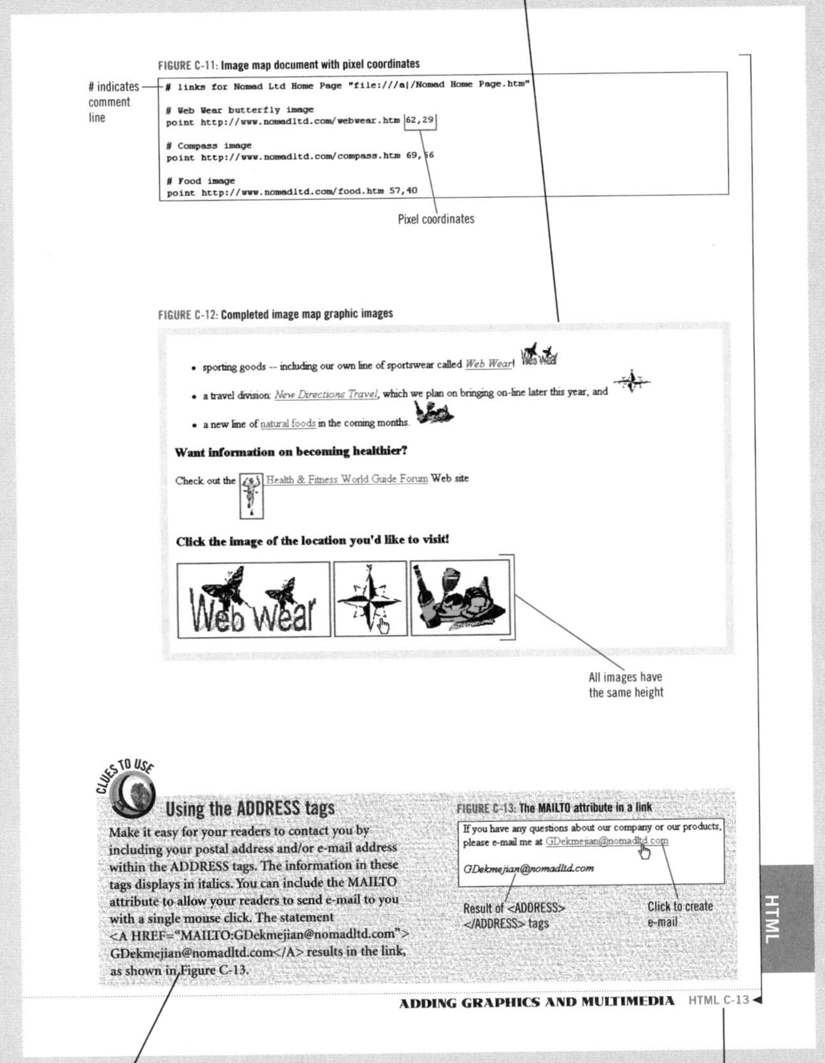

FIGURE C-11: **Image map document with pixel coordinates**

# indicates comment line

```
# links for Nomad Ltd Home Page "file:///a|/Nomad Home Page.htm"

# Web Wear butterfly image
point http://www.nomadltd.com/webwear.htm 62,29

# Compass image
point http://www.nomadltd.com/compass.htm 69,6

# Food image
point http://www.nomadltd.com/food.htm 57,40
```

Pixel coordinates

FIGURE C-12: **Completed image map graphic images**

- sporting goods -- including our own line of sportswear called *Web Wear* [Web Wear]
- a travel division: *New Directions Travel*, which we plan on bringing on-line later this year, and
- a new line of natural foods in the coming months.

Want information on becoming healthier?

Check out the [S] Health & Fitness World Guide Forum Web site

Click the image of the location you'd like to visit!

Web wear

All images have the same height

CLUES TO USE

Using the ADDRESS tags

Make it easy for your readers to contact you by including your postal address and/or e-mail address within the ADDRESS tags. The information in these tags displays in italics. You can include the MAILTO attribute to allow your readers to send e-mail to you with a single mouse click. The statement <A HREF="MAILTO:GDekmejian@nomadltd.com"> GDekmejian@nomadltd.com</A> results in the link, as shown in Figure C-13.

FIGURE C-13: **The MAILTO attribute in a link**

If you have any questions about our company or our products, please e-mail me at GDekmejian@nomadltd.com

GDekmejian@nomadltd.com

Result of <ADDRESS> </ADDRESS> tags

Click to create e-mail

HTML

Clues to Use boxes provide concise information that either expands on one component of the major lesson skill or describes an independent task that is in some way related to the major lesson skill.

The page numbers are designed like a road map. C indicates Unit C and 13 indicates the page within the unit.

Other Features

The two-page lesson format featured in this book provides the new user with a powerful learning experience. Additionally, this book contains the following features:

▶ **Real-World Case**
The skills used throughout the textbook are designed to be "real-world" in nature and representative of the kinds of activities that students encounter when working with HTML. With a real-world case, the process of solving problems will be more meaningful to students.

▶ **End of Unit Material**
Each unit concludes with a Concepts Review that tests students' understanding of what they learned in the unit. The Concepts Review is followed in each skills-based unit by a Skills Review, which provides students with additional hands-on practice of the skills they learned in the unit. The Skills Review is followed by Independent Challenges, which pose case problems for students to solve. At least one Independent Challenge in each unit asks students to use the World Wide Web to solve the problem as indicated by a Web Work icon. The Visual Workshops that follow the Independent Challenges help students develop critical thinking skills. Students are shown completed Web pages or screens and are asked to recreate them from scratch.

Instructor's Resource Kit

The Instructor's Resource Kit is Course Technology's way of putting the resources and information needed to teach and learn effectively into your hands. With an integrated array of teaching and learning tools that offer you and your students a broad range of technology-based instructional options, we believe this kit represents the highest quality and most cutting edge resources available to instructors today. Many of these resources are available at www.course.com. The resources available with this book are:

Course Test Manager   Designed by Course Technology, this cutting-edge Windows-based testing software helps instructors design, administer, and print tests and pre-tests. A full-featured program, Course Test Manager also has an online testing component that allows students to take tests at the computer and have their exams automatically graded.

Instructor's Manual   Quality assurance tested and includes:
- Solutions to all lessons and end-of-unit material
- Detailed lecture topics for each unit with teaching tips
- Extra Independent Challenges
- Task References
- Transparency Masters
- Project Files

WWW.COURSE.COM   We encourage students and instructors to visit our web site at www.course.com to find articles about current teaching and software trends, featured texts, interviews with authors, demos of Course Technology's software, Frequently Asked Questions about our products, and much more. This site is also where you can gain access to the Faculty Online Companion or Student Online Companion for this text — see below for more information.

Course Faculty Online Companion   Available at www.course.com, this World Wide Web site offers Course Technology customers a password-protected Faculty Lounge where you can find everything you need to prepare for class, including the Instructor's Manual in an electronic Portable Document Format (PDF) file and Adobe Acrobat Reader software. Periodically updated items include any updates and revisions to the text and Instructor's Manual, links to other Web sites, and access to project and solution files. This site will continue to evolve throughout the semester. Contact your Customer Service Representative for the site address and password.

Course Student Online Companion   Available at www.course.com, this book features its own Student Online Companion where students can go to gain access to Web sites that will help them complete the Web Work Independent Challenges. These links are updated on a regular basis. These sites will continue to evolve throughout the semester.

Project Files   To use this book students must have the Project Files. See the inside front or inside back cover for more information on the Project Files. Adopters of this text are granted the right to post the Project Files on any stand-alone computer or network.

X-tra files   Now it's even easier to teach the skills you want to teach! Every two-page spread in this book requiring a project file now includes a project file or an X-tra file. An X-tra file is a project file in the exact format needed to work through that one particular lesson. X-tra files are not available for lessons in which project files are not needed or in which a project file is explicitly opened or created as part of the lesson steps.

The filename of each X-tra file is the page number for the lesson with an "X" in front of it. For instance, the X-tra file for the lesson on page HTML K-6 is XHTML K-6. As the name implies, these files are "extra" and you can choose whether or not to make them available to your students. The X-tra files for this book are provided separately from the Project Files in the Instructor's Resource Kit and on the Faculty Online Companion.

Brief Contents

Contents

HTML

> **Welcome to the Nomad Ltd home page, Lydia!**   **Nomad Ltd**
>
> **Learn About Our Company's Philosophy**
>
> Nomad Ltd has been in business for over ten years. During that time, we have offered tours to exotic (and simple) lands and sold sporting equipment (for bicycling, hiking, and other activities). In all that time, we have always been aware that our employees are our corporate ambassadors, and our customers are our royalty. We know that any company can make a buck here and there, but we want to do more than that. We want you to enjoy shopping at our stores and contribute to making Nomad a fun and interesting place to shop. We also know that as a business, we are also community members. Nomad wants to contribute to community efforts and make each town we're in a better place to live and shop. How do we do that? By hiring from the community, offering educational and financial benefits to our employees, and becoming involved in various community efforts.
>
> Types Of Nomad Tours

Contents

Working with Dymamic HTML (DHTML)

window
- location
- frames
- history
- navigator
- event
- screen
- document
  - links
  - anchors
  - images
  - filters
  - forms
  - applets
  - embeds
  - plug-ins
  - frames
  - scripts
  - all
  - selection
  - stylesheets
  - body

Specifying Style Dynamically

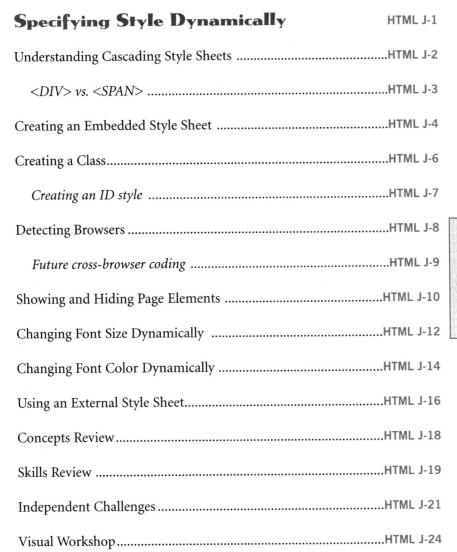

Frequently Asked Questions about

Nomad Ltd

Dynamic HTML (DHTML)

- **What is Dynamic HTML?**
  Dynamic HTML (DHTML) describes a set of new technologies for designing Web pages that allow new and more precise formatting features, along with faster access for users.

- **Is DHTML a new language?**
  DHTML is not a new language. DHTML is simply a snazzy name for a set of new features that recent Web browsers are equipped to interpret and use. DHTML features work only within the context of a standard HTML document.

- **How does DHTML work?**
  DHTML uses two new pieces in concert with HTML. The first is scripts that run on the user's browser, written in a scripting language such as JavaScript or VBScript. The other is Cascading Style Sheets, a new method of specifying exact styles for a Web page's elements.

Contents

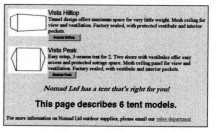

Positioning with DHTML

Contents

Implementing Advanced DHTML Features

HTML M-1

Structuring Data with XML

Contents

Scripting
for HTML

HTML allows you to create basic Web pages easily. Using many of the newest features available in Web page design, however, requires the incorporation of **scripts**, which are programs in a Web page that run on the viewer's browser. Using scripts can expand the number of features you can add to your Web pages and can simplify some HTML commands. 🖌 Lydia Burgos works in the information systems division of Nomad Ltd. Her supervisor heard about the advantages of scripts at a recent seminar and has asked Lydia to create a report on ways that scripts could enhance the company's current Web publication. Lydia begins by researching the fundamentals of **scripting**, which is the process of writing scripts.

Understanding Scripting for HTML

A **script** is a small program contained within an HTML document that can be executed by a Web browser. In the early days of the Web, scripts were separate files stored and run on a remote Web server. Today, Web page designers can place scripts within a page's standard HTML, and the scripts can run on each user's computer. This change is made possible by new techniques for data transfer on the Web as well as a new generation of more powerful home computers. Other forms of Web page programming (such as CGI files that process data from Web page forms) may also be referred to as scripts. However, scripts that run on a user's browser represent the most powerful and innovative form of scripting on the Web today. This is the definition we will use in this book. Figure H-1 shows the source code for a Web page containing a script, as well as the Web page generated by that code. In researching scripting fundamentals, Lydia Burgos has learned that using scripting in Web page development offers several advantages over using HTML alone. These advantages include the following:

Flexibility

Scripting allows you to modify your Web pages in ways that are not yet part of standard HTML. Additionally, you can combine scripting codes in many different ways, which opens the door to more variety and creativity in your pages than with HTML alone. For example, you can have a message that runs automatically when the Web page is opened and that is updated automatically, such as a current list of top headlines for a news Web site.

Simplification

You can script some tasks that you usually would code using HTML. In many cases, scripting is more efficient and allows you to create a more organized publication. One of the first areas in which scripting is replacing HTML is in assigning styles to text. Instead of adding attributes to the tags for each block of text in your publication, you can insert a small script that automatically assigns specific attributes, such as boldface type or text color, to specific blocks of text throughout an entire Web page or set of pages.

Immediate response

Traditionally, to access many features available on a Web page, your browser contacts the Web site where the page resides and requests a linked Web page or new information based on your input. Embedded scripts eliminate the lag time involved in contacting the remote server, waiting for a response, and downloading new information. This is because the scripts run on your local computer and can change what your browser displays without downloading new information from the server.

Improved interactivity

The quick response time that local scripting provides allows you to incorporate an impressive amount of user interactivity into your Web pages. Since script processing occurs locally, your script can react almost instantaneously to any user action. For example, your script could display a short summary of a link when the user simply moves the pointer over the link without clicking it.

Reduced server load

Local execution of scripts is an advantage not just for users, but for Web site administrators as well. The reduced demand on the server when some of the processing is shifted to local computers results in more free system resources. This may result in a decrease in download time for people viewing your site's pages and faster processing when a Web page does need to submit a request to the server.

```
<HTML>

<HEAD>
<TITLE>Nomad Ltd online</TITLE>

<SCRIPT LANGUAGE="javascript">
<!--
var name=prompt("For personal service, please type your first name and click
OK.","")

function submitted() {
      alert("Information submitted!")
}

function clearUp() {
      document.info.elements[0].value=""
      document.info.elements[1].value=""
      document.info.elements[2].value=""
      document.info.elements[3].value=""
      document.info.elements[4].value=""
      document.info.elements[5].value=""

}

//-->
</SCRIPT>
```

Script
embedded
in HTML
code

User
name
generated
by script

Welcome to the Nomad Ltd home page, Lydia!

Nomad Ltd

Learn About Our Company's Philosophy

Nomad Ltd is a national sporting goods retailer
dedicated to delivering high-quality sporting gear and
adventure travel.
Nomad Ltd has been in business for over ten years.
During that time, we have offered tours all over the
world and sold sporting equipment for bicycling, hiking,
and other activities. Like most companies, our main goal
is to make a profit. At the same time, we realize that as a
business, we are also community members. Nomad Ltd
is committed to contributing to community efforts and
making each town where we do business a better place
to live. We do that by hiring from the community,

Choosing a scripting language

Several languages are available when writing scripts
for an HTML document. These include **JavaScript**
and **JScript**, which are both adaptations of Sun
Microsystems' Java programming language, as well as
VBScript, which is Microsoft's adaptation of its
Visual Basic programming language for Web use.
Both Internet Explorer 4 and Netscape Navigator 4
are largely compatible with JavaScript. On the other
hand, JScript and VBScript are not universally compatible, meaning that users of certain browsers might
be unable to view the scripted elements of your page
if you used one of these languages. This text uses
JavaScript to create pages viewable by both Internet
Explorer and Netscape Navigator users.

HTML

Unit H

HTML

Creating a Script

You can add a script to a Web page just as you would add to or edit the Web page's HTML code. To do this, you can use a text editor such as WordPad or Notepad or a Web page editor such as FrontPage Express or Composer. In order for a browser to recognize a script, the script must be contained within <SCRIPT> HTML tags. It is also good practice to surround each script with a set of HTML tags to make it invisible to browsers incompatible with scripts. This second set of HTML tags tells incompatible browsers to bypass the script. ✍ While researching scripting fundamentals, Lydia found a sample script that validates a form before submitting it to a server by checking the form to be sure information has been entered in each field. If information has not been entered in each field and the user tries to send the form, then this form validation script displays a warning box which reminds the user to complete each field. Lydia decides to try adding this script to the Nomad Ltd home page in order to better understand how to insert scripts into HTML code.

Steps

QuickTip

When saving a file as HTML, be sure to select Text (.txt) as the file type to be saved and include the extension .htm in the filename.

1. Start your text editor program, open the file **HTML H-1.htm**, then save it as a text document with the filename **Scripted page.htm**

   If you use WordPad or Notepad, which are text editors built into Windows 95, the source code for the Web page appears as text in the text editor. If you use an HTML editing tool, such as Microsoft FrontPage or Netscape Composer, you will see the graphical representation of the file code. You must select the option Page Source or HTML from the View menu to see the HTML code for the page.

2. Select the text **[replace with opening script tags]** below the TITLE tag, then press **[Delete]**

3. Type **<SCRIPT LANGUAGE="javascript">** and press **[Enter]**

   Now the beginning of the script is marked with the <SCRIPT> HTML tag and an attribute specifying the scripting language you're using, which is JavaScript.

QuickTip

All browsers ignore the remainder of the line after the <!-- tag; thus, some script writers add a normal language comment here, such as "HIDE," to make the script code easier for programmers to look at and understand.

4. Type **<!--** and press **[Enter]** twice

   The tag <!-- tells an incompatible browser (one that can't process your script) to ignore the code that follows. A compatible browser (one that can interpret your script) will go ahead and process the script that follows.

5. Select the text **[replace with closing script tags]**, then press **[Delete]**

6. Type **//-->** and press **[Enter]**, then type **</SCRIPT>** and press **[Enter]**

   These tags mark the end of the script. Figure H-2 shows the Web page source code containing the opening and closing script tags and the dialog box generated by the script.

7. Check the lines you added for errors, make changes as necessary, then save Scripted page.htm as a text document

Trouble?

If the Web page does not display correctly, or if a dialog box opens describing an error in your script, click OK if necessary, read the next lesson to learn about debugging scripts, then return to look for errors in your Web page code.

8. Start your Web browser program, cancel any dial-up activities, open the page **Scripted page.htm**, scroll down to the text fields near the bottom of the page, fill in sample information, then click the **Send now! button**

   The script runs and displays the dialog box shown in Figure H-2.

9. Click the **OK button**

   The browser simulates form submission to a server. This script will save time for people using the Nomad Ltd Web page, since they do not have to wait for the form to be submitted to the server and then wait for an error message to be transmitted back to their computer.

FIGURE H-2: Source code for Web page dialog box

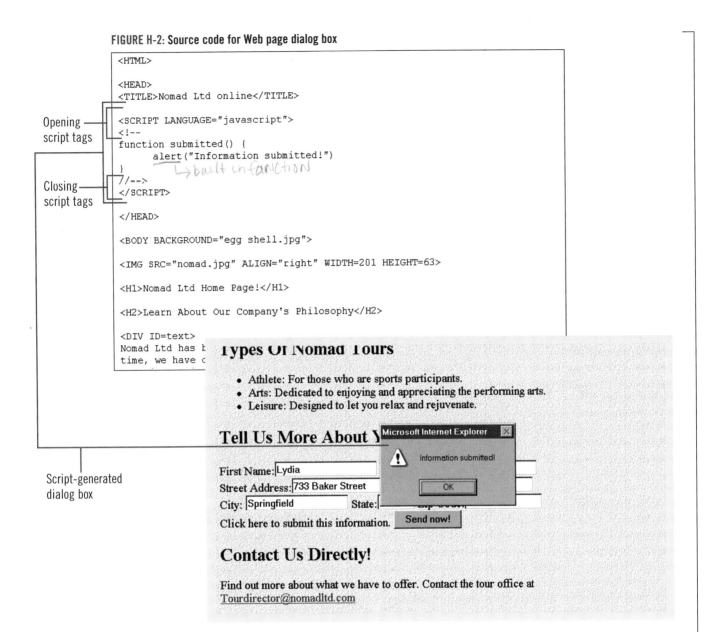

Opening script tags

Closing script tags

Script-generated dialog box

```
<HTML>

<HEAD>
<TITLE>Nomad Ltd online</TITLE>

<SCRIPT LANGUAGE="javascript">
<!--
function submitted() {
        alert("Information submitted!")
}                    └> built in function
//-->
</SCRIPT>

</HEAD>

<BODY BACKGROUND="egg shell.jpg">

<IMG SRC="nomad.jpg" ALIGN="right" WIDTH=201 HEIGHT=63>

<H1>Nomad Ltd Home Page!</H1>

<H2>Learn About Our Company's Philosophy</H2>

<DIV ID=text>
Nomad Ltd has
time, we have
```

Types Of Nomad Tours

- Athlete: For those who are sports participants.
- Arts: Dedicated to enjoying and appreciating the performing arts.
- Leisure: Designed to let you relax and rejuvenate.

Tell Us More About Y

Microsoft Internet Explorer

⚠ Information submitted!

OK

First Name: Lydia
Street Address: 733 Baker Street
City: Springfield   State:
Click here to submit this information.   Send now!

Contact Us Directly!

Find out more about what we have to offer. Contact the tour office at
Tourdirector@nomadltd.com

Linking to an external script

In addition to typing script code directly into a Web page, you can add scripts to your pages by using an HTML code that references a separate file containing script code. A script located in an external file that you can link to a Web page is known as a **scriptlet**. Scriptlets make it easier to share code and to reuse scripts on multiple pages by allowing you to use a script without needing to paste its code into each Web page.

Debugging a Script

No matter how carefully scripting code is entered, a script often contains errors, or **bugs**, the first time your browser processes it. In general, a bug causes the script to return unexpected and undesired results. These may include improper text formatting, the display of HTML or JavaScript code in the browser window, or, in the worst case, requiring you to exit and restart the browser. It's doubtful that simple errors you make entering the scripts in this book could hang your browser. However, when your results are different than those shown in this text, you can use a process called **debugging** to systematically identify and fix your script's bugs. Lydia reads up on debugging scripts and learns about several main culprits that cause undesired results. These are illustrated in Figure H-3.

Details

Capitalization

JavaScript is a **case-sensitive** language, meaning that it treats capital and lowercase versions of the same letter as different characters. Thus, depending on the script being entered, capitalizing or not capitalizing letters can result in errors. Always check that you have used capital letters where called for and that all the capital letters in your script are correct.

Spacing

When entering script code from a printed source, it is easy to add extra spaces or to leave spaces out. Some parts of JavaScript syntax allow for extra spaces, which makes code easier to view and understand. However, as in HTML, incorrect spacing in certain parts of a script can render otherwise-perfect code incomprehensible to the browser. The best way to avoid spacing errors is to pay careful attention to spacing while you enter code.

Parentheses ( ), brackets [ ], braces { }, and quotes " "

JavaScript often uses these four types of symbols to enclose arguments, values, or numbers upon which certain commands are executed. In more complex scripts, you may end up with several sets enclosing other sets, which makes it easy to forget to type one or more closing symbols. In lines or blocks of script where these symbols are concentrated, it can be difficult to check for accuracy. However, to ensure that your script will run properly, you must make sure that each one is paired with its counterpart.

Typographical errors (0 vs. O, 1 vs. l)

Another common source of errors when entering code from printed material is interchanging characters that appear similar, such as the number 0 and the letter O. Generally, the context provides good clues to figuring this out. For example, even if you don't know the function of the expression "value=0", the use of the word *value* gives you a good clue to type a number rather than a letter. Ultimately, the best way to avoid confusing these symbols is to analyze what the script is doing in the current line. Once you understand this, it should be obvious which character to type.

Others

Inevitably, various other sources of error will creep into your scripts. To help you deal with miscellaneous problems, as well as those detailed earlier, JavaScript-compatible browsers often display a JavaScript Error window, as shown in Figure H-4, when they can't interpret your code. Generally, the window describes the type of error the browser encountered and the error's location, referenced by its line number in the script. With this information, some investigation of your code, and a bit of thought, you can track down and fix most any bug that crops up.

Now that you understand the basics of working with scripts, you can begin to learn how to construct your own scripts.

FIGURE H-3: JavaScript containing common bugs

```
<HTML>

<HEAD>
<TITLE>Nomad Ltd online</TITLE>
<SCRIPT LANGUAGE="javascript">
<!--
function submit() {}

function verify() {
     if (document.info.elements[O].value == "" ||
     document.info.elements[1].value == "" ||
     Document.info.elements[2].value == "" ||
     document.info.elements[3].value == "" ||
     document._info.elements[4].value == "" ||
     document.info.elements[5].value == "" {
          alert("Please complete each field")
     } else {
          submit()
     }
}
//-->
</SCRIPT>

</HEAD>

<BODY BACKGROUND="egg shell.jpg">
```

Letter instead of number

Unclosed parentheses

Incorrect capital

Extra space

FIGURE H-4: JavaScript Error window

Description of error

Erroneous code with error indicated

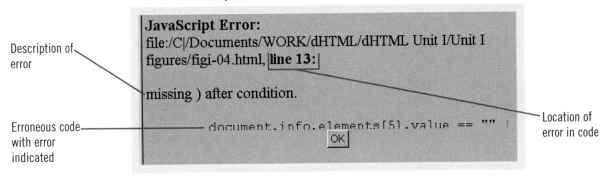

JavaScript Error:
file:/C|/Documents/WORK/dHTML/dHTML Unit I/Unit I figures/figi-04.html, **line 13:**

missing) after condition.

          document.info.elements[5].value == "" {

          [OK]

Location of error in code

Commenting a script

While writing a script, it can be useful to include comments in ordinary language to explain what the script is doing at particular places. These notes can be helpful for you when editing or debugging your script or for someone else who wants to understand how the script works. To add a comment to the end of a line of the script, type // at the end of the line's script code, then type your comment. You also can mark several lines of text in a script as a comment by typing /* at the start of the block and */ at the end.

Understanding Objects

In order to organize and work with the various parts of the browser window, including the current Web page and each of its elements, JavaScript treats each element in the window as a unit called an **object**. JavaScript gives each object a default name and set of descriptive features based on its location and function. These features include **properties**, which are qualities such as size, location, and type. In a Web page containing a graphic, the IMG tag would be an object, and the WIDTH setting would be one of its properties. Each object also has associated **methods**, which are actions the object can carry out. For example, each frame in a browser window has an associated ALERT method, which allows you to create customized dialog boxes. JavaScript organizes objects in an **object hierarchy**, much like the system of folders used by Windows to keep track of disk contents.   As Lydia researches the object hierarchy, she learns different ways to refer to the various elements in a document when writing a script.

To specify an object on a Web page, you need to detail its position in the hierarchy, beginning on the document level and then separating each level name with a period. This method of referencing objects in the hierarchy is called **dot syntax**. For example, to specify an image on a Web page, the name would begin *document.images*. Because a document can contain more than one image, each image is assigned a number, based on the order in which it appears in the Web page code. Other elements such as anchors, hyperlinks, and forms also are assigned numbers. It is important to note, however, that in JavaScript, this numbering begins with 0. Thus, when writing a script that refers to the first image in your HTML code, you would use the name *document.images[0]*. The second image in your HTML code would be called *document.images[1]* according to the object hierarchy. To specify an element such as a button or a text field contained inside a form you would use a slightly longer address. For example *document.forms[0].elements[0]* would refer to the first element created in the first form in a Web document.

You also use dot syntax to refer to an object's methods. For example, the code *document.write("Copyright Course Technology, 1999.")* calls on the *write* method of the *document* object. This code causes the information in parenthesis to be written to the document. Table H-1 lists the default objects that are part of every browser window, along with their methods.

TABLE H-1: Default JavaScript objects and methods

object name	method name	description
window	alert(message)	Displays a dialog box with a message in the window
	close()	Closes the window
	prompt(message, default_text)	Displays a dialog box prompting the user for information
	scroll(x, y)	Scrolls to the x.y coordinate in the window
frame	alert(message)	Displays a dialog box with a message in the frame
	close()	Closes the frame
	prompt(message, default_text)	Displays a dialog box prompting the user for information
history	back()	Returns to the previous page in the history list
	forward()	Goes to the next page in the history list
location	reload()	Reloads the current page
document *whole web site*	write()	Writes text and HTML tags to the current document
	writeln()	Writes text and HTML tags to the current document on a new line
form	reset()	Resets the form
	submit()	Submits the form

CLUES TO USE

Naming an object

When you initially create a page element, you can assign it an ID using the ID property. Then, you can refer to the object by its name instead of using its index number. For example, the code <FORM ID="input"> assigns the ID input to the form. You can then use the form ID input rather than forms[0] to refer to the form or any elements within it.

You could now refer to this form as document.input.elements[0] rather than document.forms[0].elements[0]. By assigning a name to each element, such as check boxes or text boxes, you could eliminate the need for index numbers in the address as well.

Using JavaScript Event Handlers

In order for your Web pages to interact with users, your scripts must be able to recognize and respond to user actions. Each action by a user is known as an **event**. JavaScript can respond to a user's actions with **event handlers**, which are terms that specify possible user actions. By including an event handler along with a set of instructions, your script can respond to certain user actions when they happen. Table H-2 lists 12 event handlers and describes the event that each one names. Lydia has read about using event handlers. She wants the Nomad Ltd home page to display a message in the status bar window when a user moves the pointer over the e-mail address. She recognizes that this pointer positioning is an event, and that she can use a script containing an event handler to display the message.

Steps

1. Open HTML H-2.htm in your text editor and save it as a text document with the filename **Event handler.htm**
Lydia wants to insert her script code in the <A> code near the bottom of the page.

2. Scroll to the end of the document, select the text **[insert event handler here]** in the <A> tag, then press **[Delete]**

Trouble?

Be sure you use two apostrophes, rather than a quotation mark, following *onMouseOut="window. status=*.

3. Type the following all on the same line, without pressing [Enter]:
onMouseOver="window.status='We will reply to your inquiry within 24 hours!';return true" onMouseOut="window.status='';return true"   → 2 single quote

The completed script is shown in Figure H-5. Even without pressing Enter, your text editor may wrap the text onto multiple lines. This will not affect the accuracy of your code. The window.status object refers to the status bar. In this script, the onMouseOver event handler instructs the browser to display the text typed between the apostrophes in the status bar when the pointer is over the hypertext link. In this script, the onMouseOut event handler instructs the browser to clear the text—that is, to display nothing in the status bar—when the mouse pointer is moved off the hypertext link. The text is cleared as indicated by the apostrophes containing no text or spaces that follow the second window.status.

4. Check the document for errors, make changes as necessary, then save Event handler.htm as a text document

5. Open the file **Event handler.htm** in your Web browser, then scroll to the bottom of the page
Notice that the status bar contains information about the loading status of the current Web page.

Trouble?

If your message does not appear correctly, check to be sure you have typed the script exactly as shown in Step 3.

6. Move the mouse pointer over the link **Tourdirector@nomadltd.com**, but do not click
The scripted message appears in the status bar, as shown in Figure H-6.

7. Move the mouse pointer off the link
The message no longer appears in the status bar.

FIGURE H-5: Completed script containing new event handlers

```
<H2>Tell Us More About Yourself!</H2>
<FORM NAME="info">
First Name:<INPUT TYPE="TEXT" SIZE=20 NAME="firstname">
Last Name: <INPUT TYPE="TEXT" SIZE=20 NAME="lastname"><BR>
Street Address:<INPUT TYPE="TEXT" SIZE=50 NAME="address"><BR>
City: <INPUT TYPE="TEXT" SIZE=20 NAME="city">
State:<INPUT TYPE="TEXT" SIZE=6 NAME="state">
Zip Code:<INPUT TYPE="TEXT" SIZE=15 NAME="zipcode">
<BR>Click here to submit this information. <INPUT TYPE="BUTTON" VALUE="Send
now!" onClick="submitted()">
</FORM>

<H2>Contact Us Directly!</H2>

Find out more about what we have to offer. Contact the tour
office at <A HREF="MAILTO:Tourdirector@nomadltd.com"
onMouseOver="window.status='We will reply to your inquiry within 24
hours!';return true" onMouseOut="window.status='';return
true">Tourdirector@nomadltd.com</A>

</BODY>
</HTML>
```

Event handler code entered

> single QUOTE

FIGURE H-6: Browser displaying status bar message

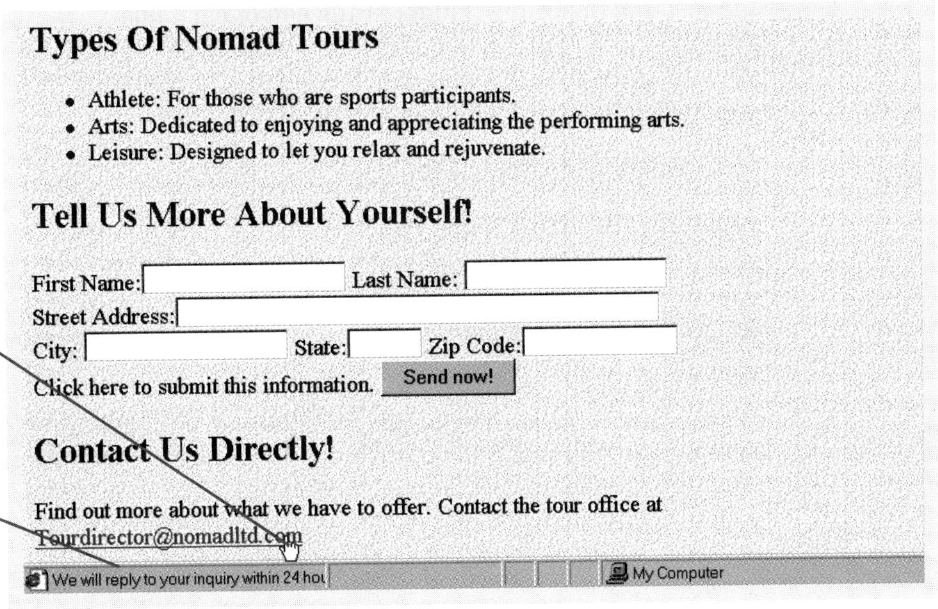

Types Of Nomad Tours

- Athlete: For those who are sports participants.
- Arts: Dedicated to enjoying and appreciating the performing arts.
- Leisure: Designed to let you relax and rejuvenate.

Tell Us More About Yourself!

First Name: [   ]   Last Name: [   ]
Street Address: [   ]
City: [   ]   State: [   ]   Zip Code: [   ]
Click here to submit this information.   [Send now!]

Contact Us Directly!

Find out more about what we have to offer. Contact the tour office at
Tourdirector@nomadltd.com

We will reply to your inquiry within 24 hou   My Computer

Event handler activated by position of pointer

Message in status bar triggered by event handler

TABLE H-2: JavaScript event handlers

event handler	triggering action	event handler	triggering action
onAbort	Page loading halted	onLoad	Page or image opens
onBlur	Object not current or highlighted	onMouseOut	Mouse pointer not over link
onChange	Object value changed	onMouseOver	Mouse pointer over link
onClick	Hyperlink or button clicked	onSelect	Text selected
onError	Error executing script	onSubmit	Form submitted
onFocus	Object current or highlighted	onUnload	Different page opened

HTML

Creating a Function

As your scripts become more complex, you will begin to incorporate many lines of code in each one to store and process information. To help keep your scripts organized, JavaScript allows you to group and name sets of script code in units called **functions**. A function is a set of code that performs a specific task. When you group the lines of your scripts into functions, the code is logically broken down into functional units, which makes it easier to understand and to debug. You usually define functions in a page's head section, which allows any programmer to quickly scan a page's code. Additionally, because each function has a name, you can easily refer to it in several different parts of a Web page. This means you do not need to duplicate code each time you want your page to repeat a procedure. Lydia wants to add a button to the Web page that will clear the user's input in the form. She writes a function to perform this task.

Steps

1. Open the file **HTML H-3.htm** in your text editor, then save it as a text document with the filename **Function.htm**
   Generally, it's best to define functions at the beginning of a Web page, to make sure they are available for all subsequent uses.

2. Select the text **[replace with clearUp function]** in the page's head section, then press **[Delete]**

3. Type the following, pressing **[Enter]** at the end of each line

   function clearUp() {

       document.info.elements[0].value=""

       document.info.elements[1].value=""

       document.info.elements[2].value=""

       document.info.elements[3].value=""

       document.info.elements[4].value=""

       document.info.elements[5].value=""

   These lines define a function that assigns the value **null**, or nothing, to each of the six text fields on the page. This null value is defined with the paired quotation marks that follow each equal sign and that contain nothing between them.

4. Type **}**
   Figure H-7 shows the completed function, including the opening and closing braces. The code for a function is always demarcated with braces {}.

5. Scroll to the end of the document, select the text **[replace with Clear button code]**, then press **[Delete]**

6. Type **<INPUT TYPE="BUTTON" value="Clear form" onClick = "clearUp()">**
   The button tag includes an event handler to trigger, or **call**, the function clearUp() when a user clicks the button. Figure H-8 shows the completed button tag in the document.

7. Check the document for errors, make changes as necessary, then save Function.htm as a text document

8. Open **Function.htm** in your Web browser, fill in the six input fields, then click the **Clear form button**
   The browser clears each of the text input fields.

FIGURE H-7: Document containing clearUp() function code

```
<HTML>

<HEAD>
<TITLE>Nomad Ltd online</TITLE>

<SCRIPT LANGUAGE="javascript">
<!--
function submitted() {
      alert("Information submitted!")
}

function clearUp() {
      document.info.elements[0].value=""
      document.info.elements[1].value=""
      document.info.elements[2].value=""
      document.info.elements[3].value=""
      document.info.elements[4].value=""
      document.info.elements[5].value=""
}


//-->
</SCRIPT>

</HEAD>
```

Code defining new function

FIGURE H-8: Document containing clearUp() function reference

```
</UL>

<H2>Tell Us More About Yourself!</H2>
<FORM NAME="info">
First Name:<INPUT TYPE="TEXT" SIZE=20 ID="firstname">
Last Name: <INPUT TYPE="TEXT" SIZE=20 ID="lastname"><BR>
Street Address:<INPUT TYPE="TEXT" SIZE=50 ID="address"><BR>
City: <INPUT TYPE="TEXT" SIZE=20 ID="city">
State:<INPUT TYPE="TEXT" SIZE=6 ID="state">
Zip Code:<INPUT TYPE="TEXT" SIZE=15 ID="zipcode">
<BR>Click here to submit this information. <INPUT TYPE="BUTTON" VALUE="Send
now!" onClick="submitted()">
<BR>Click here to clear the form and start over.
<INPUT TYPE="BUTTON" VALUE="Clear form" onClick="clearUp()">
</FORM>

<H2>Contact Us Directly!</H2>

Find out more about what we have to offer. Contact the tour
office at <A HREF="MAILTO:Tourdirector@nomadltd.com"
onMouseOver="window.status='We will reply to your inquiry within 24
hours!';return true" onMouseOut="window.status='';return
true">Tourdirector@nomadltd.com</A>

</BODY>
</HTML>
```

Code referencing new function

HTML

Assigning a Variable

In scripting, you often instruct JavaScript to perform functions on pieces of information that you specify, known as **values**. For example, the text *We will reply to your inquiry within 24 hours!*, which you used earlier in conjunction with an event handler, is a value. Values can also include "true" and "false" and information about the user's browser, such as the width of the window in pixels. JavaScript can add or manipulate any numeric value mathematically. When values are composed of many characters, such as the message text above, or when they change in different situations, such as browser window dimensions, they can be cumbersome if you need to enter them several times in your script. You can make this process easier and more efficient by assigning the value to a **variable**, which serves as a nickname. When you assign a value to a variable, you enter or look up the value only one time and then you use the variable to refer to the value. Using variables saves you time when writing scripts. Variables provide added flexibility by allowing you to modify the value in only one place and have the modifications reflected instantaneously throughout the document as indicated by the variable. ✏ Lydia has modified the Nomad Ltd home page to personalize text by displaying the user's name. To finish her changes, she needs to define the variable she will use to represent the user's name, and then insert the variable name in the scripts.

Steps

1. Open the file **HTML H-4.htm** in your text editor, then save it as a text document with the filename **Variable.htm**

2. Select the text **[replace with variable definition]** near the top of the page, then press **[Delete]**

3. Type the following text on one line, without pressing [Enter]
   var name=prompt("For personal service, please type your first name and click OK.","")
   This line of script creates a dialog box that prompts the user to enter his or her first name and assigns the user's input to a variable named "name". Figure H-9 shows the document with this line of code inserted. The command "var" tells JavaScript that you are specifying a variable. The word following var—in this case, "name"—is the name of the variable you are creating. The value of the new variable follows the name after an equals sign. In this case, the value will be the result of user input in a dialog box created by the "prompt" method.

4. Scroll down to the beginning of the page's body section, select the text **[replace with heading script]**, then press **[Delete]**
   Notice that Lydia has already inserted the opening and closing script tags.

5. Type the following text on one line, without pressing [Enter]
   document.write("<H1>Welcome to the Nomad Ltd home page, " + name + "!</H1>")
   This script writes a line of code to the Web page, containing H1 tags to format the text. Lydia uses the variable "name" to insert the user's name into the page heading.

6. Scroll down to the beginning of the form section, select the text **[replace with second heading script]**, then press **[Delete]**

7. Type the following all on one line, without pressing [Enter]
   document.write("<H2>Please tell us more about yourself, " + name + ".</H2>")
   This script places the user's name at a second location in the Web page.

8. Check the document for errors, make changes as necessary, then save **Variable.htm** as a text document

9. Open the file **Variable.htm** in your Web browser, type your first name in the prompt dialog box, then click **OK**
   The Nomad Ltd home page is now personalized. The name the user enters in the prompt dialog box is displayed. See Figure H-10.

Trouble?

Be sure you type a space after the text **page**, and before the closing ".

FIGURE H-9: **Script creating a variable**

Variable inserted in script

```
<HTML>

<HEAD>
<TITLE>Nomad Ltd online</TITLE>

<SCRIPT LANGUAGE="javascript">
<!--
var name=prompt("For personal service, please type your first name and click
OK.","")

function submitted() {
      alert("Information submitted!")
}

function clearUp() {
      document.info.elements[0].value=""
      document.info.elements[1].value=""
      document.info.elements[2].value=""
      document.info.elements[3].value=""
      document.info.elements[4].value=""
      document.info.elements[5].value=""
}

//-->
</SCRIPT>
```

FIGURE H-10: **Web page incorporating user information**

Welcome to the Nomad Ltd home page, Lydia!

Nomad Ltd

User name incorporated into Web page text generated by script

Learn About Our Company's Philosophy

Nomad Ltd has been in business for over ten years. During that time, we have offered tours to exotic (and simple) lands and sold sporting equipment (for bicycling, hiking, and other activities). In all that time, we have always been aware that our employees are our corporate ambassadors, and our customers are our royalty. We know that any company can make a buck here and there, but we want to do more than that. We want you to enjoy shopping at our stores and contribute to making Nomad a fun and interesting place to shop. We also know that as a business, we are also community members. Nomad wants to contribute to community efforts and make each town we're in a better place to live and shop. How do we do that? By hiring from the community, offering educational and financial benefits to our employees, and becoming involved in various community efforts.

Types Of Nomad Tours

Manipulating variables

In addition to simply using variable values that a user enters or that a script looks up, your scripts can process values using **arithmetic operators**, which allow you to manipulate variables mathematically to create new values. For example, to count page headings, you could create a script that reads through your Web page code, adding 1 to a variable value each time it encounters a heading tag. You also could combine several values that a user enters using a mathematical equation.

Creating a Conditional

Sometimes, you want a script to be able to create different results depending on different user actions or on the value of a certain browser attribute. JavaScript allows you to set up this situation by creating a **conditional** in your script. A conditional allows your script to choose one of two paths, depending on a condition that you specify. For example, you might want a graphic to display at a smaller size if a user's window is not maximized, to keep it fully in view. You could use a conditional to check the dimensions of the user's browser window and then set the graphic dimensions to one of two preset choices. Conditionals allow you to create flexible, interactive scripts whose output can change in different situations. ➤ Nomad Ltd has had a problem with users submitting forms missing the zip code information. Lydia wants her Web page to verify that the user has completed the zip code form field before it submits the data to the server. Using a conditional, her page can prompt the user to complete the field if it is left blank.

Steps

1. Open the file **HTML H-5.htm** in your text editor, then save it as a text document with the filename **Conditional.htm**

2. Select **[replace with verify function]** in the page's head section and press **[Delete]**

3. Type the following code, pressing **[Enter]** at the end of each line

```
function verify() {
        if (document.info.elements[5].value == "") {          →TESTING
                alert("Please complete each field.")
        }       else {
                submitted()
        }
}
```

Figure H-11 shows the document containing the verify function. The "if" statement code checks if the value of the zipcode field is null, indicating that the user has left it blank. When the "if" statement returns a value of "true," the function executes the code that immediately follows it. Here, the "true" result triggers the "alert" command to create a dialog box prompting the user to complete each field. When the "if" statement returns a value of "false," the function executes the code following the word *else*. In Lydia's script, the else command runs a function called "submitted()" that sends the user's information to the Web server.

4. Scroll to the bottom of the form section, select the text **[replace with event handler]** in the tag for the Send now! button, then press **[Delete]**

5. Type **onClick="verify()"**

6. Check scripts you added for errors, make changes as necessary, then save **Conditional.htm** as a text document

7. Open **Conditional.htm** in your Web browser, enter your name, scroll down to the form, then click the **Send now! button** without filling in any of the fields
The script runs and displays the dialog box shown in Figure H-12.

8. Click the **OK button**, then fill in each of the fields with sample information and click the **Send now! button**
The script you added verifies that the zip code field contains information and then allows the form submit function to execute.

FIGURE H-11: Web document containing completed script

Condition ————

```
            document.info.elements[5].value=""
    }

function verify() {
    if (document.info.elements[5].value == "") {
        alert("Please complete each field.")
    }
    else {
        submitted()
    }
}

//-->
</SCRIPT>

</HEAD>

<BODY BACKGROUND="egg shell.jpg">

<IMG SRC="nomad.jpg" ALIGN="right" WIDTH=201 HEIGHT=63>

<SCRIPT LANGUAGE="javascript">
<!--
document.write("<H1>Welcome to the Nomad Ltd home page, " + name + "!</H1>")
//-->
</SCRIPT>
```

Conditional terms

"false" result

"true" result

FIGURE H-12: Browser showing alert dialog box

- Athlete: For those who are sports participants.
- Arts: Dedicated to enjoying and appreciating the performing arts.
- Leisure: Designed to let you relax and rejuvenate.

Please tell us more about yourself. Lydia.

First Name:

Street Address:

City: State

Microsoft Internet Explorer

⚠ Please complete each field.

OK

Click here to submit this informati...

Click here to clear the form and start over.   Clear form

Contact Us Directly!

Find out more about what we have to offer. Contact the tour office at
Tourdirector@nomadltd.com

Testing multiple conditions

In addition to using a conditional to test a single condition, you test multiple conditions using logical comparison operators. JavaScript recognizes three logical comparison operators: && ("and"), || ("or"), and ! ("not"). A conditional using the && operator between two or more conditions returns "true" only if all conditions are true. Linking multiple conditions with the || operator, however, returns "true" if any one of the conditions is true. The ! operator returns true if its associated condition is not true.

HTML

Practice

▶ Concepts Review

Label each item shown in Figure H-13.

FIGURE H-13

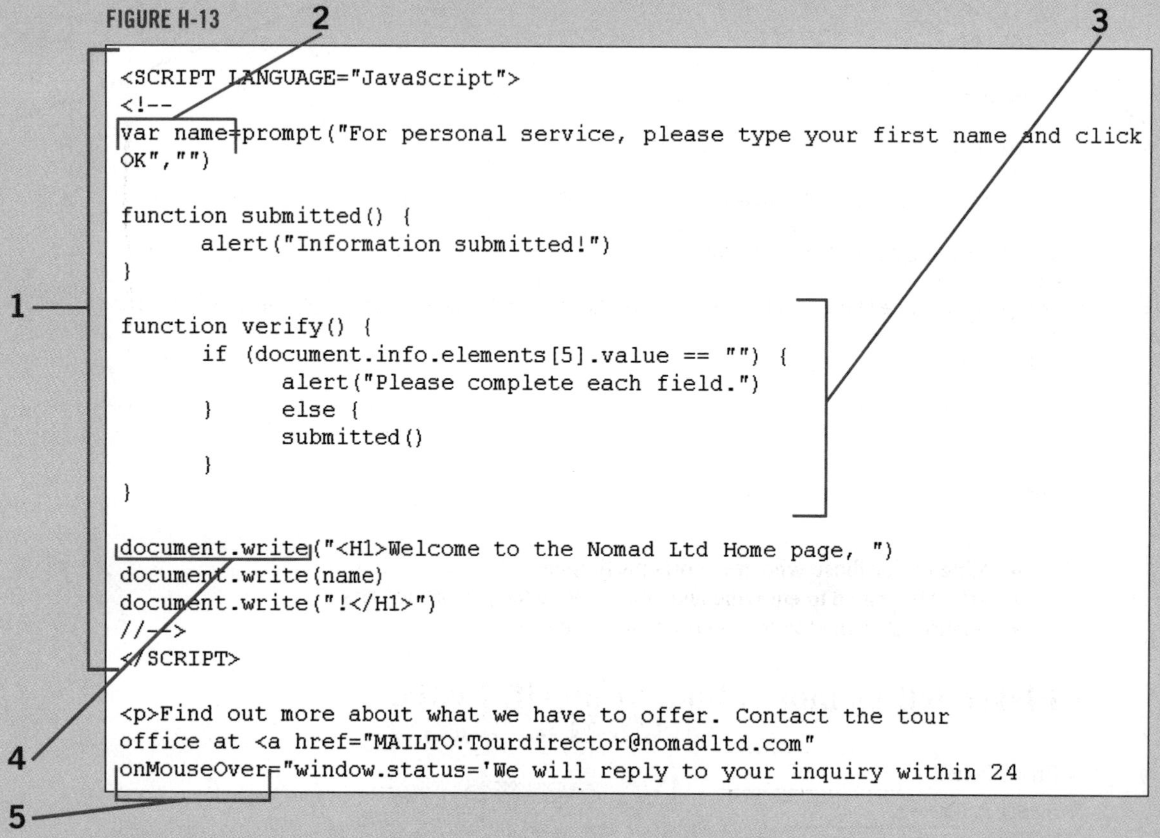

```
<SCRIPT LANGUAGE="JavaScript">
<!--
var name=prompt("For personal service, please type your first name and click
OK","")

function submitted() {
      alert("Information submitted!")
}

function verify() {
      if (document.info.elements[5].value == "") {
            alert("Please complete each field.")
      }     else {
            submitted()
      }
}

document.write("<H1>Welcome to the Nomad Ltd Home page, ")
document.write(name)
document.write("!</H1>")
//-->
</SCRIPT>

<p>Find out more about what we have to offer. Contact the tour
office at <a href="MAILTO:Tourdirector@nomadltd.com"
onMouseOver="window.status='We will reply to your inquiry within 24
```

1 **2** **3** **4** **5**

Match each statement with the term it describes.

6. Object hierarchy
7. Event handler
8. Bug
9. Method
10. JavaScript

a. Term specifying a possible user action
b. An error in a script
c. A Web page scripting language
d. JavaScript's object organization
e. Any action an object can carry out

Select the best answer from the list of choices.

11. **What HTML tagset marks the beginning and end of a script?**
    a. <JS>..</JS>
    b. <JAVASCRIPT>..</JAVASCRIPT>
    c. <SCRIPT>..</SCRIPT>
    d. <JAVASCRIPT>..<JAVASCRIPT>

12. **Which scripting language is compatible with both Netscape Navigator 4 and Microsoft Internet Explorer 4?**
    a. JScript
    b. JavaScript
    c. HTML
    d. VBScript

13. **Which of the following typing mistakes would not result in an error in your script?**
    a. Substituting the letter l for the number 1
    b. Inserting an extra space
    c. Omitting a closing bracket
    d. All of the above could result in errors.

14. **What would be the proper form of address in the object hierarchy for the second element in a form called "info"?**
    a. document.info.elements[1]
    b. document.info.elements[2]
    c. document.forms.info.elements[2]
    d. info.elements[2]

15. **What is the function of the string <!-- in scripting?**
    a. It is the HTML code for the beginning of a script.
    b. It is the HTML code for the end of a script.
    c. It tells an incompatible browser to ignore the code that follows.
    d. It tells the browser to display the text "--"

16. **Which comparison operator returns true only if the values before and after are both true?**
    a. &&
    b. ||
    c. !
    d. ==

17. **A set of script code grouped logically and named is called a(n)**
    a. Object.
    b. Variable.
    c. Hierarchy.
    d. Function.

HTML

▶ Skills Review

1. Create a script.
- **a.** Open the text editor, open the file HTML H-6.htm, then save it as a text document with the filename Script review.htm.
- **b.** Select the text [replace with script tags] in the page's head section, then press [Delete].
- **c.** Type <SCRIPT LANGUAGE="javascript"> and press [Enter].
- **d.** Type <!-- and press [Enter] twice.
- **e.** Type //--> and press [Enter], then type </SCRIPT>.
- **f.** Save Script review.htm as a text document.
- **g.** Open Script review.htm in your Web browser.

2. Debug a script.
- **a.** Open the file HTML H-7.htm in your browser, read the description of the error in the JavaScript Error dialog box, then click yes.
- **b.** Open the file HTML H-7.htm in your text editor, then save it as a text document with the filename Debug review.htm.
- **c.** Position the pointer in the third line of the clearUp() function, which begins document.info.elements[2].value, then insert a second quotation mark (") after the existing one at the end of the line.
- **d.** Save Debug review.htm as a text document, open Debug review.htm in your Web browser, enter information in the form, then click the Clear form button.

3. Use JavaScript event handlers.
- **a.** Open the file HTML H-8.htm in your text editor, then save it as a text document with the filename Event handler review.htm.
- **b.** Scroll to the bottom of the document, select the text "[replace with event handler]" in the first <A> tag, then press [Delete].
- **c.** Type the following without pressing [Enter]:
  onMouseOver="window.status='Guidelines on scheduling vacation time';return true"
  onMouseOut="window.status='';return true"
- **d.** Review your typing for errors, then save Event handler review.htm as a text document.
- **e.** Open Event handler review.htm in your Web browser, move the mouse pointer over the hypertext link "Additional vacation information" and verify that the message "Guidelines on scheduling vacation time" appears in the status bar.
- **f.** If necessary, fix any errors in your text editor, then save and preview the page.

4. Create a function.
- **a.** Open the file HTML H-9.htm in your text editor, then save it as a text document with the filename Function review.htm.
- **b.** Select the text "[replace with date function]" in the page's head section, then press [Delete].
- **c.** Type function writeDate() {
- **d.** Press [Enter], then type document.write(month + "/" + today.getDate() + "/" + today.getYear() + ".")
- **e.** Press [Enter], then type }

f. Select the text [replace with function call] near the bottom of the page, then type writeDate()

g. Save Function review.htm as a text document.

h. Open Function review.htm in your browser, verify that it displays the current date below the list of vacation dates, use your text editor to make changes if necessary, then save Function review.htm as a text document.

5. Assign a variable.

a. Open the file HTML H-10.htm in your text editor, then save it as a text document with the filename Variable review.htm.

b. Select the text [replace with variable code] in the page's head section, then type var name=prompt("Please type your first name and click OK","").

c. Select the text [replace with variable reference] at the top of the body section, then press [Delete].

d. Type document.write(name).

e. Save Variable review.htm as a text document, then open Variable review.htm in your browser.

f. Type your first name, then click OK.

g. Use your text editor to debug as needed.

6. Create a conditional.

a. Open the file HTML H-11.htm in your text editor, then save it as a text document with the filename Conditional review.htm.

b. Select the text [replace with conditional function] in the page's head section, then press [Delete].

c. Type the following code, pressing [Enter] at the end of each line:

```
function verify() {
        if (document.info.elements[0].value == "" ||
        document.info.elements[1].value == "" ||
        document.info.elements[2].value == "" ||
        document.info.elements[3].value == "" ||
        document.info.elements[4].value == "" ||
        document.info.elements[5].value == "") {
                alert("Please complete each field.")
        }       else {
                submitted()
        }
}
```

d. Review your code for typing errors, then save Conditional review.htm as a text document.

e. Open Conditional review.htm in your browser, fill in every field in the form except the last name field, click the "Submit now!" button, verify that your browser opens a dialog box asking you to complete all the fields, then click OK.

f. Close your text editor and browser.

▶ Independent Challenges

1. Green House, a local plant store, has hired you to add interactive features to their Web pages. You've decided to start by using an event handler to display link explanations in the status bar when users point to the page's links.

    To complete this independent challenge:

a. Start your text editor program, open the file HTML H-12.htm, then save it as a text document with the filename Green House home.htm.

b. To define the text strings that will be displayed as variables, select the text [replace with variable script] at the top of the page, press [Delete], and insert the following script, pressing [Enter] at the end of each line:

```
<SCRIPT LANGUAGE="javascript">
<!--
var plants="An overview of our plant stock and sources"
var tips="Helpful growing hints on common houseplants"
var services="A guide to our professional plant care services"
//-->
</SCRIPT>
```

c. Select the text "[replace with first event handlers]" in the <A> tag for the first link at the bottom of the page, press [Delete], and type the following without pressing [Enter]:

```
onMouseOver="window.status=plants;return true"onMouseOut="window.status='';return true"
```

d. Repeat Step c to modify the second link with the following insertion:

```
onMouseOver="window.status=tips;return true" onMouseOut="window.status='';return true"
```

e. Repeat Step c to modify the third link with the following insertion:

```
onMouseOver="window.status=services;return true" onMouseOut="window.status='';return true"
```

f. Save Green House home.htm as a text document, then open the file Green House home.htm in your Web browser.

g. Use your text editor to make any changes necessary, always save the file as a text document, then close your text editor and browser.

2. You have designed a Web publication for Sandhills Regional Public Transit. You want to incorporate a function you've written to tell prospective riders which fare period is in effect. A sentence stating the fare period will display at the bottom of the Web page. This sentence will change depending on the time of day.

    To complete this independent challenge:

a. Start your text editor program, open the file HTML H-13.htm, then save it as a text document with the filename SRPT home.htm.

b. Replace the text [replace with fare function] in the page's head section with the script located in the file HTML H-14.txt.

c. Scroll down immediately before the closing body section tag, delete the text [replace with function call script], enter the two opening script tags, type "schedTime()" (without the quotes) as the third line of the script, then enter the two closing script tags.

d. Save and preview your file in your Web browser program, debugging as necessary until you see no more JavaScript error messages.

3. You have been hired by Community Public School Volunteers to add advanced features to their Web publication using scripts. You have inserted a script into the home page they provided, but a JavaScript error dialog box opens when the page loads. To complete this independent challenge, preview the file HTML H-15.htm in your browser, noting the type of JavaScript error described and its location. Open the page in your text editor and save a copy as CPSV home.htm. Edit the script to fix the JavaScript error. Use the guidelines listed earlier in the unit to identify the types of errors that may be present. Continue to preview and edit the page until you no longer receive an error message, then save your work in your text editor as a text file.

4. Scripts are used in many Web pages on the WWW today to add features, as well as to create interesting formatting that is not possible with standard HTML coding. To complete this independent challenge, find two pages on the Web that contain scripts. (*Hint:* after opening a page in your browser, choose the HTML or Page Source option in your browser's View menu to check the document code for <SCRIPT> tags.) Print their HTML source code, and circle all scripts you see on your printouts. Circle and label any variables, conditionals, and functions you see in the documents.

HTML

► Visual Workshop

Open your text editor program, open the file HTML H-16.htm, and save it as a text document named Touchstone.htm. Then open Touchstone.htm in your browser. Scroll down to see the Send now! button. Click the Send now! button on the form without entering information in any of the fields. Use the form-verification script located in the file HTML H-17.txt and your text editor to modify the document Touchstone.htm. Change the event handler for the Send now! button to run the verify() function. Save the changes as a text document with the filename Touchstone.htm. Click the browser program button on the taskbar, and refresh your screen. Click the Send now! button again. Your screen should look like Figure H-14. Debug as necessary. (*Hint:* Remember to insert the verification script in the document header section between the beginning and ending script tags.)

FIGURE H-14

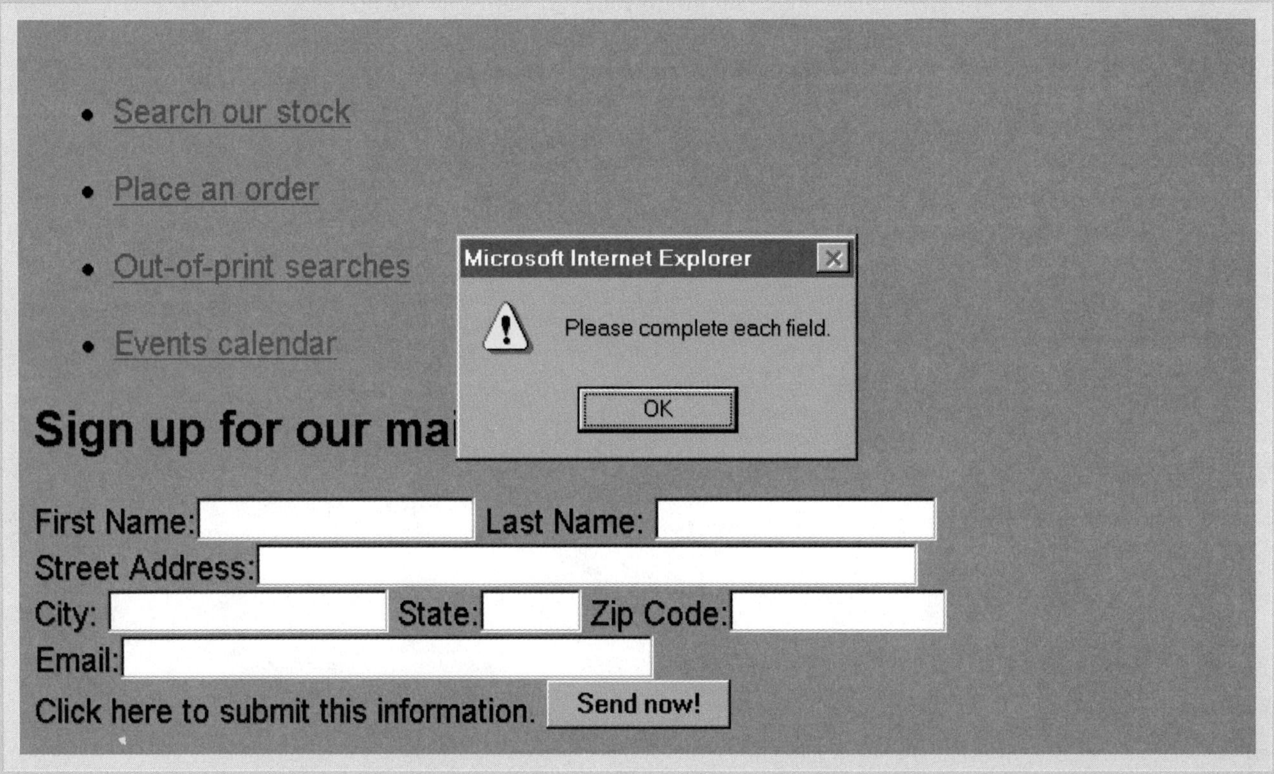

- Search our stock

- Place an order

- Out-of-print searches

- Events calendar

Microsoft Internet Explorer ☒

⚠ Please complete each field.

OK

Sign up for our mai

First Name: [   ]   Last Name: [   ]
Street Address: [   ]
City: [   ]   State: [   ]   Zip Code: [   ]
Email: [   ]
Click here to submit this information. [Send now!]

HTML

Unit I

Working
with Dynamic HTML (DHTML)

Objectives

- ▶ **Define Dynamic HTML**
- ▶ **Understand the building blocks of DHTML**
- ▶ **Tour DHTML pages**
- ▶ **Understand the DHTML Object Model**
- ▶ **Understand browser variability**
- ▶ **Design DHTML pages**
- ▶ **Research code architecture**
- ▶ **Keep up with DHTML changes**

Once you have an understanding of standard HTML and Web page design, you can create well-structured Web pages that use effective style combinations and that allow basic user input. However, recent innovations in Web page design and scripting, collectively known as **Dynamic HTML** (or **DHTML** for short), have revolutionized Web page design. DHTML has greatly increased the degree of interactivity possible in Web page design. With DHTML, your Web pages are enlivened as text and graphics change color, grow, shrink, and move on and off the page in response to user actions. ✐ Lydia Burgos, who works in the information systems department at Nomad Ltd, has read about Dynamic HTML and wants to explore using it in her company's Web pages. She starts with some research to learn about what DHTML is and how it works.

Unit I

HTML

Defining DHTML

During the early 1990's, all Web pages were simple documents that users downloaded and viewed on their local computers. Each Web page's interactivity was limited to hyperlinks, which opened other Web pages, opened new mail messages, or ran scripts on the server. Web pages that fit this description are known as **static HTML**. Today, however, many Web pages respond to and even interact with the user by changing their appearances based on user actions. Such pages use **dynamic HTML**, which describes a varied set of technologies that allow almost-immediate response to user actions in a Web page without accessing the Internet server. In her research, Lydia learns of several broad categories of design that DHTML allows.

Details

Dynamic style

When you create a page using standard HTML coding, you specify a style for each text element. These styles remain the same, regardless of user actions. The one exception to this is hyperlinks; their color may be changed by the browser if you have followed them recently. However, when you create a page using DHTML, you can incorporate styles—including font size, typeface, and color—that change immediately in response to user actions, such as moving the mouse pointer over a heading. This feature, known as **dynamic style**, allows your pages to emphasize an area when a user shows interest in it, without flooding the page with distracting large font sizes or bright colors. Figure I-1 provides an example of dynamic style. Notice on this DHTML page that the text color has changed, which is the result of DHTML. If the user selects this hyperlink, the color will change again to show that it has been viewed already.

Dynamic content

A DHTML Web page can display different content based on a user's activities, which is a feature known as **dynamic content**. Instead of taking the time to request, download, and display a new Web page (as standard HTML coding would do), DHTML utilities can simply hide or display blocks of text or other elements in the current page. This aspect of DHTML allows you to create a simple, well-organized, and visually appealing page that can instantly display extra information when the user is likely to be interested in it. Figure I-1 provides an example of dynamic content. Notice the message displayed in the status window, which is the result of DHTML.

Data-awareness

Standard HTML tools allow your Web pages to download chunks of information, such as database contents, from a Web server as a user requests access to them. With DHTML, this process is instantaneous for the user; for example, a DHTML Web page could be designed to download a complete database but then display only the information the user wants to view. A Web page equipped to work with data in this way is termed **data aware**, which means the user can work with information from a Web server without adding to Internet traffic by repeatedly requesting additional pieces of information. Also, data awareness can allow the user to manipulate and change the information right in the browser window.

Positioning

As with other formatting options, static HTML leaves many of the choices regarding the positioning of elements in a Web page to the browser's discretion. In addition to causing pages to display nonuniformly and unpredictably on different browsers, this aspect of HTML has prevented Web page design from rivaling the intricacy inherent in the best layouts of other media, such as magazines. DHTML represents an important step toward changing this by allowing Web page designers to specify precisely the location of all page elements, a feature known as **positioning**, which is unavailable in standard HTML. The Web page in Figure I-2, which is from an online tutorial on DHTML, uses DHTML to position text in combinations not possible with static HTML.

FIGURE I-1: Dynamic Web page

Classes to be offered, Fall 2000

- Introduction to Biology I
- Introduction to Biology II
- Plant Physiology
- Plant Chemistry
- Plant Field Practicum
- Marine Biology
- Introductory Microbiology
- Immunology
- Directed Study

Classes to be offered, Fall 2000

- Introduction to Biology I
- Introduction to Biology II
- Plant Physiology
- Plant Chemistry
- Plant Field Practicum
- Marine Biology
- Introductory Microbiology
- Immunology
- Directed Study

Dynamic Web page on opening

Text changes color when pointer positioned over it

Text appears in status window in response to pointer position

Fall registration begins August 15, 2000.   My Computer

FIGURE I-2: Web page formatted with DHTML positioning

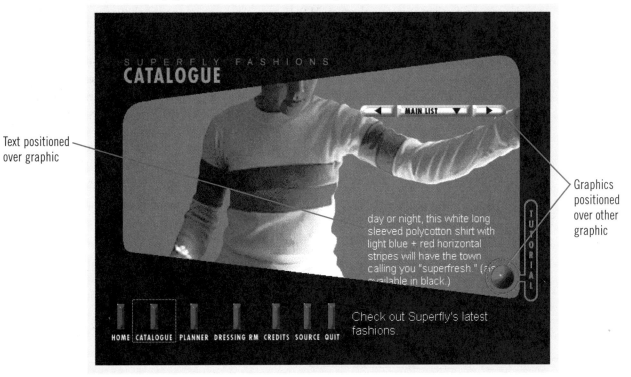

SUPERFLY FASHIONS
CATALOGUE

MAIN LIST

day or night, this white long sleeved polycotton shirt with light blue + red horizontal stripes will have the town calling you "superfresh." (also available in black.)

TUTORIAL

HOME CATALOGUE PLANNER DRESSING RM CREDITS SOURCE QUIT

Check out Superfly's latest fashions.

Text positioned over graphic

Graphics positioned over other graphic

HTML

HTML

Understanding the Building Blocks of DHTML

The creation of simple Web pages, while drawing on organization, design, and content-production skills, uses only HTML for arrangement and display in a browser. By contrast, DHTML is not a language or even a single technology, but, rather, a collection of Web page tools that, when used in various combinations, let designers create the effects specified in the previous lesson. As she reads more about DHTML, Lydia learns that DHTML is comprised of two main tools that work in tandem with standard HTML. These DHTML tools are included in the Web page source code shown in Figure I-3.

Client-side scripts

Scripts are small programs that can be triggered by a user's action on a Web page. In the early days of the Web, browsers allowed only the use of **server-side scripts**, or scripts that were stored and run on the Web server. Using these server-side scripts was similar to triggering a hyperlink. Each time a server-side script was run, the Web page sent a message to the server instructing it to run the script. Users had to wait as the browser downloaded the results of the server-side script. The lag time involved in this setup made features such as dynamic content and dynamic style impractical. Recent versions of browsers have allowed Web page designers to create **client-side scripts**, or scripts that the browser itself interprets and runs. Client-side scripts are a key element in allowing DHTML to respond immediately to user actions. For example, the client-side script at the bottom of Figure I-3 changes the text color and adds text to the status window when the mouse pointer moves over certain text.

Cascading Style Sheets (CSS)

In standard HTML, you assign styles and properties to elements of your page—text blocks, images, and other objects—through HTML tags. This system means that each element has its own set of properties. Even if two elements share the same properties, you must assign them separately and make any subsequent changes to each element. Although you can assign similar properties to groups of elements using defined styles, such as <H1>, these styles are defined on each user's browser, and thus you cannot predict exactly how a viewer will see your page in the browser window. **Cascading Style Sheets (CSS)** is a tool that allows you to specify attributes such as color and font size for all page elements marked by a specific tag, name, or ID. CSS not only gives designers a more efficient way to specify style but also more control over an object's attributes as well as how each object should be displayed in certain situations. For example, the Cascading Style Sheet in Figure I-3 assigns attributes to various tags. All text marked with these tags, such as <LI> and <P>, will display the attributes defined for this tag in the style sheet.

FIGURE I-3: Code for Web page incorporating DHTML tools

Cascading Style Sheet

Client-side script

```
<STYLE TYPE="text/css">
body {background:navy; color:white}
LI {list-style-image: none; list-style: none}
UL.toc {display:none}
UL.expanded {display:block}
A.select {color:white; background:blue}
.over {color:red}
P {margin-top:0; margin-bottom:0}
</STYLE>

<SCRIPT LANGUAGE="JavaScript">
<!--
var curSelection = null;

function setStyle(src, toClass) {
        if (null != src)
        src.className = toClass;
}

function mouseEnters() {
        if ((curSelection != event.toElement) && ("A" ==
event.toElement.tagName)) {
                setStyle(event.toElement,"over");
                window.status="Fall registration begins August 15, 2000."
        }
}
```

Proprietary features

Both Netscape and Microsoft have each introduced unique features, known as **proprietary features**, into their browsers. For example, Netscape Navigator 4 allows use of the <LAYER> tag to overlap screen elements easily. Microsoft Internet Explorer 4 supports the embedding of external tables in a Web page, as well as a set of features that affect element appearance in complex ways. Eventually, some of these technologies become part of new international Web page standards. When proprietary features become part of the industry standard, they eventually become supported by the major browsers and are then no longer considered proprietary features. However, proprietary features that are supported by only one of the two major browsers are most useful only in single-browser settings, such as intranets whose users all run the same browser.

HTML

Touring DHTML Pages

Although DHTML technology may sound intriguing, viewing and interacting with it is the only way to get a true sense of its impact and capabilities. Looking at existing pages, both successful and not, is also a useful way to begin planning the features you want to include in your own pages. ✐ Lydia has downloaded several sample Web pages that incorporate features she has researched. She opens and tests them as she begins collecting ideas for updating the Nomad Ltd Web site.

Steps 1234

Trouble?

If you are using Navigator, some text on the page may be arranged differently from that shown in the figures. However, all of the features of the page should still work.

1. **Start your Web browser program, open the file HTML I-1.htm, then scroll down the page to view its layout**
   As Figure I-4 shows, this page contains several blocks of text positioned around the page; each of these is an example of DHTML positioning. The designer of this Web page created the sidebar along the right edge of the screen by using DHTML style specifications to position the text, specify its width, and specify a background color for the text block.

2. **Scroll down the page until the heading Blue Ray appears in your document window, then move your mouse pointer over the heading Blue Ray**
   If you are using Internet Explorer 4, notice that the text color changes from black to purple and that the text size increases—an example of **dynamic style**. Netscape Navigator 4 does not support most dynamic styles and shows no change when your mouse pointer is over this heading.

3. **Click the heading Blue Ray**
   A paragraph of detailed information appears beneath the heading, without the page reloading, as shown in Figure I-5. This is an example of **dynamic content** because user activity can affect the page content.

4. **Watch the text in the status window**
   A message continuously scrolls across the status window. This feature, created by a script, is another example of dynamic content.

5. **Scroll to the top of the page, and move your mouse pointer over one of the links under the heading "Learn more about Jim's!"**
   As the pointer moves over link text or an image, the link image changes. When the pointer moves off the link, the image returns to its original appearance, which is an instance of dynamic content. Rather than simply changing a graphic's display properties, the position of the pointer over the link triggers a script that changes the source of the image in the image tag. The pointer movement causes the image to toggle between two different source files.

QuickTip

Currently, data binding is a proprietary feature of Internet Explorer 4, but an extension is available from the Microsoft Web site that allows Netscape Navigator 4 to display this and other Internet Explorer 4 features.

6. **If you are using Internet Explorer, open the file HTML I-2.htm and scroll to the bottom of the page**
   As Figure I-6 shows, this page contains a data table. Unlike standard HTML tables, however, this table was generated from an external file as the Web page opened. Linking a Web page to an external data file is known as **data binding**. If you added or changed records in the external file, they would be reflected in the Web page the next time you opened it without requiring any changes in the Web page's code. A related feature, known as **data-awareness**, allows a Web page to load all the records from a database but display only some of them. Then, a user can access any record instantly without needing to download more information to the browser.

FIGURE I-4: Sample DHTML Web page

Positioned elements

FIGURE I-5: Dynamic content and style changes

Text color changes in response to pointer position

New text appears after click

FIGURE I-6: Web page containing bound data

The following table summarizes the information on all our blueberry types. Click any table heading to sort the table by that column.

Table generated from linked external data source

Bush	Type	Height	Fruit maturity	Yield per bush	Berry size	Berries per cup
Blue Ray	high	4-6 ft.	mid/late July	10-20 lb.	large	60
Blue Jay	high	5-7 ft.	late July	7-10 lb.	small/medium	110
Jersey	high	5-7 ft.	late July	7-10 lb.	small/medium	110
Elliott	high	5-7 ft.	late Aug./early Sept.	10-20 lb	small/medium	75
Northland	medium	3-4 ft.	early July	15-20	small	135

HTML

Understanding the DHTML Object Model

Developers of early scripting languages created an **object hierarchy**, which is a system of organization that allows Web page developers to describe and work with the Web page elements in a browser window. This hierarchy, officially called the **Document Object Model (DOM)**, categorizes and groups Web page elements into a tree-like structure. Each part of this structure is referred to as an **object**. For example, in the basic JavaScript DOM, a page's images, forms, anchors, and links are all grouped beneath the document object. The document, its location, and its history are, in turn, grouped below the frame object. DOMs allow browsers to identify page elements and to make them available to scripts in Web pages that they display. Although the earliest DOMs were part of scripting languages, Navigator 4 and Internet Explorer 4 have increased the range and versatility of DHTML by including their own extended DOM versions in the browser code itself, which are sometimes referred to as **DHTML Object Models**. DHTML Object Models allow you to reference a particular object the same way in any scripting language on a particular browser. However, because Netscape and Microsoft have developed different DOMs, you must reference some objects differently in Navigator 4 than in Internet Explorer 4. Figure I-7 shows the basic structure of the DOM for Internet Explorer 4, which makes virtually all browser window elements available to scripts. In order to take full advantage of DHTML's capabilities, Lydia reviews the top level of object classes in the Microsoft DHTML Object Model.

Details

Location
The location object contains the URL of the current page.

Frames
The frames object contains a separate Window object for each frame in the current browser window. When the window is not divided into frames, this object is empty and the entire document contents are part of the document object The Microsoft DOM also contains a frames collection within the document object, to reference its <IFRAME> tag.

History
The history object allows access to the browser's list of previously visited URLs.

Navigator
The navigator object makes information about the browser available.

Event
The event object allows interaction with the event currently being processed by the browser, such as mouse movement or the press of a button.

Screen
The screen object makes information about the user's screen setup and display available.

Trouble?

Don't worry if you don't know the meaning of each element of the Document object. You will learn about some of these elements as you learn more about DHTML.

Document
The document object represents the current Web page in the browser window. A document object contains many elements as listed in Figure I-7. These elements, including links, anchors, images, and so on, are what help to give each Web page its unique characteristics.

FIGURE I-7: Microsoft DHTML Object Model

window
- location
- frames
- history
- navigator
- event
- screen
- document
  - links
  - anchors
  - images
  - filters
  - forms
  - applets
  - embeds
  - plug-ins
  - frames
  - scripts
  - all
  - selection
  - stylesheets
  - body

HTML

Understanding Browser Variability

Although DHTML has few current standards, work is underway to change this situation. The **World Wide Web Consortium**, or the **W3C**—an international body whose mission is the creation of standards for WWW technologies—is creating official guidelines for DHTML. Although the W3C has created standards for the DOM and other DHTML technologies, these agreements have not yet resulted in a uniform interpretation of DHTML on the Web. The Microsoft and Netscape corporations, as the manufacturers of the vast majority of browsers in use today, have the greatest influence in DHTML implementation on the Web because the technology depends on each user's browser to interpret and run it. This difference in implementation means that code written for use on one browser may not work on the other, which requires writing two sets of code to incorporate some features into a page. As standards evolve and new browser versions are released, it will become easier to create today's features with a uniform code. However, both companies undoubtedly will continue to incorporate new, incompatible innovations into their browsers, which means that browser variability probably will always be a factor in creating DHTML pages. Lydia researches the implications of the different browsers available on the DHTML pages she is planning.

 Some dynamic HTML code is compatible with the 3.x versions of Navigator and Internet Explorer, known as **third generation** browsers, but most features work only on the 4.x and later versions, the **fourth generation** browsers. Because many users have upgraded to fourth generation browsers already and many more will upgrade eventually, it is often easiest to create DHTML with these browsers in mind. Remember, however, that if you want your pages to reach the largest possible audience, they must still accommodate other browsers. By organizing your pages to display logically even without their DHTML features and adding a few extra tags to allow older browsers to process the code, your content can remain accessible by older browsers that can't interpret DHTML, by text-based browsers, and by Web interfaces for people with disabilities. Testing your pages on different browsers before publishing them is important because standard DHTML code could cause older browsers to stop functioning, or **hang**. Figure I-8 shows a DHTML page in a fourth-generation browser and in Lynx, a text-only browser. Notice that the text-only browser ignores all of the DHTML commands, such as those for positioning, while still displaying all the information logically.

 The differences in DHTML capabilities between fourth-generation browsers and earlier versions make writing interactive Web pages complicated because Internet Explorer 4 and Navigator 4 use and interpret DHTML differently. As you saw in the DHTML tour, therefore, they are not compatible when it comes to creating certain dynamic HTML features. Because DHTML components are still new technologies, many are not yet standardized in the software industry. For now, this incompatibility issue results in some features being available only in one browser and others being available only in the other. For some features to be available in either Web browser, DHTML Web page designers must write separate scripts to create similar features in the fourth-generation browsers.

Designing dynamic Web pages is easiest when they will reside on a network where all users run the same browser, such as a corporate intranet. When publishing to the WWW, the only way to make sure that most users can view your pages is to write **cross-platform code**, or DHTML code that works on both fourth generation browsers. This often requires two sets of code in your page, along with a script to recognize in which browser the Web page is opening. Using this technique allows you to make interesting and interactive pages without causing compatibility problems for potential users. Although cross-platform coding can be time-consuming, many Web sites freely distribute such code that they have developed for popular features, along with tutorials describing how the code works. Using existing code can save a lot of page-development time.

FIGURE I-8: One Web page as it displays in two different browsers

Web page using style sheets and positioning in a fourth generation browser

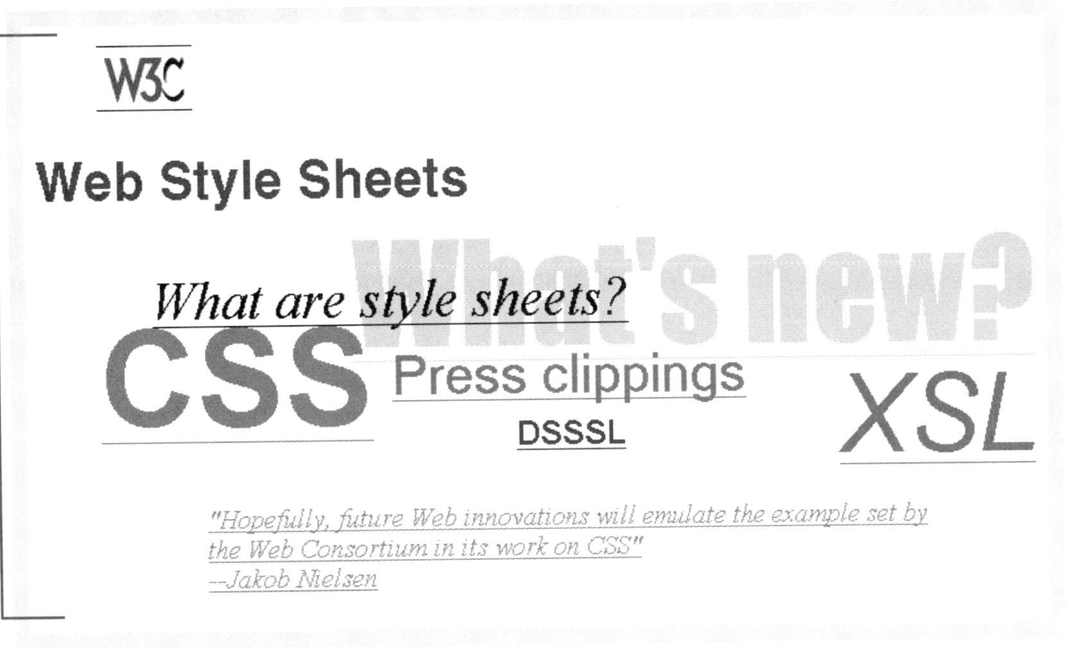

W3C

Web Style Sheets

What are style sheets? What's new?

CSS Press clippings **XSL**

DSSSL

"Hopefully, future Web innovations will emulate the example set by the Web Consortium in its work on CSS"
--Jakob Nielsen

Page structure and coding creates orderly display without DHTML features

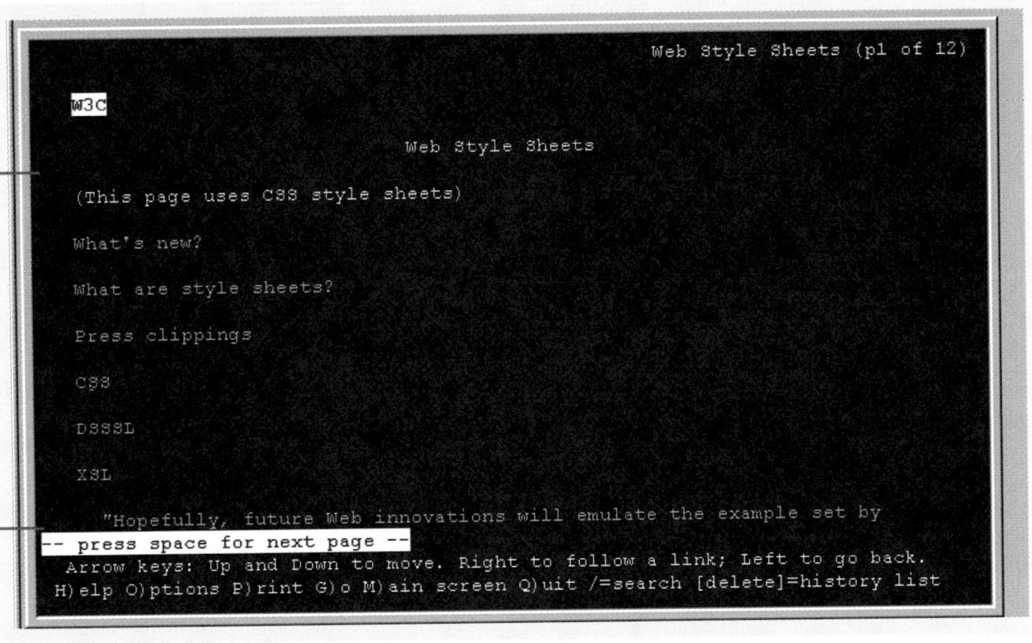

```
                                              Web Style Sheets (p1 of 12)

  W3C
                              Web Style Sheets

  (This page uses CSS style sheets)

  What's new?

  What are style sheets?

  Press clippings

  CSS

  DSSSL

  XSL

      "Hopefully, future Web innovations will emulate the example set by
-- press space for next page --
  Arrow keys: Up and Down to move. Right to follow a link; Left to go back.
  H)elp O)ptions P)rint G)o M)ain screen Q)uit /=search [delete]=history list
```

HTML

HTML

Designing DHTML Pages

Like static Web pages, those incorporating DHTML require planning and forethought. Standard HTML rules, such as careful proofreading and judicious use of headings, still apply to dynamic pages. However, DHTML has its own advantages and pitfalls, which are important to keep in mind. In addition to awareness of browser differences, several other guidelines are helpful in working with this new technology. ◢ To ensure that her Web pages follow good design principles, Lydia has made a list of recommendations, based on her DHTML research, for designing pages with DHTML.

Details

Organize for dynamic content

Remember that DHTML allows positioning of page elements and lets you show new content in response to user actions. Generally, this means that you can fit more in a dynamic page than in a static HTML page. For example, the hierarchical menu, shown in Figure I-9, allows a single page to contain information that otherwise works best as a list of links and a set of associated pages. This menu works like the one you use when you click the Start button in Windows. With DHTML, you can insert this within your Web pages, for simplified navigation, which keeps the Web page uncluttered. It also organizes the information so that the user can see the interrelationships of choices. Organizing your Web site to take advantage of DHTML capabilities can make the site easier for users to navigate and for you to manage.

Use dynamic features purposefully

Dynamic HTML features appear impressive, and you may be eager to show off your new skills by incorporating many of them into the pages you create. However, just as in static pages, the best Web pages are focused and free of distracting elements. Your Web page's content and message, rather than newly available features, should dictate which dynamic tools you use.

FIGURE I-9: Web page containing a hierarchical menu

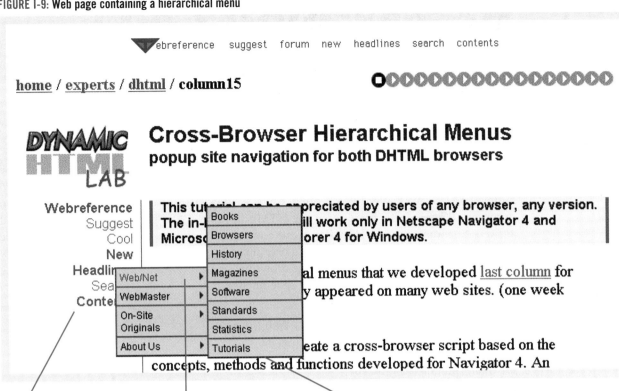

Pointing to "Contents" opens first level of menu

Pointing to "Web/Net" opens second level of menu

Second level contains list of links to open listed pages

Design resources

One advantage of the browser competition between Microsoft and Netscape is that both companies are eager to show off their browser's features. Both companies keep a list of links to well-designed pages (supporting their own proprietary features) on their corporate Web sites. Reviewing these pages can give you ideas for planning successful dynamic Web pages as well as introduce you to new features.

Researching Code Architecture

After you outline your Web page and identify the DHTML features you want to use in it, the next step is to sit down and write code to make these features work. In many cases, although you have seen a Web page incorporating a certain action, it can be difficult to determine exactly how to create the feature with scripts and style sheets. At this point, research on the Web is indispensable to creating a successful DHTML page. For example, you can use the Web to look at the page source of a Web page that uses a feature you like. You also can find well-documented sample code on Web sites, which often you are allowed to modify and use for your own purposes. ▶ Lydia has written the HTML for a new Web page that lists questions and answers. She wants to use DHTML to create a collapsible list on her Web page. In a collapsible list, explanatory text appears only when a user clicks its associated heading. Recently, Lydia saw the collapsible list feature on a page while browsing the Web, and she downloaded a copy of the Web page so that she could examine the code further.

Steps

1. Open the file **HTML I-3.htm** in your Web browser
   The page displays a list of blueberry breeds.

2. Click the phrase **Blue Jay**
   Associated text appears below the berry name, as shown in Figure I-10. Notice in the address bar that clicking the phrase did not open a new page; rather, it simply triggered a change in the appearance of the current Web page.

3. Start your text editor program, then open the file HTML I-3.htm to display the source code for the Web page
   Figure I-11 shows part of the script for creating the collapsible list.

4. Close the text editor without saving the document

5. Be sure your computer is connected to the Internet, then open a search engine of your choice

6. In the "Search" text box, type **DynamicHTML programming** and click the **Find button**, or its equivalent
   The browser returns a list of links to sites related to DHTML programming.

7. Review the links returned by the search engine, then follow one to a site that seems likely to contain tutorials or sample code
   Articles and sample scripts for dynamic HTML applications may be helpful in creating your own pages.

8. Scan the site's opening page for links to script libraries or articles about DHTML features, then follow the appropriate links

9. Locate sample code or a relevant article for an interesting DHTML feature, then download the page to your Project Disk with the name **Feature download.htm**
   This downloaded file can be a helpful reference when you plan your own DHTML applications.

FIGURE I-10: Web page containing collapsible list

Click the names of blueberry breeds below to read about our selection:

Blue Ray

Blue Jay

New text appears in response to mouse click

highbush type, 5 to 7 ft. at maturity, fruit ripening the first to middle of July, yield is 10 to 20 lbs per bush, fruit size medium/large (approx. 75 berries per cup).

Jersey

Elliott

Northland

2 T white flour
1/4 t cinnamon
1/2 t ground coriander
pinch nutmeg
3-1/2 c blueberries
Topping:
1-1/4 c blueberries

To prepare crust, mix flour and sugar. Cut butter in to mixture with pastry blender. Add 2 T water to moisten (more if required). Roll mixture and place in 9″ pie plate.

For the filling, mix sugar, flour, cinnamon, coriander, and nutmeg thoroughly. Toss with 3-1/2 c blueberries to coat

FIGURE I-11: Source code for expanding table of contents

Part of code for expanding elements in Internet Explorer

```
function expandIE(el) {
        whichEl=eval(el + "Desc");
        if (whichEl.style.display == "none") {
                whichEl.style.display="block";
                whichEl.isExpanded=true;
        }
        else {
                whichEl.style.display="none";
                whichEl.isExpanded=false;
        }
}
```

Part of code for expanding elements in Navigator

```
function expandNav(el) {
        whichEl=eval("document." + el + "Desc");
        if (whichEl.visibility == "hide") {
                whichEl.visibility="show";
                whichEl.isExpanded=true;
        }
        else {
                whichEl.visibility="hide";
                whichEl.isExpanded=false;
        }
        arrange();
}
```

CLUES TO USE

Code-borrowing etiquette

When you find existing code on the Web that fits a project you are working on, it can save you time and frustration to use the existing code in your page instead of creating it from scratch. However, to be considerate to other designers, you should follow a few simple guidelines. First, be aware that some DHTML code is copyrighted and you cannot use it without permission from its author, which usually involves paying a fee as well. Some pages and sites offer code for free re-use. In this situation, it is still considered courteous to credit the source of the code in your Web page, usually with the creator's name and the source URL. If you find code you'd like to use and are unsure whether you are allowed to, it is best to contact the creator for permission. If you don't have permission to use someone else's code, you can still use its basic framework to help you plan the creation of your page and then augment the features with your own coding.

Keeping Up with DHTML Changes

Web and software designers have already developed many ideas and methods for using DHTML in Web pages. As with any new technology, this body of knowledge will continue to grow, and in the process, will provide new uses and workarounds for DHTML programming. In addition, browser creators update and expand the capabilities of their products, resulting in ever-expanding possibilities for new DHTML applications. As a consequence of all these factors, it's important to stay current with the latest new developments in DHTML if you want to take full advantage of its possibilities for your Web pages. Predictably, the Web is a rich source of information on DHTML. Lydia wants to see what new DHTML features are on the horizon.

Steps

1. Be sure you are connected to the Internet, open your browser, then use a search engine of your choice to search the Web for the keywords **DHTML news**
The search engine returns descriptions and links to pages about DHTML.

2. Follow a link on the search results page to a site containing DHTML information

3. Scroll through and scan the opening page for tips on working with DHTML and for news about recent and upcoming developments
Figure I-12 shows a Web page offering tips and articles on using DHTML.

4. Follow links to explanations of new DHTML features or to news about upcoming additions or changes, then read one of these articles

5. Close your Web browser

FIGURE I-12: Web page containing DHTML tips

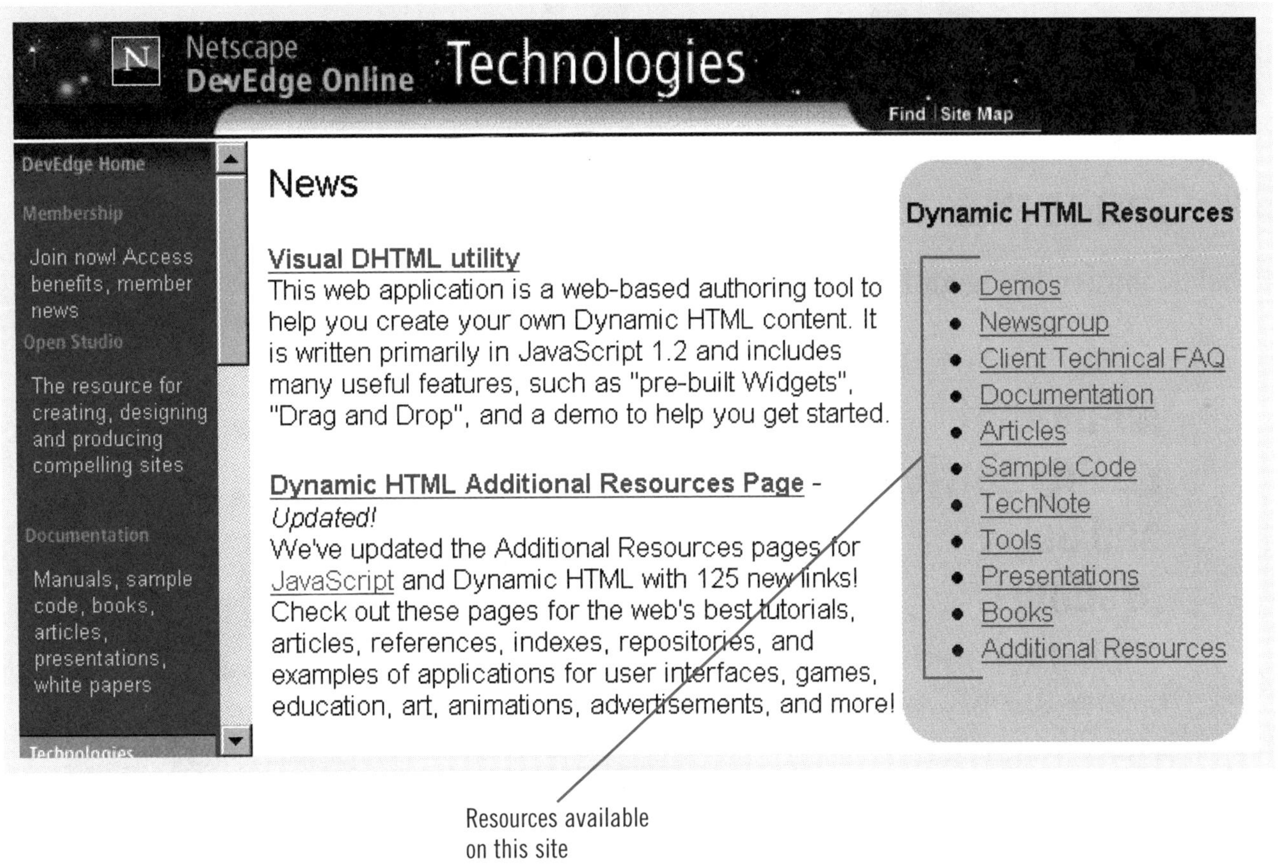

Resources available
on this site

Practice

▶ Concepts Review

Label each item in Figure I-13 with the DHTML category that best describes it.

FIGURE I-13

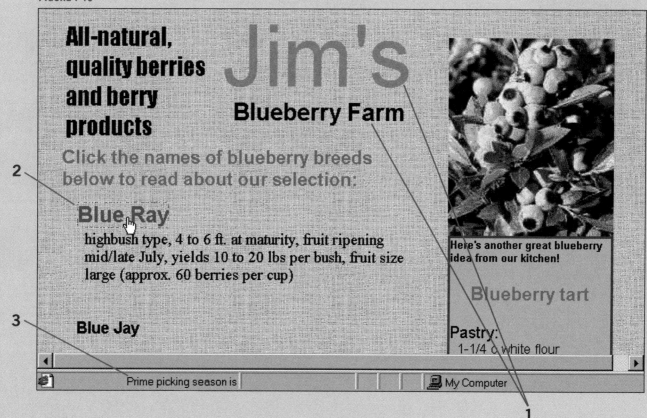

Match each term with its description.

4. **Dynamic style**
5. **Static HTML**
6. **Client-side scripts**
7. **Cascading Style Sheets (CSS)**
8. **DHTML Object Model**
9. **Cross-platform code**
10. **W3C**
11. **Positioning**
12. **Dynamic HTML**

a. Hierarchy organizing browser window elements
b. Collection of Web page technologies allowing quick response to user actions
c. Scripts that the browser itself interprets and runs
d. International body creating Web standards
e. Web page technologies allowing very limited interactivity
f. Ability to specify locations of all Web page elements
g. Component of DHTML allowing precise Web page style specification
h. Style that changes in response to user actions
i. Code that works on both fourth generation browsers

HTML

Select the best answer from the list of choices.

13. Which of the following is *not* a feature of DHTML?
a. Dynamic style
b. Dynamic content
c. Server-side scripts
d. Data awareness

14. Positioning allows Web page designers to
a. Create interactive page formatting.
b. Create predictable layouts.
c. Download Web page data.
d. Create interactive page content.

15. A collapsible list is a good example of
a. Dynamic style.
b. Dynamic content.
c. Data awareness.
d. Absolute positioning.

16. DHTML uses an object model called
a. The World Wide Web Consortium.
b. JavaScript.
c. Cascading Style Sheets.
d. The DHTML Object Model.

17. Fourth generation browsers include
a. Internet Explorer 5.0.
b. Navigator 4.0 and Internet Explorer 4.0.
c. Navigator 3.0 and Internet Explorer 3.0.
d. Lynx and other text-based browsers.

18. Creating DHTML pages for both fourth generation browsers requires
a. Excluding CSS from your pages.
b. Limiting the pages you write to working only on one browser.
c. Eliminating all dynamic features from your pages.
d. Using cross-platform code.

19. What should provide the underlying structure for your Web pages?
a. The page's content and message
b. The amount of information you want to include
c. Other pages you see on the Web
d. The dynamic features you want to include

Independent Challenges

1. The owners of the Green House plant store have asked you to add to their Web site a list of houseplant products they sell, along with a description of each. You think that a collapsible list would format and display this information easily and concisely. To begin, you design this Web page on paper.

To complete this independent challenge:

a. On a sheet of paper, write the text for one or more titles for the Web page.

b. Below the headings, copy the following list of products, along with description placeholder text:
Potting soil
[description]
Washed gravel
[description]
Peat moss
[description]
Houseplant fertilizer
[description]
Cactus soil mix
[description]

c. On your Web page outline, label each element to indicate what page elements will be part of the collapsible list and what page elements will be appear on the Web page at all times.

d. Indicate how you will format each text item.

e. Indicate next to each of the product names that it will be formatted with dynamic style and add a second style specification for how the text will display when a user interacts with it.

f. Indicate on your sketch any positioning you will use in your page.

g. Add any further text to your sketch, such as that for hypertext links, and label the text with its formatting specifications and any additional features.

2. Sandhills Regional Public Transit wants to discuss with you ways to make their Web pages more interactive. In preparation for meeting with your clients, you want to become more familiar with different DHTML formatting options.

To complete this independent challenge:

a. Log on to the Internet and open a search engine of your choice, then search on the phrase *DHTML formatting.*

b. Click one of the links provided by the search engine to open a Web site containing DHTML formatting resources.

c. Scan the opening page and navigate the site to locate articles or sample scripts for Web page features using DHTML.

d. Read and print the article or the explanatory text accompanying a script.

e. Write a paper detailing two DHTML formatting features you think would be useful in a home page that provides information to a wide range of people. Explain why you would include these features and how they would enhance the page.

3. Community Public School Volunteers has hired you to manage their Web site on an ongoing basis. To stay on top of the latest Web page design trends, you want to regularly research relevant news on the Web. Because you're preparing to create dynamic pages for CPSV, you want to research the state of W3C standards for DHTML.

To complete this independent challenge:

a. Log on to the Internet and search on the keywords *W3C DHTML standards.*

b. Investigate the sites listed on the search results page. Locate and print two articles regarding recommendations or standards released within the past six months.

c. For each article, use the Microsoft and Netscape Web sites to research whether the standard is supported in each company's fourth-generation browser or if the company has announced plans to comply with the standard in a future release.

d. Write a paragraph on each article, summarizing the area of DHTML it covers (for example, scripting or dynamic style), which browsers support it or will support it, and an overview of the article's content.

4. Explore sample DHTML pages on the Web, either at the Microsoft or Netscape Web sites, or by searching on the term *DHTML sample pages* in a search engine. Choose one Web page, print it out from your Web browser, and on the printout areas of the page that demonstrate DHTML features. On a separate sheet of paper, list these elements and, if applicable, describe briefly how they respond to user actions. Submit your printout and list to your instructor.

Specifying
Style Dynamically

► **Understand Cascading Style Sheets**
► **Create an embedded style sheet**
► **Create a class**
► **Detect browsers**
► **Show and hide page elements**
► **Change font size dynamically**
► **Control font color dynamically**
► **Use an external style sheet**

Cascading Style Sheets (CSS) and scripts form the foundation of DHTML. Whereas scripting allows the browser to alter the page, CSS lets you specify in detail how the page and its elements should appear. An understanding of CSS's simple syntax and organization opens the door to many new options for your Web pages' appearance. Lydia is looking forward to adding new effects to the Nomad Ltd Web pages. First, she will look at CSS a bit more in depth, then she will use CSS to create an interactive page for her department.

Understanding Cascading Style Sheets

With CSS, you can organize and expand the style attributes available in a Web page. CSS allows a Web page designer to easily specify attributes such as color, font size, and even position on the page for single objects or groups of objects, including text blocks, images, and all other DOM objects. CSS offers three different ways to specify style, which simplifies creating and changing Web page code. As Lydia reviews how to implement CSS in her Web pages, she studies the three levels of style available.

Inline style

Use **inline style** to take advantage of CSS's extended formatting options for a small text block or other object a single time in your document. You use inline style—the most basic level of using CSS—to specify your selected attributes in the opening tag surrounding the text itself, as shown in Figure J-1. This method allows you to specify a format different from all others on the page. However, formatting all page objects using inline style is impractical, given the amount of typing required.

Embedded style

Use **embedded style** to simplify formatting multiple page elements. Figure J-2 shows the source for a page using embedded style. To create embedded styles, you associate style attributes with HTML tags between the HEAD tags at the top of your Web page, creating a set of HTML code known as an **embedded style sheet**. Then, any place in the Web page code where you use the tags specified in the embedded style sheet, the text or object is formatted automatically with that style. Embedded style rather than inline style is a more efficient way to format an entire Web page. However, you can specify inline styles in a page that uses embedded styles when you have single objects that need their own style or style adjustment. Each inline style supersedes the embedded style defined for the object where it is used.

External style

Use **external style** to apply the global formatting of embedded style to multiple pages. External style allows you to specify formats and apply them to multiple Web pages rather than just one. External style also is known as **linked style** because, instead of listing style specifications at the top of your Web page, you create a link to an external document that contains the style code, known as an **external style sheet**. This method allows you to format a set of Web pages, such as a Web publication, with a uniform style and allows you to change the style for all pages later simply by editing the external style sheet. External style can be used in a page together with both inline and embedded styles. Just as inline style takes precedence over embedded style wherever you use it, embedded styles and inline styles both take precedence over external style. This system of precedence is known as **cascading**, and it gives CSS its name. Cascading allows you to apply a general format for a page or group of pages as well as to make local exceptions to the global style.

FIGURE J-1: Web page containing inline style

```
<LINK REL="stylesheet" HREF="nomadltd.css" TYPE="text/css">

<SCRIPT LANGUAGE="JavaScript">
<!--
NS4 = (document.layers) ? 1:0;
IE4 = (document.all) ? 1:0;
//-->
</SCRIPT>

<STYLE TYPE="text/css">
<!--
H1 {font-family: arial, sans-serif; font-size: 20pt}
H2 {font-family: "times new roman", times, serif; font-size: 14pt; font-
style: italic}
.question {font-family: "times new roman", times, serif; font-size: 12pt;
font-weight: bold}
//-->
</STYLE>

</HEAD>

<BODY BACKGROUND="Egg shell.jpg">
<DIV STYLE="font-color: navy; text-decoration:underline" ALIGN="center">
<H2>Frequently Asked Questions about</H2>
<H1>Dynamic HTML (DHTML)</H1></DIV>
```

Inline style located in formatting tag →

FIGURE J-2: Web page containing embedded style

```
<HTML>
<HEAD>
<TITLE>Nomad Ltd DHTML FAQ</TITLE>

<STYLE TYPE="text/css">
<!--
H1 {font-family: arial, sans-serif; font-size: 20pt; font-style: normal}
H2 {font-family: "times new roman", times, serif; font-size: 14pt; font-
style: italic}
//-->
</STYLE>

</HEAD>

<BODY BACKGROUND="Egg shell.jpg">
<DIV ALIGN="center"><IMG SRC="nomad.jpg" ALIGN="right">
<H2>Frequently Asked Questions about</H2>
<H1>Dynamic HTML (DHTML)</H1></DIV><BR>

<UL TYPE="disk">
<LI><DIV>What is Dynamic HTML?</DIV>

<DIV>Dynamic HTML (DHTML) describes a set of new technologies for designing
Web pages that allow new and more precise formatting features, along with
faster access for users.</DIV><BR>
```

Embedded style sheet →

CLUES TO USE

<DIV> vs. <SPAN>

Although it's often useful to assign CSS styles to standard formatting tags such as <H1> or <LI>, HTML includes two specialized tags that are especially valuable for CSS. Both the <DIV> and <SPAN> tags can enclose an element or group of elements, which allows you to specify a style for everything they contain. The <DIV> tagset always includes a line break before and after the enclosed elements, which creates a unit divided from the surrounding page. The <SPAN> tagset does not include line breaks before or after, which causes its contents to flow with the objects surrounding them in the page. When formatting text, <DIV> is best for enclosing a paragraph or group of paragraphs, whereas <SPAN> allows you to create a special style for words or sentences within a paragraph.

Creating an Embedded Style Sheet

An embedded style sheet consists of one or more lines of HTML code specifying style attributes, surrounded by tags marking the section as CSS style specifications. You can associate style attributes with any HTML structuring or formatting tag and then apply them to Web page elements simply by inserting the tags. 🗡 After completing her basic research, Lydia decides to create a **FAQ** (which is an acronym for Frequently Asked Questions, pronounced "fak") document about DHTML for her co-workers in Nomad Ltd's information systems department. Lydia wants to take advantage of CSS to specify exactly how the page will appear in a user's browser. Because she wants to create a uniform look for the page, she decides to create an embedded style sheet.

1. **Start your text editor, open the file HTML J-1.htm, then save it as a text document with the filename FAQ embedded style.htm**
   This file contains the text of the FAQ Lydia is creating, along with basic HTML structuring tags. Lydia has enclosed each unit of text in opening and closing DIV tags to make it easy for her to add style attributes later.

2. **Select the text [replace with embedded style sheet], press [Delete], type <STYLE TYPE="text/css"> and press [Enter], then type <!-- and press [Enter]**
   Embedded style sheets are placed in the Web page's head section, which allows the browser to incorporate the styles in the text it displays in the body section. A browser recognizes the code as an embedded style sheet from the beginning and ending <STYLE> tags. The TYPE property in the STYLE tag tells the browser the language and format of the style sheet it marks. In this case, the language is CSS, and the information is in text format. The <!-- tag tells browsers that are not compatible with embedded style sheets to ignore this section.

3. **Type H1 {font-family: arial, sans-serif; font-size: 20pt; font-style: normal} and press [Enter]**
   Lydia associates 20-point arial with the <H1> tag for use with the page's main heading. By putting it first in a list of two, Lydia specifies arial as her font preference. Her second choice, sans-serif, instructs the user's browser to use any sans-serif font if arial is not available.

4. **Type H2 {font-family: "times new roman", times, serif; font-size: 14pt; font-style: italic} and press [Enter]**
   Lydia has specified 14 point as the font size to associate with the <H2> tag, which is the subheading.

5. **Type //--> and press [Enter], then type </STYLE>**
   Figure J-3 shows the completed Web page source containing the style sheet.

6. **Check the document for errors, make changes as necessary, then save FAQ embedded style.htm as a text document**

7. **Start your browser program, cancel any dialup activities, then open the file FAQ embedded style.htm**
   The Web page appears as shown in Figure J-4.

QuickTip

Font names composed of multiple words, such as *times new roman*, must be listed within quotation marks for a browser to recognize them as single names.

FIGURE J-3: Completed embedded style sheet

Opening and closing embedded style sheet tags

Style specifications for heading tags

```
<HTML>
<HEAD>
<TITLE>Nomad Ltd DHTML FAQ</TITLE>

<STYLE TYPE="text/css">
<!--
H1 {font-family: arial, sans-serif; font-size: 20pt; font-style: normal}
H2 {font-family: "times new roman", times, serif; font-size: 14pt; font-
style: italic}
//-->
</STYLE>

</HEAD>

<BODY BACKGROUND="Egg shell.jpg">
<DIV ALIGN="center"><IMG SRC="nomad.jpg" ALIGN="right">
<H2>Frequently Asked Questions about</H2>
<H1>Dynamic HTML (DHTML)</H1></DIV><BR>

<UL TYPE="disk">
<LI><DIV>What is Dynamic HTML?</DIV>

<DIV>Dynamic HTML (DHTML) describes a set of new technologies for designing
Web pages that allow new and more precise formatting features, along with
faster access for users.</DIV><BR>
```

FIGURE J-4: Web page formatted with embedded style sheet

Text formatted with H2 style specified in embedded style sheet

Text formatted with H1 style specified in embedded style sheet

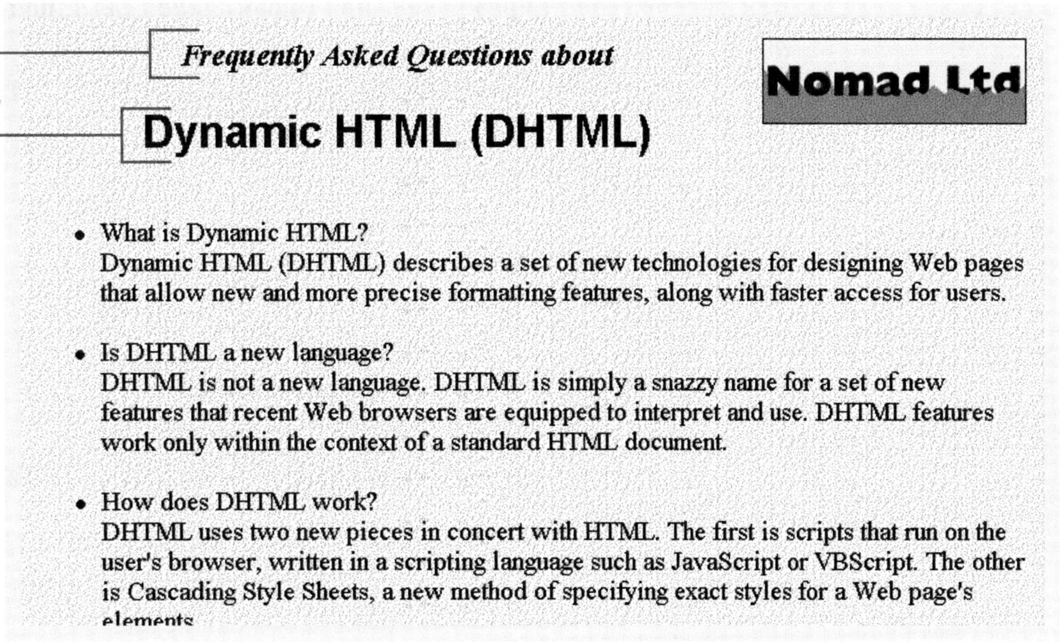

Frequently Asked Questions about

Nomad Ltd

Dynamic HTML (DHTML)

- What is Dynamic HTML?
  Dynamic HTML (DHTML) describes a set of new technologies for designing Web pages that allow new and more precise formatting features, along with faster access for users.

- Is DHTML a new language?
  DHTML is not a new language. DHTML is simply a snazzy name for a set of new features that recent Web browsers are equipped to interpret and use. DHTML features work only within the context of a standard HTML document.

- How does DHTML work?
  DHTML uses two new pieces in concert with HTML. The first is scripts that run on the user's browser, written in a scripting language such as JavaScript or VBScript. The other is Cascading Style Sheets, a new method of specifying exact styles for a Web page's elements.

HTML

Creating a Class

In addition to specifying style for all occurrences of a particular HTML tag, you also can name a set of style specifications and then associate, or **call**, this name in tags within your Web page. This named style, known as a **class**, allows you to format selected elements with an embedded style, without requiring that each element be enclosed in the same tag or that every occurrence of a certain tag display the same style. All class names begin with a period to mark them as classes. To apply a class to an element, you add the CLASS attribute to the element's opening HTML tag. ✎ Lydia's bulleted list is a series of questions and answers. Lydia wants to format the headings in her list, which are the questions, differently than the paragraph text, which are the answers. She creates a class that specifies the formatting for the questions and then calls the class within the opening <DIV> tag for each of the questions.

Steps

1. Open the file **HTML J-2.htm** in your text editor, then save it as a text document with the filename **FAQ class.htm**

2. Select the text **[replace with class style]** in the embedded style sheet, then press **[Delete]**

3. Type **.question {font-family: "times new roman", times, serif; font-size: 12pt; font-weight: bold}** and press **[Enter]**
   The dot preceding the style name "question" indicates that the style specification is for a class.

4. Select the text **[replace with class]** in the <DIV> tag for the first question, then press **[Delete]**

5. Type **CLASS="question"**
   The tag now reads <DIV CLASS="question">. This calls the class and applies the style associated with the class "question" to this text, which is the first question in the FAQ.

6. Repeat Steps 4 and 5 for the remaining six questions
   Figure J-5 shows a portion of the completed source for the bulleted list.

7. Check your document for errors, make changes as necessary, then save **FAQ class.htm** as a text document

8. Click the browser program button on the taskbar, then open the file **FAQ class.htm**
   The Web page appears as shown in Figure J-6.

FIGURE J-5: Web page source using a class

Class definition inserted in embedded style sheet

```
H2 {font-family: "times new roman", times, serif; font-size: 14pt; font-
style: italic}
.question {font-family: "times new roman", times, serif; font-size: 12pt;
font-weight: bold}
//-->
</STYLE>

</HEAD>

<BODY BACKGROUND="Egg shell.jpg">
<DIV ALIGN="center"><IMG SRC="nomad.jpg" ALIGN="right">
<H2>Frequently Asked Questions about</H2>
<H1>Dynamic HTML (DHTML)</H1></DIV><BR>

<UL TYPE="disk">
<LI><DIV CLASS="question">What is Dynamic HTML?</DIV>

<DIV>Dynamic HTML (DHTML) describes a set of new technologies for designing
Web pages that allow new and more precise formatting features, along with
faster access for users.</DIV><BR>

<LI><DIV CLASS="question">Is DHTML a new language?</DIV>

<DIV>DHTML is not a new language. DHTML is simply a snazzy name for a set of
new features that recent Web browsers are equipped to interpret and use.
DHTML features work only within the context of a standard HTML
```

Class question called in <DIV> tags

FIGURE J-6: Web page formatted with new class

Frequently Asked Questions about

Nomad Ltd

Dynamic HTML (DHTML)

- **What is Dynamic HTML?**
  Dynamic HTML (DHTML) describes a set of new technologies for designing Web pages that allow new and more precise formatting features, along with faster access for users.

Bold format added using class property

- **Is DHTML a new language?**
  DHTML is not a new language. DHTML is simply a snazzy name for a set of new features that recent Web browsers are equipped to interpret and use. DHTML features work only within the context of a standard HTML document.

- **How does DHTML work?**
  DHTML uses two new pieces in concert with HTML. The first is scripts that run on the user's browser, written in a scripting language such as JavaScript or VBScript. The other is Cascading Style Sheets, a new method of specifying exact styles for a Web page's

Creating an ID style

As well as assigning styles to tags and classes in your embedded style sheets, you can define styles for element IDs. Just as each class style name begins with a period, you preface each ID style name with a number sign (#). Because you can assign an ID to only one element, defining global ID styles is no more efficient than specifying the styles inline. However, ID styles allow you to group style information at the top of the document, rather than inline, which can help make your code less cluttered and easier to read and understand.

HTML

SPECIFYING STYLE DYNAMICALLY HTML J-7

Detecting Browsers

The combination of scripts and CSS allows you to add lag-free interactivity to your Web pages. Although both fourth-generation browsers support DHTML, each does so in a different way. Whereas the methods for creating basic effects in Internet Explorer and Netscape Navigator are the same, the code for most advanced DHTML features is different for each browser. This means that creating code offering dynamic features in both browser platforms, known as **cross-browser code**, often requires writing and integrating two different sets of code into a single page. Additionally, a cross-browser DHTML page requires a **browser-detection script**, which determines the user's browser brand and generation. The browser then uses this information to determine which of the page's DHTML scripts are appropriate for a user's browser. Lydia wants to add interactive DHTML features to control her FAQ page's display. Before adding the coding to create these features, she inserts a browser-detection script into her page.

Steps

1. Open the file **HTML J-3.htm** in your text editor, then save it as a text document with the filename **FAQ browser detect.htm**
   This copy of the FAQ page contains the CSS features Lydia created in the last lesson.

2. Select the text **[replace with browser-detection script]**, then press **[Delete]**

3. Type the following script, pressing **[Enter]** at the end of each line:

```
<SCRIPT LANGUAGE="javascript">
<!--
Nav4 = (document.layers) ? 1:0;
IE4 = (document.all) ? 1:0;
//-->
</SCRIPT>
```

This info is old but still can use it

   Lydia's completed script, shown in Figure J-7, tells the browser to check for elements of the DOM, one of which is specific to Navigator 4 and the other of which is specific to Internet Explorer 4. The question mark in each line tells the browser to evaluate the preceding condition and to assign the variable the value 1, which equals "true" if the condition is true; otherwise, assign the variable the value 0, which is "false" if it is not true. This script determines if the browser is Netscape Navigator 4 or Internet Explorer 4. Based on the results of the conditional test, the browser reads the appropriate scripts, which create DHTML features in the user's browser.

4. Check the document for errors, then make changes as necessary

5. Save FAQ browser detect.htm as a text document

6. Open the file **FAQ browser detect.htm** in your browser to ensure it displays correctly, and debug the file as necessary until it displays as expected

Browser-detection script

```
<HTML>
<HEAD>
<TITLE>Nomad Ltd DHTML FAQ</TITLE>

<SCRIPT LANGUAGE="javascript">
<!--
Nav4 = (document.layers) ? 1:0;
IE4 = (document.all) ? 1:0;
//-->
</SCRIPT>

<STYLE TYPE="text/css">
<!--
H1 {font-family: arial, sans-serif; font-size: 20pt}
H2 {font-family: "times new roman", times, serif; font-size: 14pt; font-
style: italic}
.question {font-family: "times new roman", times, serif; font-size: 12pt;
font-weight: bold}
//-->
</STYLE>

</HEAD>

<BODY BACKGROUND="Egg shell.jpg">
<DIV ALIGN="center"><IMG SRC="nomad.jpg" ALIGN="right">
<H2>Frequently Asked Questions about</H2>
```

Browser detection script → look on favorite browser & use that script

CLUES TO USE

Future cross-browser coding

Much of the difference in browser support between Navigator 4 and Internet Explorer 4 stems from the lack of a DHTML standard. As the W3C organization refines and extends the industry standard, however, future browser releases should match more closely in how they support today's basic features. Although this may make future cross-browser coding as easy as writing for a single browser today, browser-detection routines will probably never become obsolete. As long as the browsers of multiple companies are popular, each company will continue to develop and add its own features, which will be standardized later. Additionally, some Web users will continue to use earlier-generation browsers. Because advanced scripts can hang older browsers, causing them to stop working and sometimes requiring the user to reboot, a browser-detection script can help you develop pages that identify and accommodate less-advanced browsers.

HTML

Showing and Hiding Page Elements

By working together with embedded scripts, CSS can specify how page elements should display in different situations and in response to user actions, which allows you to create the interactive features that are the hallmark of DHTML. ◄━━━ Lydia wants her Web page to hide the paragraphs containing the answers and to display each answer only when the user clicks its corresponding question. Lydia can create this feature, known as an **expandable outline**, with a combination of style sheets and scripts. Lydia has already inserted the code to create this feature in Navigator 4. Now, she adds code that Internet Explorer 4 can interpret.

Steps

1. Open the file **HTML J-4.htm** in your text editor, then save it as a text document with the filename **FAQ show and hide.htm**
   Notice that this copy of the FAQ page already contains the browser detection script.

2. Scroll and select **[replace with expandIE function]**, then press **[Delete]**

Trouble?

"El" stands for element. Be sure to type *El* or *el* using the letter l and not the number 1.

3. Type the following code, pressing **[Enter]** at the end of each line

```
function expandIE(el) {
    theEl=eval(el + "Answer");
    if (theEl.style.display == "none") {
        theEl.style.display="block";
        theEl.expanded=true;
    }
    else {
        theEl.style.display="none";
        theEl.expanded=false;
    }
}
```

[handwritten: example code]
[handwritten: if hidden →display]
[handwritten: if display → hide]

   Figure J-8 shows the new code.

4. Scroll down to the <DIV> tag for the first list item "What is Dynamic HTML?", select the text **[replace with opening A tag]** and the space following it, then press **[Delete]**

5. Type **<A HREF="#" onClick="expand('one'); return false">**
   Because Lydia uses an A tag with # as a dummy href, the mouse pointer becomes a hand when it moves over the question which indicates to the user that clicking the text triggers an action. The remaining code uses the onClick event handler to call the function expand and specifies the variable 'one' for the function to process. The function expand checks which browser the user is running and, in Internet Explorer 4, calls the expandIE function you entered earlier.

6. Replace the text **[replace with closing A tag]** in the next line with **</A>**

7. Repeat Steps 4 through 6 for the remaining six list items, substituting 'two' for 'one' in item two, and so forth
   Figure J-9 shows a portion of the completed code for the expanding FAQ list.

8. Use Figures J-8 and J-9 to check the document for errors, make changes as necessary, then save FAQ show and hide.htm as a text document

Trouble?

In Navigator 4, all the text is visible briefly when the page opens.

9. Open **FAQ show and hide.htm** in your browser, then click the first question
   As Figure J-10 shows, the text for the first question is displayed.

FIGURE J-8: FAQ page with added script

```
function expand(el) {
        if (!ver4) return;
        if (IE4) {
                expandIE(el)
        }
        else {
                expandNav(el)
        }
}

function expandIE(el) {
        theEl=eval(el + "Answer");
        if (theEl.style.display == "none") {
                theEl.style.display="block";
                theEl.expanded=true;
        }
        else {
                theEl.style.display="none";
                theEl.expanded=false;
        }
}

function expandNav(el) {
        theEl=eval("document." + el + "Answer");
        if (theEl.visibility == "hide") {
```

Script to make outline expandable in IE4

Change value of display property for a clicked line

FIGURE J-9: <A> tags added to list items

```
<H3>Click any of the popular questions about DHTML below to see its
answer.</H3>

<DIV ID="oneQuestion" CLASS="question"><A HREF="#" onClick="expand('one');
return false"><P>What is Dynamic HTML?</P></A></DIV>

<DIV ID="oneAnswer" CLASS="answer"><P>Dynamic HTML (DHTML) describes a set
of new technologies for designing Web pages that allow new and more precise
formatting features, along with faster access for users.</P></DIV>

<DIV ID="twoQuestion" CLASS="question"><A HREF="#" onClick="expand('two');
return false"><P>Is DHTML a new language?</P></A></DIV>

<DIV ID="twoAnswer" CLASS="answer"><P>DHTML is not a new language. DHTML is
simply a snazzy name for a set of new features that recent Web browsers are
equipped to interpret and use. DHTML features work only within the context
of a standard HTML document.</P></DIV>

<DIV ID="threeQuestion" CLASS="question"><A HREF="#"
onClick="expand('three'); return false"><P>How does DHTML
work?</P></A></DIV>

<DIV ID="threeAnswer" CLASS="answer"><P>DHTML uses two new pieces in concert
with HTML. The first is scripts that run on the user's browser, written in a
scripting language such as JavaScript or VBScript. The other is Cascading
```

Opening <A> tag and event handler inserted

Closing </A> tag inserted

FIGURE J-10: Expanding FAQ list

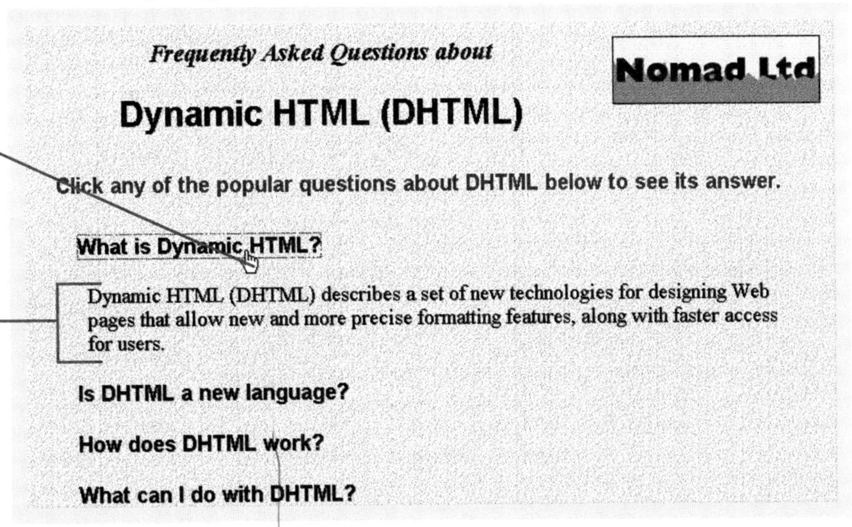

Mouse pointer becomes hand over question text

Clicking question displays answer text

Frequently Asked Questions about

Nomad Ltd

Dynamic HTML (DHTML)

Click any of the popular questions about DHTML below to see its answer.

What is Dynamic HTML?

Dynamic HTML (DHTML) describes a set of new technologies for designing Web pages that allow new and more precise formatting features, along with faster access for users.

Is DHTML a new language?

How does DHTML work?

What can I do with DHTML?

HTML

Changing Font Size Dynamically

In the last lesson, you used a script to modify the style of an element in response to a user action. Using this general formula, you can add dynamic formatting to most style aspects of any object on your Web pages. A popular application of this method has been to change the appearance of text when a user points at it, commonly referred to as a **rollover**. A rollover changes text attributes to make the text stand out. ✎ Lydia wants to change the text size of the FAQ questions when the user moves the pointer over them. Although adding this feature to graphics is straightforward in both browsers, Lydia finds that it is difficult to create for text blocks in Navigator. Because the feature is not crucial to the overall layout of her Web page, she decides to focus on creating the feature only in Internet Explorer.

Steps

1. Open the file **HTML J-5.htm** in your text editor, then save it as a text document with the filename **FAQ text size.htm**
2. Scroll down the document to the ending </SCRIPT> tag in the document's head section, select the text **[replace with text size functions]**, press **[Delete]**, then type the following functions, pressing **[Enter]** at the end of each line

```
function changeText(whichQuestion) {
    if (Nav4) {return}
    whichQuestion.style.fontSize="16pt";
}
function changeTextBack(whichQuestion) {
    if (Nav4) {return}
    whichQuestion.style.fontSize="12pt";
}
```

(handwritten annotations) if (Nav4) {return} → NOT Necessary — set it to 16 — set it to 12

   Figure J-11 shows the functions entered into the Web page source. The first function, changeText, changes the font size of the object from which it was called to 16 point. The second function, changeTextBack, changes the font size of the calling object back to 12 point.
3. Scroll down the page to the opening <A> tag for the first list item "What is Dynamic HTML?", select the text **[replace with event handlers]**, then press **[Delete]**
4. Type **onMouseOver="changeText(this)" onMouseOut="changeTextBack(this)"**
   This code adds two new arguments to the heading. The first uses the onMouseOver event handler to call the changeText function you created earlier. The "this" is scripting shorthand to tell the function to make changes to the current object. The second argument calls the changeTextBack function for the current object in response to the mouse moving off the text.
5. Repeat Steps 3 and 4 for the remaining six list items
   Figure J-12 shows source code containing the inline code for dynamically changing text size.
6. Use Figures J-11 and J-12 to check the document for errors, make changes as necessary, then save FAQ text size.htm as a text document
7. Open **FAQ text size.htm** in your browser, then move the pointer over a list item
   Figure J-13 shows the result of this step in Internet Explorer 4. Notice that the text size of the heading increased. However, if you opened FAQ text size.htm in a different browser, such as Netscape Navigator 4, no change occurs.
8. Move the mouse pointer off the first heading
   The first heading returns to its original size.

FIGURE J-11: Page containing new functions

Changes current text to larger font size ─┐

Changes larger text back to smaller font size ─┐

```
function changeText(whichQuestion) {
        if (Nav4) {return}
        whichQuestion.style.fontSize="16pt";
}
function changeTextBack(whichQuestion) {
        if (Nav4) {return}
        whichQuestion.style.fontSize="12pt";
}
//-->
</SCRIPT>
```

FIGURE J-12: Page containing code to change text size

Calls function to increase text size

Calls function to decrease text size

```
<H3>Click any of the popular questions about DHTML below to see its
answer.</H3>

<DIV ID="oneQuestion" CLASS="question" ><A HREF="#" onClick="expand('one');
return false" onMouseOver="changeText(this)"
onMouseOut="changeTextBack(this)"><P>What is Dynamic HTML?</P></A></DIV>

<DIV ID="oneAnswer" CLASS="answer"><P>Dynamic HTML (DHTML) describes a set
of new technologies for designing Web pages that allow new and more precise
formatting features, along with faster access for users.</P></DIV>

<DIV ID="twoQuestion" CLASS="question" ><A HREF="#" onClick="expand('two');
return false" onMouseOver="changeText(this)"
onMouseOut="changeTextBack(this)"><P>Is DHTML a new language?</P></A></DIV>

<DIV ID="twoAnswer" CLASS="answer"><P>DHTML is not a new language. DHTML is
simply a snazzy name for a set of new features that recent Web browsers are
equipped to interpret and use. DHTML features work only within the context
of a standard HTML document.</P></DIV>

<DIV ID="threeQuestion" CLASS="question"><A HREF="#"
onClick="expand('three'); return false" onMouseOver="changeText(this)"
onMouseOut="changeTextBack(this)"><P>How does DHTML work?</P></A></DIV>

<DIV ID="threeAnswer" CLASS="answer"><P>DHTML uses two new pieces in concert
```

FIGURE J-13: Changed text size in Internet Explorer 4

Question font size increases in response to pointer ─

Frequently Asked Questions about

Dynamic HTML (DHTML)

Click any of the popular questions about DHTML below to see its answer.

What is Dynamic HTML?

Is DHTML a new language?

How does DHTML work?

What can I do with DHTML?

What do I need to learn to use DHTML?

HTML

Changing Font Color Dynamically

Just as you can script a page to change text size in response to a user action, you can easily change or modify such scripts to change several other properties that control how text displays. In addition to the increase in text size, Lydia wants the heading font color to change in response to mouse pointing. She can modify the scripts she already created to alter font color at the same time they alter text size in Internet Explorer 4.

Steps

1. Open the file **HTML J-6.htm** in your text editor, then save it as a text document with the filename **FAQ text color.htm**

2. Scroll down the page to the changeText function in the page header, select the text **[replace with changeText color]**, then press **[Delete]**

3. Type whichQuestion.style.color="#9400D3";

4. Select the text **[replace with changeTextBack color]** in the changeTextBack function in the page header, then press **[Delete]**

5. Type whichQuestion.style.color="#000000";
   Figure J-14 shows the completed changes in the Web page source containing the color style. The changeText function increases the size of the text as well as changes the color for the selected object. The changeTextBack function returns the text to its original size and color.

6. Check the document for errors, make changes as necessary, then save FAQ text color.htm as a text document

7. Open the file **FAQ text color.htm** in your browser, then move the pointer over the first heading
   Figure J-15 shows the change, which again takes place only in Internet Explorer 4. In addition to the size increase, the text turns purple, making it stand out from the other questions on the page.

8. Move the mouse pointer off the first heading
   In Internet Explorer 4, the text size and color return to their default settings.

FIGURE J-14: Color change code inserted

New script lines to change text color

```
function changeText(whichQuestion) {
     if (Nav4) {return}
     whichQuestion.style.fontSize="16pt";
     whichQuestion.style.color="#9400D3";
}
function changeTextBack(whichQuestion) {
     if (Nav4) {return}
     whichQuestion.style.fontSize="12pt";
     whichQuestion.style.color="#000000";
}
//-->
</SCRIPT>

<STYLE TYPE="text/css">
<!--
H1 {font-family: arial, sans-serif; font-size: 20pt; font-style: normal}
H2 {font-family: "times new roman", times, serif; font-size: 14pt; font-
style: italic}
H3 {font-family: arial; font-size: 12pt; color: #4619E1; position: relative;
left: 20px; top: -10px}
.question {font-family: "times new roman", times, serif; font-size: 12pt;
font-weight: bold}
.question A {font-family: arial; font-size: 12pt; font-weight: bold; text-
decoration: none; color: black}
.rest {position: absolute; left: 25px}
```

FIGURE J-15: Color change in browser

Frequently Asked Questions about

Dynamic HTML (DHTML)

Click any of the popular questions about DHTML below to see its answer.

Changed text color —— **What is Dynamic HTML?**

Is DHTML a new language?

How does DHTML work?

What can I do with DHTML?

What do I need to learn to use DHTML?

HTML

Using an External Style Sheet

When you create or manage a group of related Web pages, it is often helpful to create an external style sheet. Just as you use hyperlinks to refer to external HTML documents, you can link each Web page to the style sheet with a simple line of code. Creating an external style sheet allows you to apply a standard style to a set of Web pages and to easily make changes that apply to all the pages. ◆━━ Because Lydia plans to create other FAQ pages for her department, she has created an external style sheet to reflect the styles she wants all the FAQs to use. She also takes into account Nomad Ltd's standard Web page style. She replaces the existing embedded style sheet with a link to the external file. The rules of cascading precedence allow her to leave in place the inline styles that help individualize the Web page by creating her dynamic effects.

QuickTip

Both fourth-generation browsers ignore the highest-level heading definition in an external style sheet. Adding an empty style definition named H0 guarantees that all other heading definitions will display correctly in your documents.

1. Open the file **HTML J-7.css**, then save it as a text document with the filename **nomadltd.css**
   This file contains the Nomad Ltd stylesheet. The document consists of text, just like an HTML document, and contains the opening and closing <STYLE> tags that tell browsers how to interpret the contents. A CSS document is formatted just like an embedded style sheet, except that it contains no HTML code outside of the <STYLE> tags. Lydia cut and pasted the styles from her FAQ page that she will apply to other pages she creates.

2. Select the text **#4619E1** in the color definition for the H3 heading, press [Delete], then type **#238E68**
   This changes the color for the H3 style, which applies to the directions in Lydia's current page, from blue to green.

3. Save **nomadltd.css** as a text document

4. Open the file **HTML J-8.htm** in your text editor, then save it as a text document with the filename **FAQ external style.htm**
   Lydia has removed the heading definitions from the embedded style sheet for her FAQ page because the external style sheet contains these specifications.

5. Scroll down and select **[replace with external style sheet link]** which is just above the embedded style sheet, then press **[Delete]**

6. Type **<LINK REL="stylesheet" HREF="nomadltd.css" TYPE="text/css">**
   Figure J-16 shows the page source containing the insertion. The LINK tag contains information about a file related to the current document. The REL attribute identifies the file type of the related file. The value assigned to HREF is the name and address of the file, just as for a hyperlink. TYPE specifies the format of the associated file because you can code associated information including style sheets in different ways.

7. Check the file for errors, make changes as necessary, then save **FAQ external style.htm** as a text document

8. Open the file **FAQ external style.htm** in your Web browser
   The Web page appears as shown in Figure J-17. Because both Navigator 4 and Internet Explorer 4 support basic CSS, the standardized Nomad Ltd format appears in both browsers. The instruction text color displays in green, which confirms that the page is using the external styles you defined. When Lydia links other FAQ Web pages to this nomadltd.css file as she develops them, then all her FAQ Web pages will have the same style. This helps ensure consistency for all her FAQ Web pages.

FIGURE J-16: Web page code containing link to external style sheet

External style sheet link text

```
}
//-->
</SCRIPT>

<LINK REL="stylesheet" HREF="nomadltd.css" TYPE="text/css">

<STYLE TYPE="text/css">
<!--
.question {font-family: "times new roman", times, serif; font-size: 12pt;
font-weight: bold}
.question A {font-family: arial; font-size: 12pt; font-weight: bold; text-
decoration: none; color: black}
.rest {position: absolute; left: 25px}
//-->
</STYLE>

</HEAD>

<BODY BACKGROUND="Egg shell.jpg">

<DIV ALIGN="center"><IMG SRC="nomad.jpg" ALIGN="right">
<H2>Frequently Asked Questions about</H2>
<H1>Dynamic HTML (DHTML)</H1></DIV><BR>

<H3>Click any of the popular questions about DHTML below to see its
answer.</H3>
```

FIGURE J-17: Web page linked to external style sheet

Text color reflects change made to external style sheet

Frequently Asked Questions about

Dynamic HTML (DHTML)

Click any of the popular questions about DHTML below to see its answer.

What is Dynamic HTML?

Is DHTML a new language?

How does DHTML work?

What can I do with DHTML?

What do I need to learn to use DHTML?

What are Cascading Style Sheets?

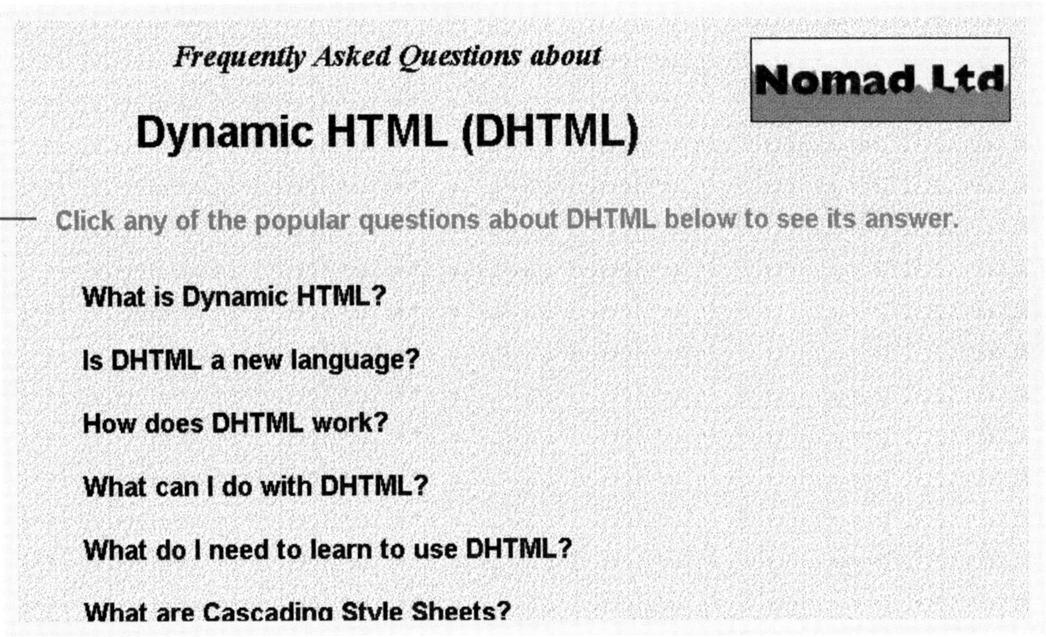

Practice

▶ Concepts Review

Label each DHTML item marked in Figure J-18.

FIGURE J-18

```
1 ──── <LINK REL="stylesheet" HREF="nomadltd.css" TYPE="text/css">

        <SCRIPT LANGUAGE="JavaScript">
        <!--
2 ──── NS4 = (document.layers) ? 1:0;
        IE4 = (document.all) ? 1:0;
        //-->
        </SCRIPT>

3 ──── <STYLE TYPE="text/css">
        <!--
        H1 {font-family: arial, sans-serif; font-size: 20pt}
        H2 {font-family: "times new roman", times, serif; font-size: 14pt; font-
        style: italic}
4 ──── .question {font-family: "times new roman", times, serif; font-size: 12pt;
        font-weight: bold}
        //-->
        </STYLE>

        </HEAD>

5 ──── <BODY BACKGROUND="Egg shell.jpg">
        <DIV STYLE="font-color: navy; text-decoration:underline" ALIGN="center">
        <H2>Frequently Asked Questions about</H2>
        <H1>Dynamic HTML (DHTML)</H1></DIV>
```

Match each term with its description.

6. **Inline style**
7. **Embedded style**
8. **External style**
9. **Cascading**
10. **Class**

a. System of precedence among style-sheet levels
b. Style associated with tags in Web page header
c. Style specified in local occurrence of tag
d. Named set of style specifications created as a tag attribute
e. Style specified in separate linked document

Select the best answer from the list of choices.

11. The most efficient method for assigning style to several text blocks marked with the same tag on one Web page is
    a. Inline style.
    b. Embedded style.
    c. External style.
    d. Linked style.

12. Embedded style sheets begin and end with which tagset?
    a. <SCRIPT> .. </SCRIPT>
    b. <STYLE> .. </STYLE>
    c. <STYLESHEET> .. </STYLESHEET>
    d. <CSS> .. </CSS>

13. **A browser-detection script**
    a. Makes your page's DHTML features viewable with any browser.
    b. Tells the user's browser which version of HTML your page uses.
    c. Tells the user's browser which version of JavaScript your page uses.
    d. Determines and stores the user's browser brand and generation.

14. **Which HTML tags does an external style sheet contain?**
    a. An external style sheet contains no HTML tags.
    b. <SCRIPT> .. </SCRIPT>
    c. <STYLE> .. </STYLE>
    d. <SCRIPT> .. </SCRIPT> and <STYLE> .. </STYLE>

15. **Which HTML tag do you use to associate an external style sheet with a Web page?**
    a. <LINK>
    b. <A>
    c. <CSS>
    d. <STYLE>

▶ Skills Review

1. **Create an embedded style sheet.**
    a. Open the file HTML J-9.htm, then save it as a text document with the filename Tours FAQ embedded style.htm.
    b. Select the text [replace with embedded style sheet], press [Delete], type <STYLE TYPE="text/css">, press [Enter], then type <!-- and press [Enter].
    c. Type H1 {font-family: "comic sans ms", arial, sans-serif; font-size: 20pt} and press [Enter].
    d. Type H2 {font-family: "times new roman", times, bookman, serif; font-size: 16pt; font-style: italic} and press [Enter].
    e. Type //--> and press [Enter], then type </STYLE>.
    f. Check the document for errors, make changes as necessary, then save Tours FAQ embedded style.htm as a text document.
    g. Open your Web browser, then open Tours FAQ embedded style.htm to view the Web page.

2. **Create a class.**
    a. Open the file HTML J-10.htm in your text editor, then save it as a text document with the filename Tours FAQ class.htm.
    b. Select the text [replace with class style] in the embedded style sheet, then press [Delete].
    c. Type .title {font-family: garamond, arial, helvetica, sans-serif; font-size: 16pt; font-weight: bold}.
    d. Select the text [replace with class] in the <DIV> tag for the first bulleted list item, then press [Delete].
    e. Type CLASS="title".
    f. Repeat Steps d and e for the remaining two bulleted titles.
    g. Check the document for errors, make changes as necessary, then save Tours FAQ class.htm as a text document.
    h. Open Tours FAQ class.htm in your browser, then view the document.

3. **Detect browsers.**
    a. Open the file HTML J-11.htm in your text editor, then save it as a text document with the filename Tours FAQ browser detect.htm.
    b. Select the text [replace with browser detection script], then press [Delete].

c. Type the following script, pressing [Enter] at the end of each line:

```
<SCRIPT LANGUAGE="javascript">
<!--
NS4 = (document.layers) ? 1:0;
E4 = (document.all) ? 1:0;
//-->
</SCRIPT>
```

d. Check the document for errors, then make changes as necessary.

e. Save Tours FAQ browser detect.htm as a text document.

f. Open Tours FAQ browser detect.htm in your browser, then debug if necessary.

4. Show and hide page elements.

a. Open the file HTML J-12.htm in your text editor, then save it as a text document with the filename Tours FAQ show and hide.htm.

b. Scroll down and select the text [replace with expandIE function], then press [Delete].

c. Type the following code, pressing [Enter] at the end of each line

```
function expandIE(el) {
        theEl=eval(el + "ExpI");
        if (theEl.style.display == "none") {
                theEl.style.display="block";
                theEl.expanded=true;
        }
        else {
                theEl.style.display="none";
                theEl.expanded=false;
        }
}
```

d. Scroll down to the <DIV> tag for the first list item "Athlete", select the text [replace with opening A tag] and the space following it, then press [Delete].

e. Type <A HREF="#" onClick="expand('one'); return false">

f. Replace the text [replace with closing A tag] on the next line with </A>.

g. Repeat Steps d through f for the remaining two tour titles, substituting 'two' for 'one' in item two, and so forth.

h. Check the document for errors, making changes as necessary, then save Tours FAQ show and hide.htm as a text document.

i. Open Tours FAQ show and hide.htm in your browser, then click the first title "Athlete".

5. Change font size dynamically.

a. Open the file HTML J-13.htm in your text editor, then save it as a text document with the filename Tours FAQ text size.htm.

b. Scroll down the page, select the text [replace with text size functions], press [Delete], then type the following functions, pressing [Enter] at the end of each line

```
function changeText(whichTitle) {
        if (Nav4) {return}
        whichTitle.style.fontSize="24pt";
}
function changeTextBack(whichTitle) {
        if (Nav4) {return}
```

```
                  whichTitle.style.fontSize="12pt";
              }
```

   c. Scroll down the page to select the text [replace with event handlers] in the opening <A> tag for the first tour title "Athlete", then press [Delete].

   d. Type onMouseOver="changeText(this)" onMouseOut="changeTextBack(this)".

   e. Repeat Steps c and d for the remaining two list items.

   f. Check the document for errors, make changes as necessary, then save Tours FAQ text size.htm as a text document.

   g. Open the file Tours FAQ text size.htm in your browser, then move the pointer over the first heading.

6. Control font color dynamically.

   a. Open the file HTML J-14.htm in your text editor, then save it as a text document with the filename Tours FAQ text color.htm.

   b. Select the text [replace with changeText color] in the changeText function in the page header, then press [Delete].

   c. Type whichTitle.style.color="#236B8E";

   d. Select the text [replace with changeTextBack color] in the changeTextBack function in the page header, then press [Delete].

   e. Type whichTitle.style.color="#000000";

   f. Check the document for errors, making changes as necessary, then save Tours FAQ text color.htm as a text document.

   g. Open the file Tours FAQ text color.htm in your browser, then move the pointer over the first heading.

7. Use an external style sheet.

   a. Open the file HTML J-15.htm, then save it as a text document with the filename Tours FAQ external style.htm.

   b. Scroll down the page, select the text [replace with LINK tag] before the opening <STYLE> tag, then press [Delete].

   c. Type <LINK REL="stylesheet" HREF="nomadltd.css" TYPE="text/css">.

   d. Check the file for errors, make changes as necessary, then save Tours FAQ external style.htm as a text document.

   e. Open the file FAQ external style.htm in your Web browser and notice the green color added to the instruction text.

▶ Independent Challenges

1. As you update and expand the Sandhills Regional Public Transit Web site, you decide to incorporate DHTML features into your pages. Currently, you are working to make a page on rider tips more interactive and easier to read. You decide to add dynamic size and color to the items on this page.

   To complete this independent challenge:

   a. Open the file HTML J-16.htm in your text editor, then save it as a text document with the filename SRPT rider tips.htm.

   b. Select the text [replace with style sheet link] in the head section, press [Delete], then type <LINK REL=stylesheet HREF="HTML J-17.css" TYPE="text/css"> and save SRPT rider tips.htm as a text document.

   c. Select the text [replace with script], press [Delete], and type the following script, pressing [Enter] at the end of each line.

```
<SCRIPT LANGUAGE="javascript">
<!--
Nav4 = (document.layers) ? 1:0;
IE4 = (document.all) ? 1:0;

function changeText(whichTitle) {
```

```
        if (Nav4) {return}
        whichTitle.style.fontSize="24pt";
        whichTitle.style.color="#FF6347"
    }


    function changeTextBack(whichTitle) {
        if (Nav4) {return}
        whichTitle.style.fontSize="16pt";
        whichTitle.style.color="#000000";
    }


    //-->
    </SCRIPT>
```

d. Select the text [replace with event handlers] in the opening <DIV> tag for each of the five tips, press [Delete], then type onMouseOver="changeText(this)" onMouseOut="changeTextBack(this)"

e. Save SRPT rider tips.htm as a text document.

f. Start your browser, cancel any dial-up activities, open SRPT rider tips.htm, then move the cursor over the tips to verify that they change color and increase in font size.
Note: This change will only be noticeable if you are using Internet Explorer 4.

g. If necessary, edit the code in your text editor until the DHTML features work in IE4, and save SRPT rider tips.htm as a text file.

2. While reorganizing the Community Public School Volunteers Web publication, you decide that the pages should have a uniform style. You think the easiest way to create and apply this style would be to make an external style sheet and link each page to it.

To complete this independent challenge:

a. Open the file HTML J-18.htm in your text editor, then save it as a text document with the filename CPSV home.htm.

b. Select the text of the embedded style sheet in the head section, including the opening and closing <STYLE> tags, then copy it to the Clipboard.

c. Open a new text file in your text editor, paste the style sheet from the Clipboard into it, then save this file as a text document with the name CPSV style.css.

d. Reopen CPSV home.htm in your text editor, delete the embedded style sheet from the head section, replace it with <LINK REL=stylesheet HREF="CPSV style.css" TYPE="text/css"> and save CPSV home.htm as a text document.

e. Open CPSV home.htm in your Web browser and notice the formatting created by the external style sheet.

f. If necessary, use your text editor to edit and save your document until it displays correctly.

3. The Green House plant store's most heavily viewed Web page lists popular items available at the store, along with descriptions and prices. The owners would like you to add DHTML features to this page. You decide to convert the list to an expanding outline.

To complete this independent challenge:

a. Open the file HTML J-19.htm in your text editor, then save it as a text document with the filename Green House supplies.htm.

b. Select the text [replace with LINK tag], press [Delete], then type <LINK REL="stylesheet" HREF="HTML J-20.css" TYPE="text/css"> and save Green House supplies.htm as a text document.

c. Select the text [replace with script], press [Delete], then type the following script, pressing [Enter] at the end of each line
Nav4 = (document.layers) ? 1:0;
IE4 = (document.all) ? 1:0;

```
ver4 =(Nav4 || IE4)?1:0;

function expandIE(el) {
    theEl=eval(el + "Desc");
    if (theEl.style.display == "none") {
            theEl.style.display="block";
            theEl.expanded=true;
    }
    else {
            theEl.style.display="none";
            theEl.expanded=false;
    }
}

function changeText(whichProduct) {
    if (Nav4) {return}
    whichProduct.style.fontSize="24pt";
    whichProduct.style.color="#215E21";
}

function changeTextBack(whichProduct) {
    if (Nav4) {return}
    whichProduct.style.fontSize="14pt";
    whichProduct.style.color="#000000";
}
```

d. In the <DIV> tag for the first product name, Potting soil, select the text [replace with opening A tag], press [Delete], then type <A HREF="#" onClick="expand('one'); return false"; onMouseOver="changeText(this)" onMouseOut="changeTextBack(this)">

e. Replace the text [replace with closing A tag] on the next line with </A>.

f. Repeat Steps d and e for the remaining four product names, replacing 'one' with 'two' for the second item, and so forth, then save Green House supplies.htm as a text document.

g. Open your browser, open Green House supplies.htm, then move the cursor over a heading and click it. *Note*: The text size and color events work only in Internet Explorer 4.

h. If necessary, edit the code in your text editor until the expanding outline works and the text size and color changes work in IE4, then save Green House supplies.htm as a text document.

WEB WORK

4. Even though it's complicated, many Web page designers have created cross-browser code to create text-rollover effects in both major fourth-generation browsers. To complete this independent challenge, open a search engine and search on one or more keywords, such as DHTML, cross-browser, or rollover. Using the results from the search engine, open and investigate Web sites that provide tutorials or articles on creating DHTML to find a sample of cross-browser text-rollover code. Print the code, along with any accompanying explanation. After reading the article and scanning the code, make a list on a separate sheet of paper of the compromises the designer found necessary when creating the code. Count the number of code lines necessary to create this feature and, if possible, total those used exclusively by each browser. Submit your printouts and your list to your instructor.

HTML

▶ **Visual Workshop**

Add the dynamic size and color features shown in Figure J-19 to each of the five bulleted items in the file HTML J-21.htm. Open HTML J-21 in your text editor, then save it as a text document with the filename Books.htm. Use the script listed in Independent Challenge 1, Step 3 in the page's head section. Use the code from Independent Challenge 1, Step C, in the opening <DIV> tags for the elements that will change color and size. Substitute the color #8E2323 (firebrick), or another color of your choice, to provide contrast to the background.

FIGURE J-19

Book ordering guidelines

In order to search for a book we don't have in stock, we need as much information as you have about it. At a minimum, we recommend one of the following:

- Author's name

- **Full book title**

⌈HTML⌋

Unit K

Controlling
Content Dynamically

▶ **Understand dynamic content**
▶ **Insert content dynamically**
▶ **Delete content dynamically**
▶ **Modify content dynamically**
▶ **Incorporate an advanced content function**
▶ **Replace graphics dynamically**
▶ **Bind data**
▶ **Manipulate bound data dynamically**

Just as dynamic HTML (DHTML) allows you to create pages whose style changes instantly based on user actions, it also provides tools that allow users to immediately modify a page's content. You can use this feature, known as **dynamic content**, to generate all or part of the page when it is opened, or even to alter the page's contents in response to user events. ✎ The manager of Nomad Ltd's retail division has heard about dynamic HTML and has asked Lydia to add dynamic content features to some of their Web pages to increase their interactivity. Lydia plans to use dynamic content features that will allow users to adapt the pages to their needs.

Unit K HTML

Understanding Dynamic Content

Dynamic HTML includes many tools for altering a Web page's appearance in response to user actions. Using scripts to change text attributes such as color and font size alter the style of elements, leaving the elements themselves, such as text or images, unchanged. Dynamic content tools, however, allow your Web page elements to move or change based on user input. These changes can include the elements themselves as well as the HTML tags associated with elements. Dynamic content can create an effect similar to an expanding outline. The outline actually uses a style attribute, "display" or "appearance," to simply show or hide text while the text remains part of the Web page. True dynamic content involves element reordering and replacing. As she learns about dynamic content, Lydia identifies several of its main uses and thinks about ways she can use it on the Nomad Ltd Web site.

Pointing

Dynamic content allows you to change an element in response to a user's mouse pointer movements. You already have learned about the formatting changes you can create using dynamic style. Now, using dynamic content, you can make your page's text and graphic contents available to user changes. Figure K-1 shows a Web page displaying an alternate graphic in response to user pointing.

Run-time activities

Dynamic content tools can create portions of your Web pages for you at **run time**, the period when a browser first interprets and displays the Web page and runs scripts. A simple case would be a script that displays the text "Good Morning!" or "Good Evening!" based on the time of day according to your computer's clock. You also can program a page to generate a table of contents for the page at run time, which allows you to change the page's structure and contents without also revising the TOC each time you make a change.

HTML tables

In addition to standard tools for working with Web page text, dynamic content includes special features for easily creating and working with tables. You can use dynamic content tools to associate an external database with a Web page, a process known as **data binding**. Data binding allows the user's browser to generate a Web page table from an external data file at run time. By adding some lines of script, you also can allow users to sort the table right on your Web page. Figure K-2 shows a dynamically generated table in a Web page that has been sorted by the Web page user.

FIGURE K-1: Dynamic content responding to user pointing

Color graphic replaces original line art in response to pointer

As you narrow your choices, click the Remove button for each tent that you're no longer considering, to remove it from the page.

Tent footprints and descriptions

XTC Starlite
One of the lightest, most compact three-season tents available. Featuring two-pole clip design with a built-in vestibule.

[Remove Starlite]

Line art of tent design

Amano Brevifolia
The simple, vaulted design characterized by two doors and two vestibules returns with the 2000 Brevifolia model. New features include: ground level, rainfly with vents, and vaulted sleeves for smoother pole feeding.

[Remove Brevifolia]

Amano Trifolia

FIGURE K-2: Table sorted by user

Bound data not sorted

Tent	Catalog number	Area (sq ft)	Vestibule (sq ft)	Description	Capacity	Weight	Price
XTC Starlite	BR-370	34	10	Staked	1 person	4 lbs. 3 oz.	$150
Amano Brevifolia	BT-356	38.5	19.6	Freestanding	2 people	5 lbs. 8 oz.	$215
Amano Trifolia	BT-358	49	25.7	Freestanding	2 people	7 lbs.	$250
Vista Hillside	BZ-339	32	15.3	Staked	1 person	4 lbs.	$120
Vista Hilltop	BZ-367	37.5	19.5			5 lbs. 3	
Vista Peak	BZ-323	42.5	24.4				
Vista Summit	BZ-334	51.5	28				

For more information on Nomad Ltd outdoor sup

Table sorted in response to click on column head

Tent	Catalog number	Area (sq ft)	Vestibule (sq ft)	Description	Capacity	Weight	Price
XTC Starlite	BR-370	34	10	Staked	1 person	4 lbs. 3 oz.	$150
Vista Hillside	BZ-339	32	15.3	Staked	1 person	4 lbs.	$120
Vista Hilltop	BZ-367	37.5	19.5	Staked	1 person	5 lbs. 3 oz.	$160
Amano Brevifolia	BT-356	38.5	19.6	Freestanding	2 people	5 lbs. 8 oz.	$215
Vista Peak	BZ-323	42.5	24.4	Freestanding	2 people	6 lbs. 3 oz.	$210
Amano Trifolia	BT-358	49	25.7	Freestanding	2 people	7 lbs.	$250
Vista Summit	BZ-334	51.5	28	Freestanding	2 people	7 lbs. 10 oz.	$275

For more information on Nomad Ltd outdoor supplies, please email our sales department

CLUES TO USE

Dynamic HTML features are not discrete

Although you can divide dynamic HTML effects into categories, such as dynamic style and dynamic content, the tools you use to create these effects often overlap. For example, to implement cross-browser dynamic style, you often need to identify the brand of the user's browser and then add lines to the embedded style sheet that are appropriate for the browser. Because you are adding code to the Web page at run time, this is a use of dynamic content to create dynamic style! As you learn more DHTML features and tools, their implementation will overlap increasingly.

HTML

Inserting Content Dynamically

Adding content at run time with scripts can allow you to create impressively customized and versatile Web pages. Because the DOM provides access to all the elements of a Web page, you can use scripts to alter any page elements based on conditions on the user's computer or on the page's current contents. Lydia's first project for the retail department is a Web page that compares the tents that Nomad Ltd sells. She wants to add a statement announcing the number of tent models that users can read about on the page. She can use a script to count the number of tent descriptions on the page and then insert the number dynamically in the page header statement that appears at the bottom of the page when the page loads. This means that the page header statement will still show the correct number even after the sales department adds to or removes tents and their descriptions from its tent selection.

Steps

1. Start your Web browser program and cancel any dial-up activities, then open the file **HTML K-1.htm**

   The page shows each tent's floor plan, or footprint, along with the tent's description.

2. Start your text editor program, open the file **HTML K-1.htm**, then save it as text document with the filename **Tent count.htm**

   Lydia has included a function in the page header that counts the number of tent-description headings in the page and assigns the number to the variable totalTents.

3. Scroll to the bottom of the page code, highlight the text **[replace with tent count code]**, then press **[Delete]**

   QuickTip

   Be sure to type a space after the word *describes* and a space before the word *tent*.

   browser detection - internet explorer

4. Type the following code, pressing **[Enter]** at the end of each line

   ```
   <SCRIPT>
   <!--
   if (IE4) {
       countHeaders()
       document.write("<H1 ALIGN='center'>This page describes ")
       document.write(totalTents)
       document.write(" tent models.</H1>")
   }
   //-->
   </SCRIPT>
   ```

   Figure K-3 shows the completed Web page code containing the script. The code formats the text "This page describes" and "tent models." as centered on the page with an H1 format. Between the two bits of text, the script uses the document.write method to insert the value counted by the countHeaders function, which is assigned to the variable "totalTents." Because the script that counts the headers works only in Internet Explorer 4, the script begins by checking the browser version.

5. Check your document for errors, make changes as necessary, then save Tent count.htm as a text document

6. Open **Tent count.htm** in your Web browser, then scroll to the bottom of the page

   Figure K-4 shows the Web page in Internet Explorer 4. The H1 text Lydia added appears near the bottom of the page. The statement includes the number of tents counted by the countHeaders function and inserted with a script.

FIGURE K-3: Completed Web page code

```
<DIV ID="tent7" name="tent">

<DIV CLASS="tenthead"><IMG SRC="summit.jpg" ALIGN="left">Vista Summit</DIV>

<DIV>Comfortable, rugged, 4-season tent. Quick setup, full rainfly, integral
vestibule, large door. Factory sealed, mesh window and door for
ventilation.</DIV><BR><BR>

<H2 ALIGN="center">Nomad Ltd has a tent that's right for you!</H2>

<SCRIPT>
<!--
if (IE4) {
      countHeaders()
      document.write("<H1 ALIGN='center'>This page describes ")
      document.write(totalTents)
      document.write(" tent models.</H1>")
}
//-->
</SCRIPT>

<DIV>For more information on Nomad Ltd outdoor supplies, please email our <A
HREF="MAILTO:sales@nomadltd.com">sales department</A></DIV>

</BODY>
</HTML>
```

Text and script for tent count statement

FIGURE K-4: Web page displaying tent count

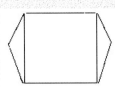
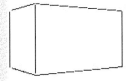

pockets.

Vista Peak
Easy setup, 3-season tent for 2. Two doors with vestibules offer easy access and protected sotrage space. Mesh ceiling panel for view and ventilation. Factory sealed, with vestibule and interior pockets.

Vista Summit
Comfortable, rugged, 4-season tent. Quick setup, full rainfly, integral vestibule, large door. Factory sealed, mesh window and door for ventilation.

Nomad Ltd has a tent that's right for you!

This page describes 7 tent models.

For more information on Nomad Ltd outdoor supplies, please email our <u>sales department</u>

Total calculated by counting script

Deleting Content Dynamically

In addition to adding Web page elements dynamically at run time, you can script your Web page to allow users to tailor it to suit their needs. For example, some scripts can allow users to delete elements from a Web page, including text and graphics. This feature—especially useful in a content-laden page—allows the user to pare down the content in order to view only pertinent elements or sections. ▟▆▅▆▅▖ Because users of the tent comparison page will be trying to select a tent based on their needs, Lydia thinks it would be helpful to allow users to remove information they are not interested in from the page for tents.

1. Open the file **HTML K-2.htm** in your text editor, then save it as a text document with the filename **Tent delete.htm**

2. Scroll down the page to view the body text describing the first tent, the XTC Starlite, select the text **[insert button code for tent1]**, then press **[Delete]**

3. Type the following code, pressing **[Enter]** at the end of each line
   ```
   <SCRIPT LANGUAGE="javascript">
   <!--
   if (IE4) {
   ```

Trouble?

To specify the null value, be sure to type single quotes after HTML=.

4. Press **[Tab]**, then type **document.write("<BUTTON CLASS='button' onClick=tent1.outerHTML=''>Remove Starlite</BUTTON>")** and press **[Enter]**
   The <BUTTON> tag set creates a button with a customized function in Internet Explorer 4 only. The text between the tags is the label that appears on the button. Lydia has inserted a class definition called .button in the page's embedded style sheet. She uses the onClick event handler to change the outerHTML property of the object named tent1, which includes the description and graphic for the first tent. An element's outerHTML property includes the element contents and the tags surrounding it, so changing the property to a null value removes the element and its surrounding tags from the Web page.

5. Type **}** and press **[Enter]**, then type the following closing script tags, pressing **[Enter]** at the end of each line
   ```
   //-->
   </SCRIPT>
   ```

6. Repeat Steps 2 through 5 for the remaining six tent descriptions, substituting the button object names and tent names as listed in Table K-1
   Figure K-5 shows the Web page containing the button code for the first two tent descriptions.

7. Check the document for errors, make changes as necessary, then save Tent delete.htm as a text document

8. Open **Tent delete.htm** in your Web browser and scroll down the page until the Amano Brevifolia description appears in the document window
   Internet Explorer 4 displays the "Remove Brevifolia" button, but other browsers do not show the buttons. Even though the function for deleting content only works in Internet Explorer 4, your cross-browser Web page still displays the basic tent information in other browsers without causing JavaScript errors.

9. If you are using Internet Explorer, click the **Remove Brevifolia button**
   As Figure K-6 shows, the Web browser removes the tent's description and graphic. Next, Lydia will need to be sure the counter reflects this change by updating the number of tent descriptions displayed.

FIGURE K-5: Web page containing code for delete buttons

Code for first delete button —

Tent ID —

Code for second delete button —

Button text —

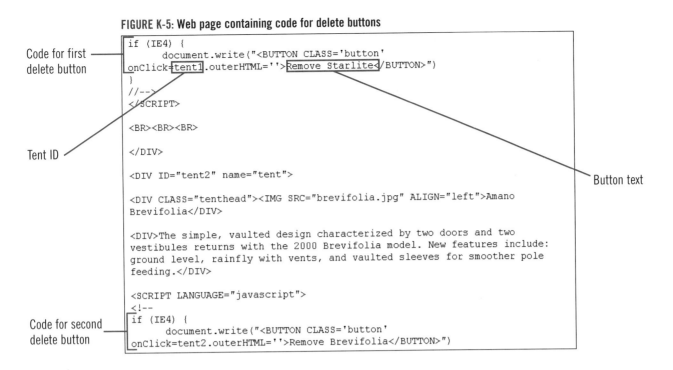

```
if (IE4) {
        document.write("<BUTTON CLASS='button'
onClick=tent1.outerHTML=''>Remove Starlite</BUTTON>")
}
//-->
</SCRIPT>

<BR><BR><BR>

</DIV>

<DIV ID="tent2" name="tent">

<DIV CLASS="tenthead"><IMG SRC="brevifolia.jpg" ALIGN="left">Amano
Brevifolia</DIV>

<DIV>The simple, vaulted design characterized by two doors and two
vestibules returns with the 2000 Brevifolia model. New features include:
ground level, rainfly with vents, and vaulted sleeves for smoother pole
feeding.</DIV>

<SCRIPT LANGUAGE="javascript">
<!--
if (IE4) {
        document.write("<BUTTON CLASS='button'
onClick=tent2.outerHTML=''>Remove Brevifolia</BUTTON>")
```

FIGURE K-6: Web page with Brevifolia removed

Brevifolia deleted from position between Starlite and Trifolia —

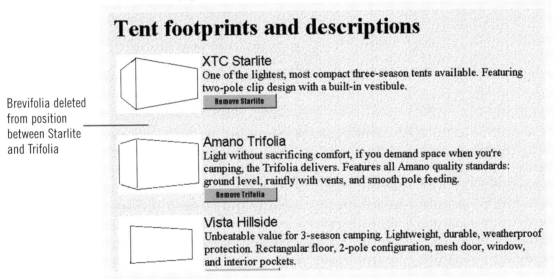

TABLE K-1: Tent description IDs and button text

description number	substitute for "tent1"	substitute for "Starlite"
2	tent2	Brevifolia
3	tent3	Trifolia
4	tent4	Hillside
5	tent5	Hilltop
6	tent6	Peak
7	tent7	Summit

Modifying Content Dynamically

Dynamic content doesn't stop at adding or deleting static Web page content. Also, you can create pages that allow their contents to change in response to various events. You can use this feature to create a basic useful function, such as a DHTML clock, as part of a Web page. A DHTML clock function changes the contents of a text element displaying the time (for example, once per second) in response to the passing of time. You also can add interactivity by modifying page content in response to user actions. Because her page allows users to remove descriptions for tents that don't fit their needs, Lydia wants to ensure that the statement showing the number of tents available displays the correct number after user deletions.

Steps 1 2 3 4

Span use to make as object

1. Open the file **HTML K-3.htm** in your text editor, save it as a text document with the filename **Tent update.htm**, then scroll down the page until the function reCount appears in the document window

   not include tags & only contents

   Notice that Lydia has added the function named reCount. The function reCount subtracts 1 from the total count of tent descriptions on the page and then uses the **innerHTML** property to update the number that appears in the statement at the bottom of the page. InnerHTML replaces an element but leaves its enclosing HTML tags intact. Lydia uses innerHTML because she wants to replace only the number, which is within HTML tags, and not any of the surrounding text or HTML tags. Lydia has written the code so that each of the buttons that removes a tent description from the page triggers the reCount function.

2. Scroll down the page until the opening <BUTTON> tag for tent1 appears

   Notice that Lydia has added a reference to the reCount function in the onClick event handler. She has added this reference for each of the buttons.

3. Scroll to the bottom of the Web page code, select the text **[replace with code to write opening SPAN tag]**, then press **[Delete]**

4. Type **document.write("<SPAN ID='textnum'<>")**   *Type*

5. Select the text **[replace with code to write closing SPAN tag]**, press **[Delete]**, then type **document.write("</SPAN>")**

   Figure K-7 shows the completed code containing the SPAN tags. By inserting the SPAN tags with an ID value, you create an inline object named "textnum" that you can manipulate with scripts. Lydia's reCount function changes textnum's innerHTML property each time the user clicks one of the delete buttons. This use of dynamic content keeps the contents of the Web page statement current with page changes produced by user actions.

6. Check your document for errors, make changes as necessary, then save **Tent update.htm** as a text document

7. Open **Tent update.htm** in your Web browser, then scroll to the bottom of the page

   In Internet Explorer 4, notice that the tent description total, which is currently 7, displays in the statement.

8. If you are using Internet Explorer, click the **Remove Summit button**

   The browser removes the description for the Vista Summit tent. Simultaneously, it updates the tent description total to 6, as Figure K-8 shows.

9. If you are using Internet Explorer, click the **Remove Hilltop button**

   The browser removes the Vista Hilltop description, and again changes the tent total to reflect the current number of descriptions on the page.

FIGURE K-7: **Code containing SPAN tags**

JavaScript to write opening and closing SPAN tags inserted

```
</SCRIPT>

<BR><BR>

</DIV>

<H2 ALIGN="center">Nomad Ltd has a tent that's right for you!</H2>

<SCRIPT>
<!--
if (IE4) {
      countHeaders()
      document.write("<H1 ALIGN='center'>This page describes ")
      document.write("<SPAN ID='textnum'>")
      document.write(totalTents)
      document.write("</SPAN>")
      document.write(" tent models.</H1>")
}
//-->
</SCRIPT>

<DIV>For more information on Nomad Ltd outdoor supplies, please email our <A
HREF="MAILTO:sales@nomadltd.com">sales department</A></DIV>

</BODY>
</HTML>
```

FIGURE K-8: **Web page displaying updated total**

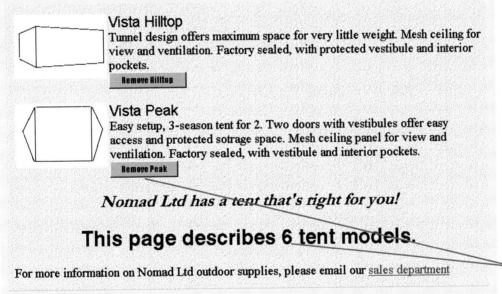

Vista Hilltop
Tunnel design offers maximum space for very little weight. Mesh ceiling for view and ventilation. Factory sealed, with protected vestibule and interior pockets.

Remove Hilltop

Vista Peak
Easy setup, 3-season tent for 2. Two doors with vestibules offer easy access and protected sotrage space. Mesh ceiling panel for view and ventilation. Factory sealed, with vestibule and interior pockets.

Remove Peak

Nomad Ltd has a tent that's right for you!

This page describes 6 tent models.

For more information on Nomad Ltd outdoor supplies, please email our sales department

Tent total updated to 6 because Summit tent description deleted

CLUES TO USE

Tool Tips and other floating help

In both Internet Explorer and Netscape Navigator, you can create floating windows that display text relevant to an element when the user moves the cursor over it. This effect is similar to ToolTips in Microsoft applications. These windows are dynamic modifications of the page content in response to user actions. For images, you can use the ALT property to specify the text that displays in a floating window when the user holds the mouse pointer over the image. For other Web page elements, Netscape Navigator versions 3 and 4 require a script to add this effect. However, you can add this effect in Internet Explorer 4 by adding TITLE="text" to the opening tag for the element. Because these floating windows add and remove Web page text, they are part of your set of dynamic content tools.

HTML

Incorporating an Advanced Content Function

Combining different DHTML tools in your scripts allows for a great variety of possible new dynamic content effects, including different ways of presenting or changing your page elements. You can make your Web page unique as well as make it easier for users to read and navigate by incorporating special features into your Web page. These features also can increase your Web page readership. ~~〰️~~ Lydia sees a page on the Web containing a script that cycles through different Web page elements in the same spot. This effect is like a slide show, with each new segment of text appearing after a short interval. She decides to use this feature on the tent page she is developing to display some additional information about Nomad Ltd's products.

Steps

1. Open the file **HTML K-4.htm** in your text editor, save it as a text document with the filename **Tent cycle.htm**, then scroll down the page until the code for the function cycle appears in the document window

   Notice that Lydia entered the function cycle in the page head script. This function replaces an object's contents at regular intervals by using the innerHTML property in conjunction with the script for counting time.

2. Scroll down the Web page code until the top of the body section appears in the document window, select the text **[replace with text cycle script]**, then press **[Delete]**

3. Type the following script, pressing **[Enter]** at the end of each line:

   ```
   <SCRIPT LANGUAGE="javascript">
   <!--
   function addCycle() {
   ```

4. Press **[Tab]**, the type **cycle(txt1, "Hiking,Bicycling,Camping,Kayaking,Climbing, find all your gear at,nomadltd.com", 30)** and press **[Enter]**

   This line defines the display parameters for the text you want to cycle as follows: txt1 indicates the name of the object whose value will be cycled; the text in quotes separated by commas specifies the different words and phrases that should cycle; and the number 30 tells how long one word or phrase should display before cycling to the next word or phrase.

5. Type the remaining code, pressing **[Enter]** at the end of each line

   ```
   }
   if (IE4) {window.onload = new Function("addCycle()")}
   //-->
   </SCRIPT>
   ```

   Figure K-9 shows the Web page source code containing the completed script. This script triggers the function cycle, which begins to cycle text after the page loads.

6. Check your document for errors, make changes as necessary, then save Tent cycle.htm as a text document and open it in your Web browser

   In Internet Explorer 4, the cycling text appears in the top right corner of the page, as shown in Figure K-10. The text cycles at a regular 3-second interval as specified by 30 in the script.

FIGURE K-9: Page source containing script to call cycle function

```
<IMG SRC="nomad.jpg" ALIGN="left">

<DIV ID="txt1" ALIGN="right" CLASS="tenthead" STYLE="font-size: 18pt"></DIV>

<SCRIPT LANGUAGE="javascript">
<!--
function addCycle() {
      cycle(txt1, "Hiking,Bicycling,Camping,Kayaking,Climbing,find all your
gear at,nomadltd.com", 30)
}

if(IE4) {window.onload = new Function("addCycle()")}
//-->
</SCRIPT>

<BR><BR><BR>
<DIV ALIGN="center" STYLE="font-size: 24pt; font-weight: bold; font-family:
arial; font-style: normal">Tents</DIV>
<H2 ALIGN="center">Selecting one that's right for you</H2>
<BR>

<DIV>Choosing a quality tent that meets your needs can be an intimidating
task. To help you out with this important decision, we've added features to
this page to make it easier to compare the characteristics of our tents.
<BR><BR>
As you narrow your choices, click the Remove button for each tent that
```

Script to invoke text cycling function

Text content changes every few seconds

FIGURE K-10: Web page displaying cycling text

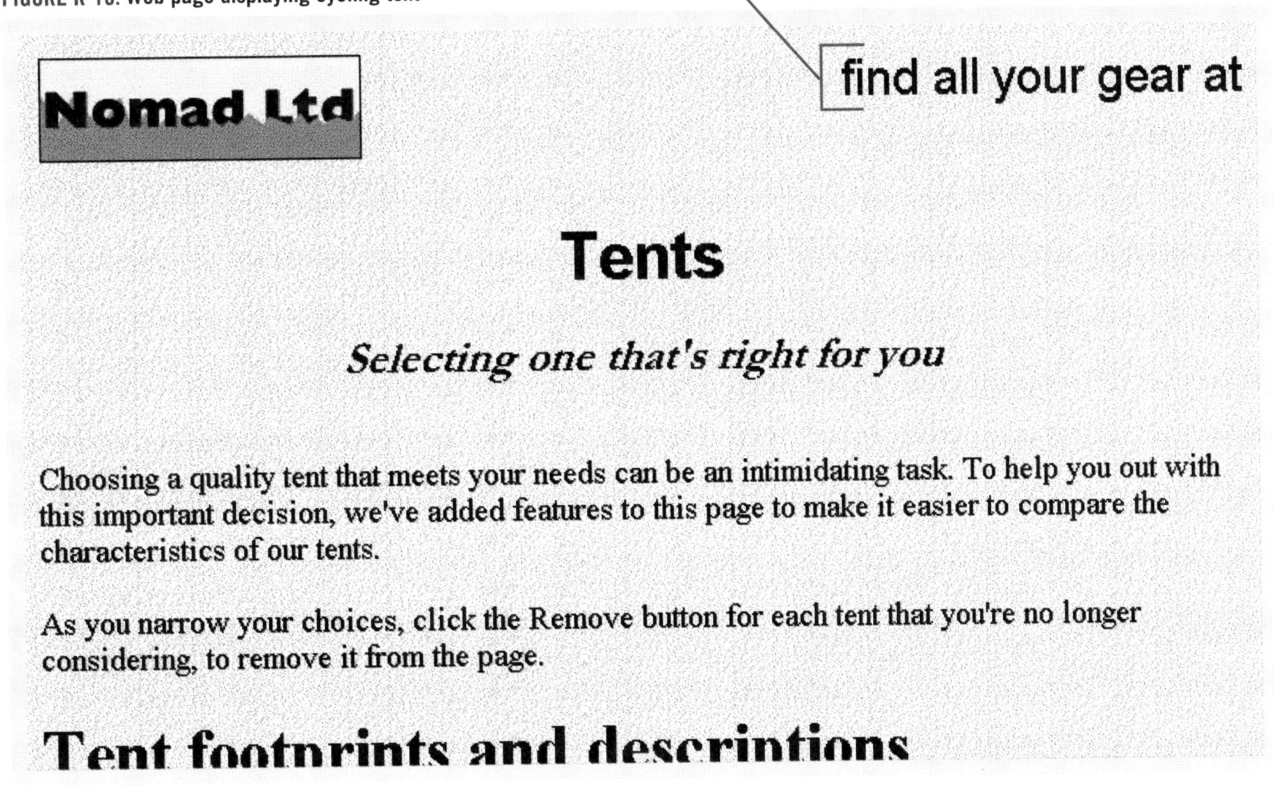

find all your gear at

Nomad Ltd

Tents

Selecting one that's right for you

Choosing a quality tent that meets your needs can be an intimidating task. To help you out with this important decision, we've added features to this page to make it easier to compare the characteristics of our tents.

As you narrow your choices, click the Remove button for each tent that you're no longer considering, to remove it from the page.

Tent footprints and descriptions

Replacing Graphics Dynamically

HTML

All the examples so far have used dynamic content tools to modify a Web page's text, but these features are equally valid for other page elements, including graphics. In a simple scenario, you can use dynamic content features to change the graphic displayed using the onMouseOver event handler. In a more complex scenario, you could gradually change a graphic's size to create the effect of animation. ✐ Lydia wants to use color to highlight the element that the user is currently pointing to. However, rather than using dynamic style, she creates colored versions of each of the tent footprint graphics. The color version of a text footprint graphic will appear in response to mouse movement over each graphic or its associated text.

Steps

1. Open the file **HTML K-5.htm** in your text editor, then save it as a text document with the filename **Tent color.htm**

2. Scroll down the Web page code until <DIV CLASS="tenthead"> appears in the document window, select the text [replace with star event handlers], then press [Delete]

3. Type onMouseOver="star.src='starcolor.jpg'" onMouseOut="star.src='starlite.jpg'"

4. Scroll down the Web page code, select the text [replace with brev event handlers], press [Delete], then type onMouseOver="brev.src='brevcolor.jpg'" onMouseOut="brev.src='brevifolia.jpg'"

   Figure K-11 shows the completed code for the first two tent items. Notice that the IMG tag for each tent has a unique ID attribute. The onMouseOver event swaps a color graphic of the tent floorplan for the original image source. The onMouseOut event replaces the color image with the original black and white graphic.

5. Repeat Step 4 for the remaining five list items, using the IDs and graphic files listed in Table K-2

6. Check your document for errors, make changes as necessary, then save **Tent color.htm** as a text document

7. Open **Tent color.htm** in your browser

8. Scroll down to the list of tent descriptions, then move your mouse pointer over the heading or graphic for the XTC Starlite

   See Figure K-12. When you move the cursor over the black and white outline or its associated heading in Internet Explorer 4, the image is replaced with a color graphic. Even though you are simply swapping one graphic for another, this action creates the illusion of modifying the original graphic, much like changing text color using style sheets.

9. Move the mouse pointer off the first list item

   The graphic changes back to the black and white version. Notice that if you move the mouse pointer over other tent graphics, they change color in response to the mouse movement.

use concept in design

FIGURE K-11: Event handlers for first and second list items

Event handlers
for Starlite
inserted in
DIV tag

ID attribute

IMG source

```
<DIV ID="tent1" name="tent">

<DIV CLASS="tenthead" onMouseOver="star.src='starcolor.jpg'"
onMouseOut="star.src='starlite.jpg'"><IMG SRC="starlite.jpg" ALIGN="left"
ID="star">XTC Starlite</DIV>
<DIV>One of the lightest, most compact three-season tents available.
Featuring two-pole clip design with a built-in vestibule.</DIV>

<SCRIPT LANGUAGE="javascript">
<!--
if (IE4) {
        document.write("<BUTTON CLASS='button'
onClick=tent1.outerHTML='',reCount()>Remove Starlite</BUTTON>")
}
//-->
</SCRIPT>

<BR><BR><BR>

</DIV>

<DIV ID="tent2" name="tent">

<DIV CLASS="tenthead" onMouseOver="brev.src='brevcolor.jpg'"
onMouseOut="brev.src='brevifolia.jpg'"><IMG SRC="brevifolia.jpg"
ALIGN="left" ID="brev">Amano Brevifolia</DIV>
```

Event handlers
for Brevifolia
inserted in
DIV tag

FIGURE K-12: Web page showing substituted graphic

Color graphic
replaces
original in
response to
pointer

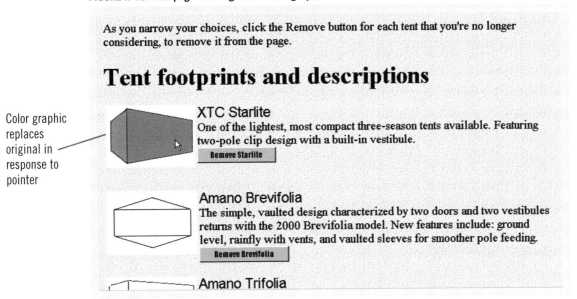

TABLE K-2: List item IDs and graphic filenames

list item	id	color graphic name (onMouseOver)	black and white graphic name (onMouseOut)
1	star	starcolor.jpg	starlite.jpg
2	brev	brevcolor.jpg	brevifolia.jpg
3	tri	trifolia.jpg	tricolor.jpg
4	hillside	hillsidecolor.jpg	hillside.jpg
5	hilltop	hilltopcolor.jpg	hilltop.jpg
6	peak	peakcolor.jpg	peak.jpg
7	summit	summitcolor.jpg	summit.jpg

HTML

HTML

Binding Data

DHTML's dynamic content tools offer specialized features for working with tables in your Web pages. One of the most powerful is dynamic table generation, first introduced in Internet Explorer 4. Instead of creating a table using a tag for each element, you can simply create the headers, then add code to reference data located in an external file. Linking an external database with a Web page is known as **data binding**. When the page loads, the browser creates the table at run time. Because the table is re-created each time a user opens the page, you can change the contents of the external data source without changing the Web page code. ◀▬▬ Because it's helpful for tent shoppers to be able to compare the details of different models, such as area and weight, Lydia decides to add a tent data table to the Web page. The sales department has provided a text file containing the appropriate information. Lydia binds the file to her Web page to create a dynamic table.

Steps

1. Open the file **HTML K-6.htm** in your text editor, then save it as a text document with the filename **Tent comparison table.htm**

2. Scroll to near the end of the code until the <OBJECT> tags and list of tent descriptions appears in the document window
   Figure K-13 shows the code including the OBJECT tags. These tags, which Lydia entered earlier, set up the external file containing the data for her table as a Web page object. The CLASSID attribute calls the Internet Explorer routine for dynamic table generation to format the linked data. The PARAM tags within the beginning and ending OBJECT tags denote parameters for this object. The DataURL parameter identifies the name of the external file to be bound, which is named tents.txt. The True value for the UseHeader attribute specifies that the data in the external file includes a row of information identifying the contents of each column.

3. Select the text **[replace with opening TABLE tag]**, press **[Delete]**, and type **<TABLE BORDER="1" ID="elemtbl" DATASRC="#tentlist">**
   The TABLE tag formats the code that follows as rows in a table. The DATASRC attribute refers to the preceding object, named "tentlist." The number sign indicates that the source is an object in the same Web page.

4. Scroll down, select the text **[replace with closing TABLE tag]**, press **[Delete]**, then type **</TABLE>**
   The rows within the TABLE tags contain row header display information and links to the columns in the external source. The DATAFLD attribute in each DIV tag names the column header in the external file that marks the column to be associated with the tag. Notice that below the closing TABLE tag, Lydia has inserted a script to display extra information for users not running IE4. Because these browsers will not display the bound data, Lydia provides another method for them to obtain the table information.

5. Check your document for errors, make changes as necessary, then save **Tent comparison table.htm** as a text document

6. Open **Tent comparison table.htm** in your browser, then scroll to the bottom of the page
   The tent comparison information from the bound data file appears in a table, as shown in Figure K-14. The sales department can add, remove, or edit lines from the external file, and the Web page table will automatically reflect the most current information each time the Web page is loaded.

FIGURE K-13: **OBJECT tags in Web page source**

Code to
format
imported
data

```
<OBJECT ID="tentlist" CLASSID="clsid:333C7BC4-460F-11D0-BC04-0080C7055A83">
      <PARAM NAME="DataURL" VALUE="tents.txt">
      <PARAM NAME="UseHeader" VALUE="True">
</OBJECT>

[replace with opening TABLE tag]

<THEAD>
<TR>
<TD><B><DIV ID=tent>Tent</DIV></B></TD>
<TD><B><DIV ID=catno>Catalog number</DIV></B></TD>
<TD><B><DIV ID=area>Area (sq ft)</DIV></B></TD>
<TD><B><DIV ID=vest>Vestibule (sq ft)</DIV></B></TD>
<TD><B><DIV ID=desc>Description</DIV></B></TD>
<TD><B><DIV ID=cap>Capacity</DIV></B></TD>
<TD><B><DIV ID=weight>Weight</DIV></B></TD>
<TD><B><DIV ID=price>Price</DIV></B></TD>
</TR>
</THEAD>
<TBODY>
<TR>
<TD><DIV DATAFLD="tent"></DIV></TD>
<TD><DIV DATAFLD="catno"></DIV></TD>
<TD><DIV DATAFLD="area"></DIV></TD>
```

FIGURE K-14: **Tent comparison table**

Browser-
generated
table based
on external
data source

Tent	Catalog number	Area (sq ft)	Vestibule (sq ft)	Description	Capacity	Weight	Price
XTC Starlite	BR-370	34	10	Staked	1 person	4 lbs. 3 oz.	$150
Amano Brevifolia	BT-356	38.5	19.6	Freestanding	2 people	5 lbs. 8 oz.	$215
Amano Trifolia	BT-358	49	25.7	Freestanding	2 people	7 lbs.	$250
Vista Hillside	BZ-339	32	15.3	Staked	1 person	4 lbs.	$120
Vista Hilltop	BZ-367	37.5	19.5	Staked	1 person	5 lbs. 3 oz.	$160
Vista Peak	BZ-323	42.5	24.4	Freestanding	2 people	6 lbs. 3 oz.	$210
Vista Summit	BZ-334	51.5	28	Freestanding	2 people	7 lbs. 10 oz.	$275

For more information on Nomad Ltd outdoor supplies, please email our sales department

Manipulating Bound Data Dynamically

In addition to dynamic table creation, Internet Explorer 4 introduced other cutting-edge tools for working with tables in Web pages. Perhaps one of the most useful is dynamic sorting, which enables users to sort the data in a table simply by clicking the relevant column heading. ✐━━━ To allow users to compare tent statistics based on the most important categories, Lydia adds a script that sorts the tent information on a given column when a user clicks that column heading.

Steps 1 2 3 4

1. Open the file **HTML K-7.htm** in your text editor, then save it as a text document with the filename **Tent sortable comparison table.htm**

2. Scroll down to the script beneath the table code near the bottom of the page until function tentClick() { is visible
   Notice that Lydia has already entered scripts to sort the table. She created a separate script for each column. Each script sorts the table by the contents of that column using the tentlist.Sort= command, and then regenerates the table to show the sort, with tentlist.Reset(). Accompanying each script is a line of code triggering the script in response to the onclick event for the given column header.

3. Scroll to the bottom of the page, select the text **[replace with price script]**, then press **[Delete]**

4. Type the following script, pressing **[Enter]** at the end of each line:
   ```
   function priceClick() {
       tentlist.Sort="price";
       tentlist.Reset();
   }
   price.onclick=priceClick;
   ```
   Figure K-15 shows the completed Web page containing the script.

5. Check the script you entered for errors, then save **Tent sortable comparison table.htm** as a text document

6. Open **Tent sortable comparison table.htm** in your Web browser, then scroll to the bottom of the page
   The tent comparison table displays in its default order. Notice that the Vestibule (sq ft) column is not displayed in any particular order.

7. Click the **Vestibule (sq ft)** column heading, then scroll down to see the regenerated table
   The table disappears, then regenerates to show the records in ascending order by vestibule area, as shown in Figure K-16.

8. Click the **Price** column heading, then scroll down
   The table displays the records in order by price, using the script you entered.

9. Close the Web browser and text editor

FIGURE K-15: Web page containing price-sorting script

Script for
sorting table
on the price
column

price Column ID for
column to be sorted

```
            tentlist.Sort="weight";
            tentlist.Reset();
    }

    weight.onclick=weightClick;

    function priceClick() {
        tentlist.Sort="price";
        tentlist.Reset();
    }

    price.onclick=priceClick;

    if (!IE4) {
        document.write("If your browser does not display the above table,
please email us at the address below for up-to-date tent details and
prices.<BR><BR>")
    }
    //-->
    </SCRIPT>

    <DIV>For more information on Nomad Ltd outdoor supplies, please email our <A
    HREF="MAILTO:sales@nomadltd.com">sales department</A></DIV>

    </BODY>
    </HTML>
```

Sorts column
in ascending
order by price

Regenerates
the table to
show the sort

FIGURE K-16: Table sorted on vestibule area column

Tent	Catalog number	Area (sq ft)	Vestibule (sq ft)	Description	Capacity	Weight	Price
XTC Starlite	BR-370	34	10	Staked	1 person	4 lbs. 3 oz.	$150
Vista Hillside	BZ-339	32	15.3	Staked	1 person	4 lbs.	$120
Vista Hilltop	BZ-367	37.5	19.5	Staked	1 person	5 lbs. 3 oz.	$160
Amano Brevifolia	BT-356	38.5	19.6	Freestanding	2 people	5 lbs. 8 oz.	$215
Vista Peak	BZ-323	42.5	24.4	Freestanding	2 people	6 lbs. 3 oz.	$210
Amano Trifolia	BT-358	49	25.7	Freestanding	2 people	7 lbs.	$250
Vista Summit	BZ-334	51.5	28	Freestanding	2 people	7 lbs. 10 oz.	$275

For more information on Nomad Ltd outdoor supplies, please email our sales department

Table sorted in response
to click on column head

Suppressing errors

When creating cross-browser code, you may want to add features to your pages that generate error messages in some browsers. To allow your information to get out to everyone who wants to view it without alarming viewers, you can include a script that keeps error messages from appearing in incompatible browsers. By setting the value of the object window.onerror to "null", you prevent error windows from opening when scripts have problems completing. Take care not to add error suppression until you have completed and debugged your page because error suppression removes an important debugging aid.

Practice

► Concepts Review

Label the code segments marked in Figure K-17.

FIGURE K-17

```
<DIV ID="tent1" name="tent">

<DIV CLASS="tenthead" onMouseOver="star.src='starcolor.jpg'"
onMouseOut="star.src='starlite.jpg'"><IMG SRC="starlite.jpg" ALIGN="left"
ID="star">XTC Starlite</DIV>
<DIV>One of the lightest, most compact three-season tents available.
Featuring two-pole clip design with a built-in vestibule.</DIV>

<SCRIPT LANGUAGE="javascript">
<!--
if (IE4) {
        document.write("<BUTTON CLASS='button'
onClick=tent1.outerHTML='',reCount()>Remove Starlite</BUTTON>")
}
//-->
</SCRIPT>

<BR><BR><BR>

</DIV>

<DIV ID="tent2" name="tent">

<DIV CLASS="tenthead" onMouseOver="brev.src='brevcolor.jpg'"
onMouseOut="brev.src='brevifolia.jpg'"><IMG SRC="brevifolia.jpg"
ALIGN="left" ID="brev">Amano Brevifolia</DIV>
```

5 — 2 — 4 — 1 — 3

Match each statement with the term that it decribes.

6. DHTML features that make immediate modifications to a page's actual content
7. Period when a browser first interprets and displays a Web page
8. Associating an external database with a Web page
9. HTML property for replacing an element and the HTML tags enclosing it
10. HTML property for replacing an element but leaving its enclosing HTML tags

a. Data binding
b. InnerHTML
c. Run time
d. OuterHTML
e. Dynamic content

Select the best answer from the list of choices.

11. The outerHTML for the code <DIV>Welcome to the Nomad Ltd home page!</DIV> is
    a. <DIV>Welcome to the Nomad Ltd home page!</DIV>.
    b. <DIV>Welcome to the Nomad Ltd home page!
    c. Welcome to the Nomad Ltd home page!.
    d. Welcome to the Nomad Ltd home page!</DIV>.

12. **A DHTML clock would be an example of**
   a. Deleting content.
   b. Modifying content.
   c. Adding content.
   d. Dynamic table generation

13. **Which HTML tag set do you use to list the properties for a dynamically generated table?**
   a. <TBL>..</TBL>
   b. <TABLE>..</TABLE>
   c. <THEAD>..</THEAD>
   d. <OBJECT>..</OBJECT>

 # Skills Review

1. **Insert content dynamically.**
   a. Open the file HTML K-8.htm in your text editor, then save it as a text document with the filename Pack count.htm.
   b. Scroll to the bottom of the Web page code, highlight the text [replace with pack count code], then press [Delete].
   c. Type the following code, pressing [Enter] at the end of each line:
   ```
   <SCRIPT>
   <!--
   if (IE4) {
        countHeaders()
        document.write("<H1 ALIGN='center'>This page describes ")
        document.write(totalPacks)
        document.write(" pack models.</H1>")
   }
   //-->
   </SCRIPT>
   ```
   d. Check your document for errors, make changes as necessary, then save Pack count.htm as a text document.
   e. Open Pack count.htm in your Web browser, then scroll down to the bottom of the page.

2. **Delete content dynamically.**
   a. Open the file HTML K-9.htm, then save it as a text document with the filename Pack delete.htm.
   b. Scroll down below the body text describing the first pack, the Nomad Moonlight, select the text [replace with button code for pack1], then press [Delete].
   c. Type the following code, pressing [Enter] at the end of each line:
   ```
   <SCRIPT LANGUAGE="javascript">
   <!--
   if (IE4) {
   ```
   d. Press [Tab], then type document.write("<BUTTON CLASS='button' onClick=pack1.outerHTML="">Remove Moonlight</BUTTON>") and press [Enter].
   e. Type } and press [Enter], then enter the two closing SCRIPT tags.
   f. Repeat Steps b through e for the remaining six pack descriptions, substituting the object names and pack names, as listed in Table K-3.

TABLE K-3

description number	substitute for "pack1"	substitute for "Moonlight"
2	pack2	Blue Moon
3	pack3	Harvest Moon
4	pack4	New Moon
5	pack5	Full Moon
6	pack6	Trekker
7	pack7	Long Haul

    g. Check the document for errors, make changes as necessary, then save Pack delete.htm as a text document.

    h. Open Pack delete.htm in your Web browser, then scroll down the Web page until the Nomad Blue Moon pack description appears in the document window.

    i. If you are using Internet Explorer, click the Remove Blue Moon button.

3. Modify content dynamically.

    a. Open the file HTML K-10.htm in your text editor, then save it as a text document with the filename Pack update.htm.

    b. Scroll to the bottom of the Web page code, select the text [replace with opening SPAN tag], then press [Delete].

    c. Type document.write("<SPAN ID='textnum'>")

    d. Select the text [replace with closing SPAN tag], press [Delete], type document.write("</SPAN>")

    e. Check your document for errors, make changes as necessary, then save Pack update.htm as a text document.

    f. Open Pack update.htm in your Web browser, then scroll to the bottom of the page.

    g. If you are using Internet Explorer, click the Remove Long Haul button.

    h. If you are using Internet Explorer, click the Remove Trekker button.

4. Incorporate an advanced function.

    a. Open the file HTML K-11.htm in your text editor, then save it as a text document with the filename Pack scroll.htm.

    b. Scroll down until the opening body tag appears in the document window, select the text [replace with text scroll script], then press [Delete].

    c. Type onload="scrollit('Find all your outdoor supplies at nomadltd.com!');"

    d. Check your document for errors, make changes as necessary, then save Pack scroll.htm as a text document.

    e. Open Pack scroll.htm in your Web browser and watch the status bar to see the scrolling text that the new function creates. (*Note*: this feature functions in both Internet Explorer and Navigator.)

5. Replace graphics dynamically.

    a. Open the file HTML K-12.htm in your text editor, then save it as a text document with the filename Pack color.htm.

    b. Scroll down until the line <DIV CLASS="packhead" appears in the document window, select the text [replace with light event handlers], then press [Delete].

    c. Type onMouseOver="light.src='lightcolor.jpg'" onMouseOut="light.src='moonlight.jpg'"

    d. Scroll down and select the text [replace with blue event handlers], press [Delete], then type onMouseOver="blue.src='bluecolor.jpg'" onMouseOut="blue.src='bluemoon.jpg'"

    e. Repeat Step d for the remaining five list items, using the IDs and graphic files listed in Table K-4.

TABLE K-4

list item	id	color graphic name (onMouseOver)	black and white graphic name (onMouseOut)
3	harvest	harvestcolor.jpg	harvest.jpg
4	newmoon	newcolor.jpg	newmoon.jpg
5	full	fullcolor.jpg	fullmoon.jpg
6	trek	trekcolor.jpg	trekker.jpg
7	long	longcolor.jpg	longhaul.jpg

  f. Check your document for errors, make necessary changes, then save Pack color.htm as a text document.

  g. Open Pack color.htm in your Web browser.

  h. If you are using Internet Explorer 4, scroll down to the list of pack descriptions, then move your mouse pointer over the heading or graphic for the Nomad Moonlight.

  i. Move your mouse pointer off the selected item.

6. Bind data.

  a. Open the file HTML K-13.htm in your text editor, then save it as a text document with the filename Pack comparison table.htm.

  b. Scroll to the end of the code for the list of pack descriptions until the <OBJECT> tags appear in the document window.

  c. Select the text [replace with opening TABLE tag], press [Delete], then type <TABLE BORDER="1" ID="elemtb" DATASRC="#packlist">

  d. Scroll down, select the text [replace with closing TABLE tag], press [Delete], then type </TABLE>

  e. Check your document for errors, make necessary changes, then save Pack comparison table.htm as a text document.

  f. Open Pack comparison table.htm in your browser, then scroll to the bottom of the page. (*Note*: remember that you will see the bound data only in IE 4.)

7. Manipulate bound data dynamically.

  a. Open the file HTML K-14.htm in your text editor, then save it as a text document with the filename Pack sortable comparison table.htm.

  b. Scroll to the bottom of the page, select the text [replace with price script], then press [Delete].

  c. Type the following script, pressing [Enter] at the end of each line:

```
function priceClick() {
   packlist.Sort="price";
   packlist.Reset();
}
price.onclick=priceClick;
```

  d. Check the script you entered for errors, make necessary changes, then save Pack sortable comparison table.htm as a text document.

  e. Open Pack sortable comparison table.htm in your Web browser, then scroll to the bottom of the page.

  f. If you are using Internet Explorer 4, click the Price column heading, then scroll down to see the regenerated table.

  g. Close the Web browser and text editor.

▶ Independent Challenges

1. The owners of the Green House plant store want to allow online ordering on their Web page. On the page listing the Green House plant store's products, you have started adding a check box next to each item. Users can click on a check box next to each item they want to buy. Also, you have begun to add a line that reports the total number of items the user has marked for purchase.

To complete this independent challenge:

a. Open the file HTML K-15.htm in your text editor, then save it as a text document with the filename "Green House supply purchase.htm".

b. Scroll down to the end of the page's head section, select the text [replace with countChecks and reCount functions], then press [Delete].

c. Type the following lines of script, pressing [Enter] at the end of each line:

```
function countChecks() {
    items = 0;
    for (var i = 0; i < document.all.length; i++){
    var el = document.all[i];
    if (el.checked){
            items++;
            }
    }
}
```

```
function reCount() {
    countChecks()
    textnum.innerHTML=" " + items;
}
```

d. Check the script you entered for errors, make changes as necessary, then save Green House supply purchase.htm as a text document. *Hint*: To view a model of this script refer to the lesson "Modifying content dynamically" and the student files associated with that lesson.

e. Open "Green House supply purchase.htm" in your browser, then, if you are using Internet Explorer 4, click one of the check boxes and observe the value displayed for total number of items marked for purchase.

f. Check for errors, then use the text editor to make corrections as needed.

g. Close the browser and text editor.

2. You are creating a Web page containing route information for Sandhills Regional Public Transit. You want to allow riders to compare routes that different bus lines follow; and you want to ensure users can remove from the screen lines that do not apply to them.

To complete this independent challenge:

a. Open the file HTML K-16.htm in your text editor, then save it as a text document with the filename "SRPT route comparison.htm".

b. Scroll down to the first list item in the body section, delete the text "[replace with rt11 button code]", then type the following code, pressing [Enter] at the end of each line:

```
<SCRIPT LANGUAGE="javascript">
<!--
if (IE4) {
```

c. Press [Tab], type document.write("<BUTTON CLASS='button' onClick=rt11.outerHTML="">Remove Route 11</BUTTON>")

d. Press [Enter], type } and press [Enter], then add the two closing script tags.

e. Repeat Steps 2 through 4 for the remaining four buttons, replacing the text as indicated in Table K-5.

TABLE K-5

route	replace "rt11" with	replace "Route 11" with
12	rt12	Route 12
13	rt13	Route 13
14	rt14	Route 14
15	rt15	Route 15

f. Check your work, then save SRPT route comparison.htm as a text document.

g. Open "SRPT route comparison.htm" in the browser, and if you are using Internet Explorer, test the buttons to be sure they work.

h. Check for errors, use the text editor to make corrections as needed.

i. Close the browser and text editor.

3. The Community Public School Volunteers organization would like to add a page to their Web site listing schools that currently need volunteers. They also want to include contact information for each school so that potential volunteers can get started immediately. The organization maintains a database of the different schools' volunteer needs. They would like their Web page to reflect the current contents of the database.

To complete this independent challenge:

a. Open the file HTML K-17.htm in your text editor, then save it as a text document with the filename "CPSV volunteer opportunities.htm".

b. Select the text [replace with opening TABLE tag], press [Enter], then type the following code:
```
<TABLE BORDER="1" ID="elemtbl" DATASRC="#schools">
```

c. Add the following lines of script after the opening script tags and before the sorting function scripts:
```
if (!IE4) {
    document.write("If your browser does not display the above table, please contact us to find out about volunteer opportunities.")
}
```

d. Check your work, make changes as necessary, then save CPSV volunteer opportunities.htm as a text document.

e. Open CPSV volunteer opportunities.htm in the browser, and, if you are using Internet Explorer 4, test the table to verify that the table-generation and table-sorting functions work correctly.

f. Check for errors, use the text editor to make corrections as needed. *Hint*: To view model code, refer to the lessons "Generating a table dynamically" and "Manipulating table contents dynamically" as well as all student files associated with these files.

g. Close the browser and text editor.

4. By creating more complex scripts, you can adapt dynamic content features for a wide range of applications. To complete this independent challenge, connect to the Internet and find two Web pages that incorporate dynamic content in ways that are different than those you learned in this unit. Because you can write cross-browser code for some dynamic content features, you can complete this exercise using either Internet Explorer or Netscape Navigator. Print a copy of each page and circle the area of the page where the content changes dynamically. On another sheet of paper, briefly describe how the content changes, what triggers the change, and what qualifies the feature you circled as dynamic content.

HTML

▶ Visual Workshop

You have created a Web page for Touchstone Booksellers that makes their book-inventory database available online. They have provided you a preliminary text file that lists several books. Your task is to bind the text file to the Web page to create a dynamically generated table. The client has asked that you make the table sortable by users, as Figure K-18 illustrates. Open the file HTML K-18.htm, save it as a text document with the filename Touchstone sortable inventory.htm, then replace the text "[replace with sorting script]" with the necessary script to make the list sortable. You need to create a set of script code for each column in the database, as you did in the lesson "Manipulating table contents dynamically" in this unit. The script for the first column is:

```
function titleClick() {
        booklist.Sort="title";
        booklist.Reset();
}
title.onclick=titleClick;
```

Table K-6 shows the variables to substitute to create the remaining script segments. Remember to include the opening and closing SCRIPT tags.

TABLE K-6

column	replace all four occurrences of "title" with
2	alast
3	afirst
4	year
5	bind
6	copies

FIGURE K-18

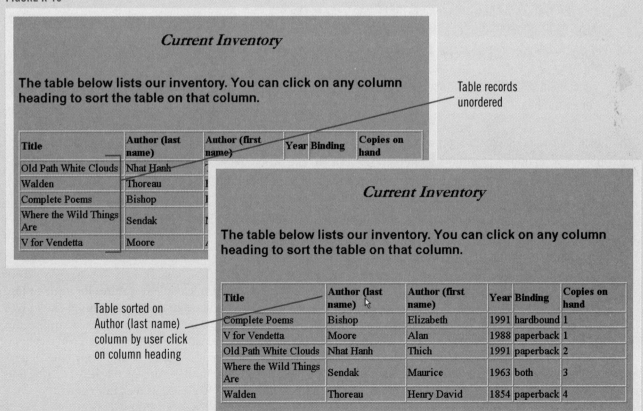

Table records unordered

Table sorted on Author (last name) column by user click on column heading

Positioning
with DHTML

Objectives

- ► **Understand DHTML positioning**
- ► **Position an element absolutely**
- ► **Position an element relatively**
- ► **Size an element manually**
- ► **Stack screen elements**
- ► **Add a scroll bar**
- ► **Create a sidebar**
- ► **Incorporate an advanced positioning function**

One of DHTML's greatest contributions to Web page design is a tool for **positioning,** or specifying the precise placement of elements within the page. Just like other DHTML components, DHTML positioning opens doors to many possibilities for new Web page features. Other DHTML features, such as scroll bars, complement positioning to help create effective page layouts. Lydia wants to enrich the Web page design for the Nomad Ltd Web publication. She will use positioning and other DHTML layout features to create a sophisticated, attractive style.

Understanding DHTML Positioning

A fundamental difference between document layouts in traditional media, such as posters and magazines, and document layouts in HTML is HTML's lack of tools for precise placement of page elements. DHTML allows precise positioning of page elements through an extension of cascading style sheets called **Cascading Style Sheets - Positioning (CSS-P)**. CSS-P allows you to position elements either **absolutely**, at fixed coordinates on a user's screen, or **relatively**, based on the position of other screen elements. To specify positioning, you use the **position** attribute, which is a style sheet property. Although some advanced page layout is possible with basic HTML, CSS-P makes the task much easier to code and offers features not possible with HTML alone. ◢◣◤ As Lydia researches CSS-P, she learns about several new features that she would like to include in her Web pages, including columns, overlap, and scripted effects.

Columns

Many Web page designers have created advanced layout features using basic HTML formatting. For example, HTML-only pages can use tables to display text in columns, rather than in one single block. However, adding these features in HTML can be difficult and limiting because the tags were not designed originally to provide advanced formatting. CSS-P makes this type of formatting much simpler by allowing you to easily specify each element's width and location on a Web page. CSS-P also places elements more predictably in different screen resolutions. Lydia plans to use the CSS-P float feature to add a sidebar to the Nomad Ltd tents page, similar to the one shown in Figure L-1.

Overlap

A design feature not found in HTML but available in CSS-P, is the ability to overlap screen elements, which facilitates adding labels over graphics. Also, it allows you to create complex layouts such as ones that superimpose words in different colors or that overlap parts of images. The Web page in Figure L-2 uses CSS-P to overlap text and graphics. Lydia wants to use the overlap feature to create a distinctive design effect in her Web pages for Nomad Ltd. She plans to place the general category name for each Web page in large, light-colored text behind the page headings.

Scripted features

As with other DHTML tools, combining CSS-P with scripts allows you to create many new display features for your Web pages. For example, by changing a graphic's dimensions slightly at regular intervals, you can animate with DHTML. You also can use scripting to allow users to drag elements to new positions on the Web page. Lydia plans to add some draggable elements to her tents page to help users visualize the placement of sleeping bags in various tent designs.

FIGURE L-1: **Web page containing sidebar**

webmonkey/dynamic_html/

Resources

- - - - - - - - - -

Inside DHTML

This site by Scott Isaacs, a member of the Internet Explorer design team, provides lots of juicy coverage of Dynamic HTML and excerpts his book - you guessed it, Inside Dynamic HTML.

Toolbox

- - - - - - - - - -

Dreamweaver
Platform: Win 95, Power Mac
Cost: not yet set
Company: Macromedia

Taylor's Tutorial

- - - - - - - - - -

Taylor's Dynamic HTML Tutorial - Day 1
Dynamic HTML is how Netscape's and Microsoft's 4.0 browsers are pushing the Web to new limits. In the first of five parts, Taylor looks at what dHTML is all about and what skills you need to code for it. *9 Mar 1998*

Taylor's Dynamic HTML Tutorial - Day 2
Taylor digs into dynamic HTML, showing you the basics of using CSS-P to lay out your pages. He even looks at the elusive z-index. *10 Mar 1998*

Taylor's Dynamic HTML Tutorial - Day 3
Today Taylor's series gets tricky: By the end of the day, he'll have you scripting dHTML and making monkeys run around

Sidebar created
using CSS-P

FIGURE L-2: **Web page displaying element overlap**

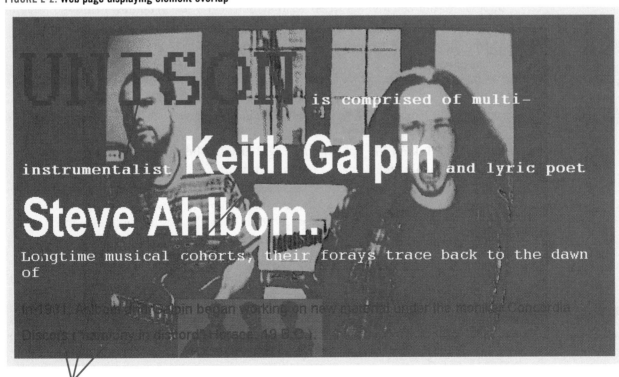

Text overlaps
graphic

Positioning an Element Absolutely

With CSS-P, you can specify an element's position in several different ways. The most straightforward way is to use **absolute positioning**, which lets you specify the left and top coordinates of an element on the Web page. You use the CSS-P **left** and **top** properties to specify an element's location relative to the top-left corner of its **parent**, or the object enclosing it. For example, a <SPAN> element nested within <DIV> tags would be positioned relative to the <DIV> element, its parent. In this case, the <SPAN> element is known as a **child** of the <DIV> element. Any element not enclosed by another element is a child of the browser window and is absolutely positioned with respect to the top-left corner of the window. You can specify left and top values in points (pt), pixels (px), inches (in), millimeters (mm), or centimeters (cm). If you don't specify units, the browser defaults to **pixels**, which are the tiny units of light that create the display on a monitor. The number of pixels visible on a user's screen varies depending on its resolution. However, even when using pixels, it is a good idea to specify units in order to make your code clearer when debugging it and when others read it. As she develops a Web page describing tents available from Nomad Ltd, Lydia wants to reposition the elements located at the top of the page to decrease the amount of blank space in her original design. She adds absolute position information to the elements to create a more compact layout.

Doesn't care about flow will place exact where specified

Steps 1 2 3 4

1. Start your Web browser, cancel any dial-up activities, then open the file **HTML L-1.htm**
   Notice how the text flows around the image. In this version of the Web page, because Lydia was using only HTML, she made the text flow by grouping the image and the text together in a DIV tagset. However, text flow created in HTML can be unpredictable depending on the user's display font size and resolution settings.

2. Start your text editor program, open the file **HTML L-1.htm**, then save it as a text document with the filename **Tent absolute position.htm**

3. Scroll to the document's HEAD section, select the text **[replace with logo absolute position code]** in the embedded style sheet, then press **[Delete]**

4. Type **#logo {position: absolute; top: 30px; left: 30px}**
   The name #logo associates this style with the ID "logo". Figure L-3 shows the document containing the absolute position code. Lydia placed the logo so that it is 30 pixels from the top of the browser window and 30 pixels from the left edge of the browser window. By positioning the Nomad Ltd logo using absolute positioning, Lydia's headers can move up to fill in the empty area at the top of the page.

5. Scroll down until the opening DIV tag above the IMG tag for nomad.jpg appears in the document window, select the text **[replace with ID]**, then press **[Delete]**
   Lydia wants her layout to work on both fourth-generation browsers. Because Netscape Navigator does not recognize absolute positioning referenced in an IMG tag, she has enclosed the IMG tag in DIV tags. By referencing the position information in the DIV element, Lydia positions the graphic element.

6. Type **ID="logo"**

7. Check your document for errors, make any necessary changes, then save **Tent absolute position.htm** as a text document

8. Open **Tent absolute position.htm** in your Web browser
   As Figure L-4 shows, the Nomad Ltd logo appears in the top-left corner of the window, moved slightly down and to the right from its position in the file HTML L-1.htm. Because the graphic is placed absolutely at a fixed location in the window, the remaining screen elements flow beginning at the top of the window. The presence of the graphic to the left of the headings has no effect on their alignment or flow. As Figure L-4 shows, the result is overlap between the logo and the heading text. Next, Lydia will adjust the position of the heading text to keep it from overlapping the logo.

FIGURE L-3: Web document containing absolute position code

```
<HTML>
<HEAD>

<TITLE>Nomad Ltd - Selecting a tent</TITLE>

<LINK REL=stylesheet HREF="nomadltd.css" TYPE="text/css">

<STYLE>
<!--
.tenthead {font-family: arial, sans-serif; font-size: 14pt}
.button {font-family: impact, arial; font-size: 8pt}
.norm {font-weight: normal}
.noital {font-style: normal}
#logo {position: absolute; top: 30px; left: 30px}
//-->
</STYLE>

<SCRIPT LANGUAGE="javascript">
<!--
Nav4 = (document.layers) ? 1:0;
IE4 = (document.all) ? 1:0;

if(!IE4) {window.onerror=null}

totalTents = 0;
function countHeaders() {
```

Code to position logo at top-left corner of page

Name associates style with ID "logo"

FIGURE L-4: Web page displaying absolutely positioned logo

Logo placed at precise coordinates

Tents
Selecting one that's right for you

Choosing a quality tent that meets your needs can be an intimidating task. To help you out with this important decision, we've added features to this page to make it easier to compare the characteristics of our tents.

As you narrow your choices, click the Remove button for each tent that you're no longer considering, to remove it from the page.

Tent footprints and descriptions

XTC Starlite
One of the lightest, most compact three-season tents available. Featuring two-pole clip design with a built-in vestibule.
Remove Starlite

Cross-browser positioning

Both fourth-generation browsers interpret and display CSS-P formatting, but as with the other parts of DHTML, each browser processes CSS-P differently. This disparity results in unique code to create features in each browser that you need to remember when creating cross-browser code. The main challenge is that Navigator 4 does not correctly interpret positioning information inserted directly in a tag. In fact, inline coding for position removes the style information from all elements in the page that follow the inline code. You can remedy this problem by defining all your positioning code in either embedded or external style sheets. Fortunately, grouping style information at the top or in a separate file brings other benefits because it organizes your code and makes it easier to read and understand.

Positioning an Element Relatively

In addition to placing elements at fixed screen coordinates, CSS-P allows you to simply offset elements from their default positions in the page flow. This format, called **relative positioning**, is useful when you want your document to always display an element before or after other elements, but at a specified horizontal or vertical offset. ◄━━━ Lydia wants to indent the page headings, while leaving them in the general page flow. She uses relative positioning to specify the new placement for the headings.

Steps

1. Open the file **HTML L-2.htm** in your text editor, then save it as a text document with the filename **Tent relative position.htm**

2. In the embedded style sheet, select the text **[replace with head relative position code]**, then press **[Delete]**

3. Type **#head {position: relative; left: 250px}**
   Figure L-5 shows the document containing the relative position code. Similar to the absolute position of the logo, the left property that Lydia used to position the text moves it left in relation to the parent element, which is the browser window. Absolute positioning removes an element from the flow of the document, which causes the elements below it to move up and to overlap its former position in the page flow. This caused the headings to move up in the last lesson. Relatively positioning leaves an element in the document flow. A relatively positioned element moves relative to its default location in the page, but the elements that follow a relatively positioned element do not move up to take that position. This is what Lydia wants to do in her document because she wants the headings indented from the left to appear next to the graphic, but she does not want the text that follows to overlap the headings and graphic.

4. Scroll until **<DIV ALIGN="center"** appears in the document window, select the text **[replace with ID]**, then press **[Delete]**

5. Select the adjacent text **ALIGN="center"** and press **[Delete]**

6. Type **ID="head"**
   Lydia references the position information in the DIV element to position the headings.

7. Check your document for errors, make any necessary changes, then save **Tent relative position.htm** as a text document

8. Open **Tent relative position.htm** in your Web browser
   As Figure L-6 shows, the main heading and the subheading are indented far enough from the left edge of the window to allow room for the logo. Because the indent was specified using relative positioning, the text after the headings does not move up into the positions previously held by the headings but, rather, continues to flow below them.

FIGURE L-5: Relative position code in Web document

Code to
position
heading
within
document
flow

```
<HTML>
<HEAD>

<TITLE>Nomad Ltd - Selecting a tent</TITLE>

<LINK REL=stylesheet HREF="nomadltd.css" TYPE="text/css">

<STYLE>
<!--
.tenthead {font-family: arial, sans-serif; font-size: 14pt}
.button {font-family: impact, arial; font-size: 8pt}
.norm {font-weight: normal}
.noital {font-style: normal}
#logo {position: absolute; top: 30px; left: 30px}
#head {position: relative; left: 250px}
//-->
</STYLE>

<SCRIPT LANGUAGE="javascript">
<!--
Nav4 = (document.layers) ? 1:0;
IE4 = (document.all) ? 1:0;

if(!IE4) {window.onerror=null}

totalTents = 0;
```

FIGURE L-6: Web page displaying relatively positioned headings

Headings
indented
within
main text
flow

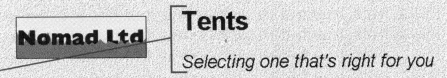

Tents

Selecting one that's right for you

Choosing a quality tent that meets your needs can be an intimidating task. To help you out with this important decision, we've added features to this page to make it easier to compare the characteristics of our tents.

As you narrow your choices, click the Remove button for each tent that you're no longer considering, to remove it from the page.

Tent footprints and descriptions

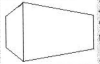

XTC Starlite
One of the lightest, most compact three-season tents available. Featuring two-pole clip design with a built-in vestibule.

Remove Starlite

Sizing an Element Manually

In addition to position on the page, DHTML style properties allow you to specify an element's dimensions using the **height** and **width** properties. You can specify the two dimensions separately by using the same units available for the positioning properties. Additionally, you can size the element relative to its parent by using percentages. If you choose not to specify the height or the width, the browser sizes the element automatically. ◄▬▬ Lydia wants to reformat the description text for each tent model, so it displays indented and in a narrower column. Because she is changing style information for several screen elements, she adds properties to the page's embedded style sheet.

Steps 1 2 3 4

1. Open the file **HTML L-3.htm** in your text editor, then save it as a text document with the filename **Tent element size.htm**

2. Select the text **[replace with tentbody class description]** in the embedded style sheet, then press **[Delete]**

3. Type **.tentbody {position: relative; left: 100px; width: 300px}**
   Figure L-7 shows the document code including the new width property.

4. Scroll down until the **<DIV ID="tent1" name="tent">** tag appears in the document window, then read through the code within this DIV element
   Notice that, in addition to the new style properties, Lydia has inserted CLASS="tentbody" in the DIV tag already, which applies the position information from the tenthead class description she created. She has added this information for each tent.

5. Check your document for errors, make any necessary changes, then save **Tent element size.htm** as a text document

6. Open **Tent element size.htm** in your Web browser, then scroll down until the tent descriptions appear in the document window
   As Figure L-8 shows, each description is indented from the left margin and the paragraph width is narrowed, which creates a column.

FIGURE L-7: Web document including width property code

```
<HTML>
<HEAD>

<TITLE>Nomad Ltd - Selecting a tent</TITLE>

<LINK REL=stylesheet HREF="nomadltd.css" TYPE="text/css">

<STYLE>
<!--
.tenthead {font-family: arial, sans-serif; font-size: 14pt; position:
relative; left: 100px}
.button {font-family: impact, arial; font-size: 8pt}
.norm {font-weight: normal}
.noital {font-style: normal}
#logo {position: absolute; top: 30px; left: 30px}
#head {position: relative; left: 250px}
.tentbody {position: relative; left: 100px; width: 300px}
//-->
</STYLE>

<SCRIPT LANGUAGE="javascript">
<!--
Nav4 = (document.layers) ? 1:0;
IE4 = (document.all) ? 1:0;

if(!IE4) {window.onerror=null}
```

Width property for tentbody class

FIGURE L-8: Web page displaying adjusted width

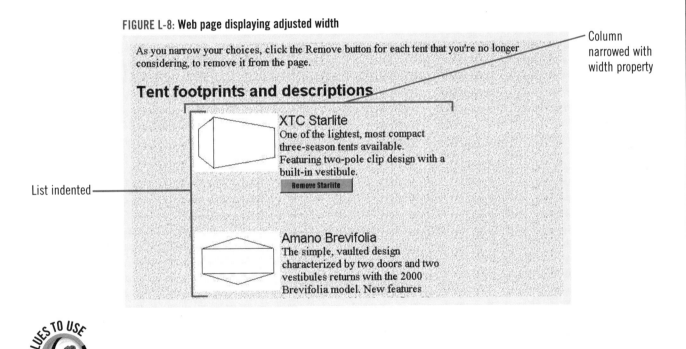

Column narrowed with width property

List indented

Positioning and sizing using percentages

Although standard measurement units, such as pixels and points, are most familiar to Web page designers, the ability to use percentage as a positioning and sizing unit offers advantages for some screen elements. Because monitors of different screen resolutions display the document window with a larger or smaller area, a size in pixels or points appears at a different position on the screen at different resolutions. While a column of 150px may fit perfectly in an 800 x 600 display, that same column may be surrounded by space at 1024 x 768, reducing the effectiveness of your layout. Elements sized with percentages, however, automatically adjust to the size of their parent elements. Thus, if you size a graphic element that is a child of the document window at 35%, that graphic element will maintain the same size relative to the document window in different resolutions. You can use the same method to absolutely or relatively position an element as a percentage of its parent. For some applications, specifying an exact measurement is important, but percentage sizing and positioning are important tools in your Web page design toolbox.

HTML

Stacking Screen Elements

Because an absolutely positioned element can appear anywhere on a Web page, including the space occupied by other elements, the browser can't format pages containing these elements as it would standard HTML pages. Instead, each absolutely positioned element is considered to be on a separate layer, which is a transparent virtual page that determines overlap order. Web page layers are like sheets of clear plastic with writing or images on them in different areas. When the sheets are superimposed, as layers are in the browser window, all the contents of all sheets are visible; but some contents may block out others, depending on their order in the stack. Each layer's z-index property determines its position in the stack. Higher numbers are located closer to the top of the stack, and elements on these layers will block out elements in the same position on lower layers of the stack. An element that is positioned using absolute positioning is placed on a separate layer. An element positioned using relative positioning remains on the same layer as the rest of the standard page elements. ◤◢◤ Lydia plans to label each page in Nomad Ltd's Web publication based on its content category. She wants to place the category name at the top of the page so that it appears behind the headings. For the tent page, she wants to add the word *camping* to the heading background in large, light-colored type.

Steps 1 2 3 4

1. Open the file **HTML L-4.htm** in your text editor, then save it as a text document with the filename **Tent layers.htm**

2. In the embedded style sheet, select the text [replace with backtext layer code], then press [Delete]

3. Type **#backtext {position: absolute; left: 250px; font-size: 64pt; font-family: arial; color: #7093DB; z-index: -1}**
   Figure L-9 shows the document code, including the new background text. The first element positioned in a Web page receives a z-index value of 0. Subsequently placed elements receive higher z-index values, resulting in later elements appearing on top of older elements by default. Because Lydia wants to make sure the word *CAMPING* appears behind the headings, she assigns it a z-index of -1, which is lower than all other default z-index values.

4. Scroll down and select the text [replace with background text], then press [Delete]

5. Type **<DIV ID="backtext">** and press [Enter]

6. Type **CAMPING** and press [Enter], then type **</DIV>**

7. Check your document for errors, make any necessary changes, then save **Tent layers.htm** as a text document

8. Open **Tent layers.htm** in your Web browser
   As Figure L-10 shows, the text *CAMPING* appears behind the headings in a large and light-colored font. This stacked layout allows Lydia to add extra information to the Web page without disrupting the flow of the page. It also adds an interesting, unusual visual effect.

FIGURE L-9: Web document including background text code

```
<HTML>
<HEAD>

<TITLE>Nomad Ltd - Selecting a tent</TITLE>

<LINK REL=stylesheet HREF="nomadltd.css" TYPE="text/css">

<STYLE>
<!--
.tenthead {font-family: arial, sans-serif; font-size: 14pt; position:
relative; left: 100px}
.button {font-family: impact, arial; font-size: 8pt}
.norm {font-weight: normal}
.noital {font-style: normal}
#logo {position: absolute; top: 30px; left: 30px}
#head {position: relative; left: 250px}
.tentbody {position: relative; left: 100px; width: 300px}
#backtext {position: absolute; left: 250px; font-size: 64pt; font-family:
arial; color: #7093DB; z-index: -1}
//-->
</STYLE>

<SCRIPT LANGUAGE="javascript">
<!--
Nav4 = (document.layers) ? 1:0;
IE4 = (document.all) ? 1:0;
```

z-index property for background text

FIGURE L-10: Web page displaying background text

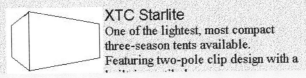

z-index value places background text behind headings

Choosing a quality tent that meets your needs can be an intimidating task. To help you out with this important decision, we've added features to this page to make it easier to compare the characteristics of our tents.

As you narrow your choices, click the Remove button for each tent that you're no longer considering, to remove it from the page.

Tent footprints and descriptions

XTC Starlite
One of the lightest, most compact three-season tents available. Featuring two-pole clip design with a

HTML

Adding a Scroll Bar

You can use CSS-P to associate a scroll bar with an element when the element is too large to fit its defined size. This effect, which you create using the **overflow** property, allows you to create the equivalent of an independent frame anywhere within your browser window. Of the fourth-generation browsers, only Internet Explorer accommodates the overflow property. To make the tent page layout more concise, Lydia formats the list of tent outlines and descriptions in a box with a scroll bar. This allows users to scroll from top to bottom in the page more quickly and still easily view the tent descriptions if they wish.

Steps

1. Open the file **HTML L-5.htm** in your text editor, then save it as a text document with the filename **Tent scroll.htm**

2. In the embedded style sheet, select the text **[replace with list scroll code]**, then press **[Delete]**

3. Type **#list {height: 300px; width: 600px; overflow: auto}**
   Figure L-11 shows the Web page code in the embedded style sheet. Because the list of tent descriptions is much longer than 300 pixels, the height specification creates a display area smaller than the object size. The "auto" value for the "overflow" property instructs the browser to display scroll bars only where necessary. Because the text in this case is longer than 300 pixels, the browser will create a vertical scroll bar for the object. The width of this DIV is not constrained by a style setting, so a horizontal scroll bar is not needed.

4. Scroll until the code for the heading Tent footprints and descriptions appears in the document window, select the text **[replace with opening DIV tag]**, then press **[Delete]**

5. Type **<DIV ID="list">**

6. Scroll to the end of the tent description list which is after the description for tent 7, select the text **[replace with closing DIV tag]**, press **[Delete]**, then type **</DIV>**

7. Check your document for errors, make any necessary changes, then save **Tent scroll.htm** as a text document

8. Open **Tent scroll.htm** in your Web browser, then scroll down to view the list of tent outlines and descriptions
   As Figure L-12 shows, in IE 4 the tent-description list displays in a limited area with a vertical scroll bar on the right edge.

9. Use the scroll bar for the list to view all of the tent descriptions

Trouble?

The amount of text displayed in your scroll bar box will depend on the size of the font you are using and your screen resolution.

FIGURE L-11: Web document including scroll bar code

```
<HTML>
<HEAD>

<TITLE>Nomad Ltd - Selecting a tent</TITLE>

<LINK REL=stylesheet HREF="nomadltd.css" TYPE="text/css">

<STYLE>
<!--
.tenthead {font-family: arial, sans-serif; font-size: 14pt; position:
relative; left: 100px}
.button {font-family: impact, arial; font-size: 8pt}
.norm {font-weight: normal}
.noital {font-style: normal}
#logo {position: absolute; top: 30px; left: 30px}
#head {position: relative; left: 250px}
.tentbody {position: relative; left: 100px; width: 300px}
#backtext {position: absolute; left: 250px; font-size: 64pt; font-family:
arial; color: #7093DB; z-index: -1}
#list {height: 300px; width: 600px; overflow: auto}
//-->
</STYLE>

<SCRIPT LANGUAGE="javascript">
<!--
Nav4 = (document.layers) ? 1:0;
```

overflow property adds scroll bar

FIGURE L-12: List formatted with scroll bar

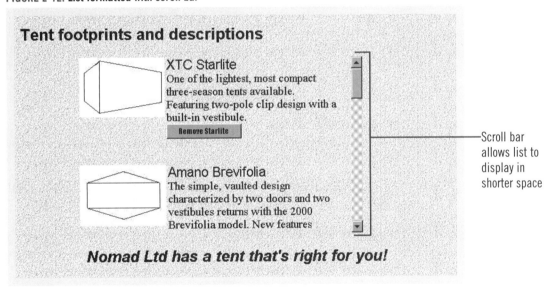

Scroll bar allows list to display in shorter space

Creating a clip region

Sometimes, you want to put a large element on your Web page but don't have room for the full element; other times, you only want to display a portion of a large element. CSS-P's **clip** property allows you to control how much of an element is visible on your Web page by acting as a layer above the element, covering all of it except for a hole you define, called a **clip region**. (Note that Netscape Navigator 4 does not support this property.) To create a clip region, you specify the coordinates of a rectangle, usually with an area smaller than the element, using the syntax **clip: rect(top right bottom left)**. The abbreviation "rect" stands for rectangle, which is the only shape currently supported by this property. Substitute each of the terms in parentheses with a coordinate value, or enter **auto** to leave the default. When the element appears in your Web page, the only portion of the element that will be visible is the section within the rectangle you specified.

Creating a Sidebar

Using CSS-P's placement and sizing properties, you can create and position text blocks independently of each other. You can use the **float** property to remove an element from the main text flow and display it to the side of the flow. The **left** and **right** values allow you to specify whether the element is positioned on the right or left side of the main document flow. The float feature allows you to create many text effects, including sidebars, which are difficult to create with HTML alone. Lydia wants to add scale outlines of backpacks and sleeping bags to the tents page to give users a better feel for the relative sizes of the tents. To make this area stand out from the page's main text, she creates a sidebar.

Steps

1. Open the file **HTML L-6.htm** in your text editor, then save it as a text document with the filename **Tent sidebar.htm**

2. In the embedded style sheet, select the text **[replace with sidebar code]**, then press **[Delete]**

3. Type **#sidebar {width: 350px; float: right; position: absolute; left: 400px; font-family: arial; font-size: 11pt; background: #8FBC8F}** and press **[Enter]**
   The "float" property removes the section from the document flow, and the "right" value specifies that it floats to the right of the flow. Lydia could specify the height, but the height property works in conjunction with the float property only in Internet Explorer. Navigator always adjusts the height of a sidebar to fit its contents, regardless of the height setting. By not assigning the height property, Lydia allows both browsers to automatically adjust the height to ensure uniform appearance.

4. Type **.expl {width: 375px}**
   To keep the paragraph to the left of the sidebar from overlapping it, Lydia associates it with a fixed width. Figure L-13 shows the Web page code containing the new style specifications.

5. Scroll until the DIV tag before the IMG tags appears in the document window, select the text **[replace with ALIGN and ID codes]**, then press **[Delete]**

6. Type **ALIGN="left" ID="sidebar"**
   Sidebars that float to the right of the main text also automatically align text along the right edge. You can override this setting using the HTML ALIGN property.

7. Check your document for errors, make any necessary changes, then save **Tent sidebar.htm** as a text document

Trouble?

If you are using Netscape Navigator 4 and the sidebar is slow to appear, simply scroll down the page and back to the top to see the scrollbar more quickly.

8. Open **Tent sidebar.htm** in your Web browser
   As Figure L-14 shows, the text displays in a rectangle with a colored background to the right of the main text flow. Lydia specified absolute positioning settings for the graphics to position them just below the sidebar text.

FIGURE L-13: Web document containing style specifications for sidebar

float property creates sidebar effect

Code added to adjust layout for new text

Absolute position code for pack and bag icons

```
.tentbody {position: relative; left: 100px; width: 300px}
#backtext {position: absolute; left: 250px; font-size: 64pt; font-family:
arial; color: #7093DB; z-index: -1}
#list {height: 300px; width: 600px; overflow: auto}
#sidebar {width: 350px; float: right; position: absolute; left: 400px; font-
family: arial; font-size: 11pt; background: #8FBC8F}
.expl {width: 375px}
#pack1 {position: absolute; left: 505px}
#pack2 {position: absolute; left: 535px}
#pack3 {position: absolute; left: 425px}
#pack4 {position: absolute; left: 460px}
#bag1 {position: absolute; left: 565px}
#bag2 {position: absolute; left: 670px}
//-->
</STYLE>

<SCRIPT LANGUAGE="javascript">
<!--
Nav4 = (document.layers) ? 1:0;
IE4 = (document.all) ? 1:0;

if(!IE4) {window.onerror=null}

totalTents = 0;
function countHeaders() {
    for (var i = 0; i < document.all.length; i++){
```

FIGURE L-14: Web page displaying sidebar

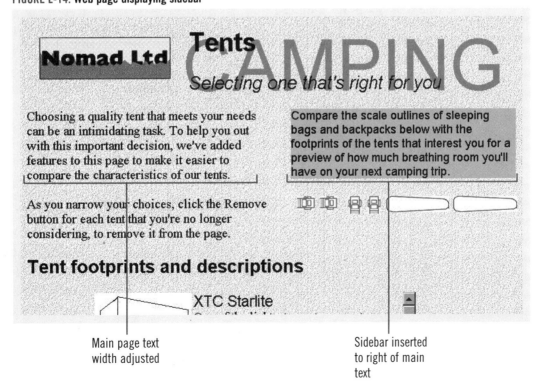

Main page text width adjusted

Sidebar inserted to right of main text

Incorporating an Advanced Positioning Function

By creating scripts to interact with position and layer information, you can add many advanced features to your Web pages. One exciting result of scripting position in Internet Explorer is dragging. A script enabling the drag feature can adjust the position of the selected element based on the coordinates of the pointer and then assign the element to its final position once the user releases the mouse button. This drag feature allows users to rearrange elements into an order that is more useful for them than the page's default organization or to interact with Web page models and games. ✎ Lydia wants to let Internet Explorer users drag the scale outlines of sleeping bags and backpacks over the tent outlines so they can explore how much each tent holds.

1. Open the file **HTML L-7.htm** in your text editor, then save it as a text document with the filename **Tent drag.htm**
   Notice that Lydia has created the class description .drag in the embedded style section for a draggable element.

2. Scroll down until the var elDrag=null code appears in the document window
   Notice that Lydia has created a script in the header section that handles dragging of absolute-positioned elements.

QuickTip

You also can format text elements to be draggable, using DIV or SPAN tags as containers.

3. Scroll down until the IMG SRC code for the first draggable image appears in the document window, select the text **[replace with drag code]** in the opening DIV tag for the image tag, then press **[Delete]**

4. Type **CLASS="drag" canDrag**
   This code associates the image with the "drag" class that Lydia defined in the embedded style sheet, which specifies a z-index of 10. The script Lydia inserted earlier in the code identifies draggable images through the "canDrag" attribute.

5. Repeat Steps 2 and 3 for the remaining five IMG tags
   Figure L-15 shows the draggable image codes for this page.

6. Check your document for errors, make any necessary changes, then save **Tent drag.htm** as a text document

7. Open **Tent drag.htm** in your Web browser

8. If you are using IE4, drag some of the backpack and sleeping bag outlines onto a tent footprint
   Look at Figure L-16, and notice that the images move with the mouse pointer. The user can display the images on top of the tent outlines.

FIGURE L-15: Web document containing draggable image codes

```
features to this page to make it easier to compare the characteristics of
our tents.<BR><BR></DIV>

<DIV ID="pack1" CLASS="drag" canDrag>
<IMG SRC="pack.jpg">
</DIV>

<DIV ID="pack2" CLASS="drag" canDrag>
<IMG SRC="pack.jpg">
</DIV>

<DIV ID="pack3" CLASS="drag" canDrag>
<IMG SRC="pack2.jpg">
</DIV>

<DIV ID="pack4" CLASS="drag" canDrag>
<IMG SRC="pack2.jpg">
</DIV>

<DIV ID="bag1" CLASS="drag" canDrag>
<IMG SRC="bag.jpg">
</DIV>

<DIV ID="bag2" CLASS="drag" canDrag>
<IMG SRC="bag.jpg">
</DIV>
```

Image codes formatted for dragging

Attribute marks element as draggable

Class property associates z-index value with each element

FIGURE L-16: Web page showing dragged images

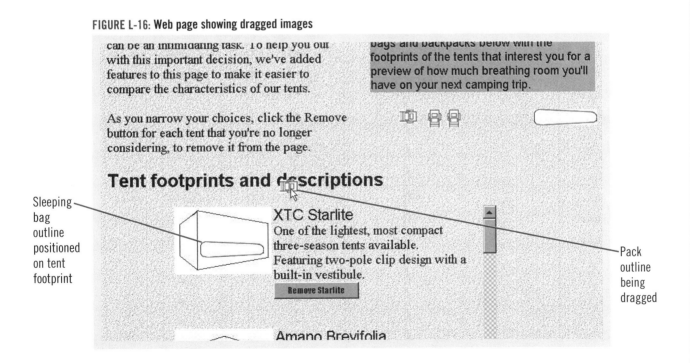

can be an intimidating task. To help you out with this important decision, we've added features to this page to make it easier to compare the characteristics of our tents.

As you narrow your choices, click the Remove button for each tent that you're no longer considering, to remove it from the page.

bags and backpacks below with the footprints of the tents that interest you for a preview of how much breathing room you'll have on your next camping trip.

Tent footprints and descriptions

XTC Starlite
One of the lightest, most compact three-season tents available. Featuring two-pole clip design with a built-in vestibule.
Remove Starlite

Amano Brevifolia

Sleeping bag outline positioned on tent footprint

Pack outline being dragged

Practice

► Concepts Review

Label the elements marked in figure L-17 with the CSS-P properties used to create them.

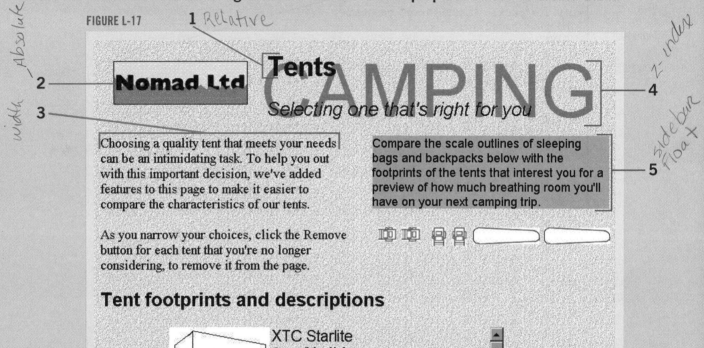

FIGURE L-17

(handwritten annotations on figure:)
1 Relative
2 — width / Absolute
3
4 — z-index
5 — sidebar / float

Match each term with its description.

6. Absolute positioning *b*
7. Relative positioning *e*
8. Float *d*
9. Height and width *a*
10. Top and left *c*

a. Properties for specifying element dimensions
b. Places element at fixed coordinates outside page flow
c. Properties for specifying location
d. Property used to create sidebar
e. Places element relative to parent element's coordinates within page flow

Select the best answer from the list of choices.

11. **An absolutely positioned element is located**
    a. On a separate layer from the rest of the Web page, offset from the parent element.
    b. On a separate layer from the rest of the Web page, offset from the top-left corner of the browser window.
    c. On the same layer as the rest of the page, offset from the parent element.
    d. On the same layer as the rest of the page, offset from the top-left corner of the browser window.

12. **DHTML allows precise positioning of page elements through an extension of Cascading Style Sheets called**
    a. Absolute positioning.
    b. Cascading Style Sheets - Positioning.
    c. The "Position" style property.
    d. Tables.

13. **The browser always places absolutely positioned text**
    a. At the top-left corner of the browser window.
    b. At the specified coordinates relative to the top-left corner of the browser window.
    c. Behind the main page elements in z-index.
    d. At the specified coordinates relative to its parent element.

14. **Which is not a valid measurement unit for specifying dimension and coordinate properties?**
    a. Feet
    b. Inches
    c. Points
    d. Pixels

15. **As you add new layers to a Web page, the elements on the most recent layers receive**
    a. The same z-index value as earlier layers.
    b. Smaller z-index values than earlier layers.
    c. Larger z-index values than earlier layers.
    d. Negative z-index values.

16. **Which property allows you to add scroll bars to specific elements?**
    a. Scroll bar
    b. Float
    c. Layer
    d. Overflow

17. **When adding a scroll bar to an element, assigning the value "auto" results in**
    a. A scroll bar only when the element size requires it.
    b. Both horizontal and vertical scroll bars always appearing .
    c. No scroll bars.
    d. Addition of a vertical scroll bar only.

▶ Skills Review

1. **Position an element absolutely.**
   a. Open the file HTML L-8.htm in your Web browser.
   b. Open the file HTML L-8.htm in your text editor, then save it as a text document with the filename Pack absolute position.htm.
   c. Scroll to the top of the document's HEAD section, select the text [replace with logo absolute position code] in the embedded style sheet, then press [Delete].
   d. Type #logo {position: absolute; top: 30px; left: 30px}
   e. Scroll and select the text [replace with ID] in the opening DIV tag above the IMG tag for nomad.jpg, then press [Delete].
   f. Type ID="logo"
   g. Check your document for errors, make any necessary changes, then save Pack absolute position.htm as a text document.
   h. Open Pack absolute position.htm in your Web browser.

2. **Position an element relatively.**
   a. Open the file HTML L-9.htm in your text editor and save a copy as Pack relative position.htm.
   b. In the embedded style sheet, select the text [replace with head relative position code], then press [Delete].
   c. Type #head {position: relative; left: 275px}
   d. Scroll and select the text [replace with ID], then press [Delete].
   e. Select the adjacent text ALIGN="center" and press [Delete].
   f. Type ID="head"
   g. Check your document for errors, make any necessary changes, then save Pack relative position.htm as a text document.
   h. Open Pack relative position.htm in your Web browser.

3. **Size an element manually.**
   a. Open the file HTML L-10.htm in your text editor, and save it as a text document with the filename Pack element size.htm.
   b. Select the text [replace with packbody class description] in the embedded style sheet, then press [Delete].
   c. Type .packbody {position: relative; left: 100px; width: 300px}
   d. Check your document for errors, make any necessary changes, then save Pack element size.htm as a text document.
   e. Open Pack element size.htm in your Web browser and scroll down to the pack descriptions.

4. **Stack screen elements.**
   a. Open the file HTML L-11.htm in your text editor, then save it as a text document with the filename Pack layers.htm.
   b. In the embedded style sheet, select the text [replace with backtext layer code], then press [Delete].
   c. Type #backtext {position: absolute; left: 275px; font-size: 64pt; font-family: arial; color: #7093DB; z-index: -1}
   d. Scroll and select the text [replace with background text], then press [Delete].
   e. Type <DIV ID="backtext"> and press [Enter].
   f. Type HIKING and press [Enter], then type </DIV>
   g. Check your document for errors, make any necessary changes, then save Pack layers.htm as a text document.
   h. Open Pack layers.htm in your Web browser.

5. Add a scroll bar.

   a. Open the file HTML L-12.htm in your text editor, and save it as a text document with the filename Pack scroll.htm.

   b. In the embedded style sheet, select the text [replace with list scroll code], then press [Delete].

   c. Type #list {height: 300px; width: 600px; overflow: auto}

   d. Scroll and select the text [replace with opening DIV tag], then press [Delete].

   e. Type <DIV ID="list">

   f. Scroll, and select the text [replace with closing DIV tag], press [Delete], then type </DIV>

   g. Check your document for errors, make any necessary changes, then save Pack scroll.htm as a text document.

   h. Open Pack scroll.htm in your Web browser, and scroll down to view the list of pack outlines and descriptions.

   i. Use the scroll bar for the list to view all of the pack descriptions.

6. Create a sidebar.

   a. Open the file HTML L-13.htm in your text editor, then save it as a text document with the filename Pack sidebar.htm.

   b. In the embedded style sheet, select the text [replace with sidebar code], then press [Delete].

   c. Type #sidebar {width: 350; float: right; position: absolute; left: 400px; font-family: arial; font-size: 11pt; background: #8FBC8F}

   d. Scroll and select the text [replace with ID], then press [Delete].

   e. Type ALIGN="left" ID="sidebar"

   f. Check your document for errors, make any necessary changes, then save Pack sidebar.htm as a text document.

   g. Open Pack sidebar.htm in your Web browser.

7. Incorporate an advanced positioning function.

   a. Open the file HTML L-14.htm in your text editor, then save a copy as Pack drag.htm.

   b. Scroll and select the text [replace with drag code] in the first image tag, then press [Delete].

   c. Type CLASS="drag" canDrag

   d. Repeat Steps b and c for the remaining five IMG tags.

   e. Check your document for errors, make any necessary changes, then save Tent drag.htm as a text document.

   f. Open Tent drag.htm in your Web browser.

   g. If you are using Internet Explorer, drag some of the water bottle and tent outlines onto a backpack outline.

▶ Independent Challenges

1. You are revising the Popular supplies page for the Green House plant store. You have incorporated positioning using style sheets to improve the appearance of the Web page and to make sure it displays similarly in different screen resolutions. Also, you have removed some of the features you added earlier to keep the page from overwhelming users with features. The owners would like to add additional information to the page about how to use it. You think this would fit best in a sidebar next to the headings.

To complete this independent challenge:

a. Open the file HTML L-15.htm in your text editor, then save a copy as "Green House supplies with sidebar.htm".

b. In the embedded style sheet, select the text [replace with #sidebar definition], then press [Delete].

c. Type #sidebar {position: relative; width: 25%; float: right; font-family: arial; font-size: 11pt; background: #8FBC8F}

d. Scroll down to the opening DIV tag for the sidebar text, select the text [replace with ID], then press [Delete].

e. Type ALIGN="left" ID="sidebar"

f. Check your document for errors and make any necessary changes, save Green house supplies with sidebar.htm as a text document and close it, then open it in your Web browser. If necessary, edit your code until the page displays appropriately.

2. You are adding CSS positioning information to the rider tips page for Sandhills Regional Public Transit. To superimpose part of the heading text on the logo graphic, you would like to rearrange the heading section.

To complete this independent challenge:

a. Open the file HTML L-16.htm in your Web browser, then explore the page.

b. Open the file HTML L-16.htm in your text editor, then save a copy as "SRPT positioned rider tips.htm".

c. Create an embedded style sheet, define a style in the embedded style sheet named #logo specifying absolute position, top at 25px, left at 25px, and z-index of -1, then scroll down to the opening DIV tag above the IMG tag for bus.jpg and replace the text [replace with ID] with ID="logo".

d. Define a style in the embedded style sheet named #headtop specifying absolute position, left at 30px, and top at 25px, then scroll down to the opening DIV tag for the first line of the page heading and replace the text [replace with ID] with ID="headtop".

e. Define a style in the embedded style sheet named #headbtm specifying absolute position, left at 60 px, and top at 325px, then scroll down to the opening DIV tag for the second line of the page heading and replace the text [replace with ID] with ID="headbtm".

f. Define a style in the embedded style sheet named #sidetext specifying absolute position, text floating on the right, left at 400px, top at 25px, and width of 350px, then scroll down to the opening DIV tag for the instructions section and replace the text [replace with ID] with ALIGN="left" ID="sidetext".

g. Add style code to the UL tag for the bulleted list specifying relative position and top at 0px.

h. Check your document for errors and make any necessary changes, save and close it, then open it in your Web browser. If necessary, edit your code until the page displays appropriately.

3. You are updating Web pages for the Community Public School Volunteers organization by adding CSS positioning information. You want to improve the layout by placing the CPSV logo graphic behind the heading text.
   To complete this independent challenge:

a. Explore the file HTML L-17.htm in your Web browser, then explore the file.

b. Open HTML L-17 in your text editor, then save a copy as "CPSV positioned home.htm".

c. Create a style in the embedded style sheet to place the new, widened logo (which is the colored letters CPSV) behind the heading text at the top of the page with absolute positioning. Use the left and top properties to position it so that it appears centered behind the text. (*Hint*: The heading is positioned relatively to allow it to be displayed in front of the logo in Navigator. Be sure to set a z-index for the logo to place it behind the text.) Reference the style you created in the opening DIV tag for the logo graphic, which is named cpsvlog3.jpg.

d. Create a style in the embedded style sheet for the DIV tagset enclosing the H3 heading and the links to narrow the width of the text area to 50% of the page width, position the section relatively, 25% to the left, change the background color to white (#FFFFFF), and add a 1pt black solid border (the style code for this feature is border: 1pt black solid). Reference the style you created in the opening DIV before the <H3> heading.

e. Save your changes, preview the page in your Web browser, and make any changes necessary to improve the appearance of the Web page.

4. The World Wide Web Consortium (W3C) has included a new set of positioning specifications in its revised Cascading Style Sheet guidelines, known as CSS2. Many of the new features that the W3C has outlined are supported in Microsoft and Netscape fifth-generation browsers. To complete this independent challenge, log on to the Internet, open your Web browser, and use a search engine to locate and open the Web site for the W3C. Locate information about the CSS2 guidelines, then print details of two new positioning features in CSS2. Write a paragraph on each feature, including what it allows a Web programmer to do and suggested syntax for implementing it. Check the Microsoft and Netscape Web sites to find out if their fifth-generation browsers will support either of the features you selected and include this information in your paragraphs. Submit your printout and paragraphs to your instructor.

▶ Visual Workshop

You are improving the layout of the Web pages for Touchstone Booksellers using CSS positioning. Using the file HTML L-18.htm as a starting point, position the heading elements to create the layout in Figure L-18. (*Hint:* Think of the text blocks on the left and right sides of the graphic as two floating sidebars. You should add code only to the two sidebar text blocks.) Save your changes as a text document with the filename Touchstone positioned home.htm.

FIGURE L-18

Touchstone Booksellers

Specializing in nonfiction of all types  *a locally-owned, independent bookstore since 1948*

You can use our Web site to search our current stock, place an order, request a search for an out-of-print book, or find out about upcoming events at our store.

- Search our stock

- Place an order

HTML

Unit M

Implementing
Advanced DHTML Features

Objectives

▶ Understand advanced features
▶ Filter content
▶ Scale content
▶ Animate element position
▶ Create 3D animation
▶ Transition elements
▶ Create a slideshow
▶ Transition between pages

Using tools such as CSS, dynamic style, dynamic content, and CSS positioning, you can create interactive Web pages with print-quality formatting and layout. By combining these tools and writing scripts to work with them, you can continually create new features. The companies making browsers also continue to simplify the process by adding browser-native features that require little code and no scripting. Lydia Burgos's supervisor has asked her to create a Web-based presentation about Nomad Ltd. In addition to incorporating CSS formatting and positioning to make the page attractive and easy to read, she plans to add advanced effects to keep her users' interest.

Understanding Advanced Features

In addition to the many effects that the basic DHTML tools offer, you can create complex-looking visual features through a combination of proprietary effects and simple scripts. Although overuse of any dynamic feature can overload users visually and slow down their computers, the limited and precise use of these advanced features can help users focus on the most important aspects of each page. Many proprietary advanced features work only on Internet Explorer 4. However, these innovations will likely be supported by both fifth-generation browsers. Learning these features now is a good way to stay current with trends in Web page design. As Lydia organizes her presentation, she notes different advanced features that she can use for different effects.

Modifying an element's appearance

In addition to basic color and sizing formatting for text and graphics alike, Internet Explorer offers predefined element formats that affect appearance in complex ways. These formats, known as **filters**, allow you to create many effects, such as a shadow or glow, as shown in Figure M-1. Another way to affect element appearance is by combining a script with CSS position or size information to create the effect of movement, or **animation**. By slowly changing an element's placement or size with a script, you can create the effect of movement without requiring special software or extensive system resources. To help ensure your page layouts remain attractive at different screen resolutions and browser window sizes, you also can include simple scripts to resize elements, depending on each user's browser size.

Open and close effects

You can effectively draw attention to a particular page element by scripting its appearance when the page opens. Internet Explorer offers predefined effects called **transitions**, which cause elements to appear gradually and in specific patterns when the page opens or exits. You can apply these effects to selected elements or to the entire page, as shown in Figure M-2. By using an animation script with offscreen starting coordinates and a timer, you can create **presentation effects** in which elements appear on the screen gradually and in a specific order.

FIGURE M-1: Web page displaying a filtered element

Glow filter adds colored halo to text

Nomad Ltd

Nomad Ltd
MISSION
Corporate goals

Our mission

Nomad Ltd is a national sporting goods retailer dedicated to delivering high-quality sporting gear and adventure travel.

Achieving our mission

Nomad Ltd has been in business for over ten years. During that time, we have offered tours all over the world and sold sporting

Tour types:
Art
Leisure
Athlete

FIGURE M-2: Web page opening using a transition effect

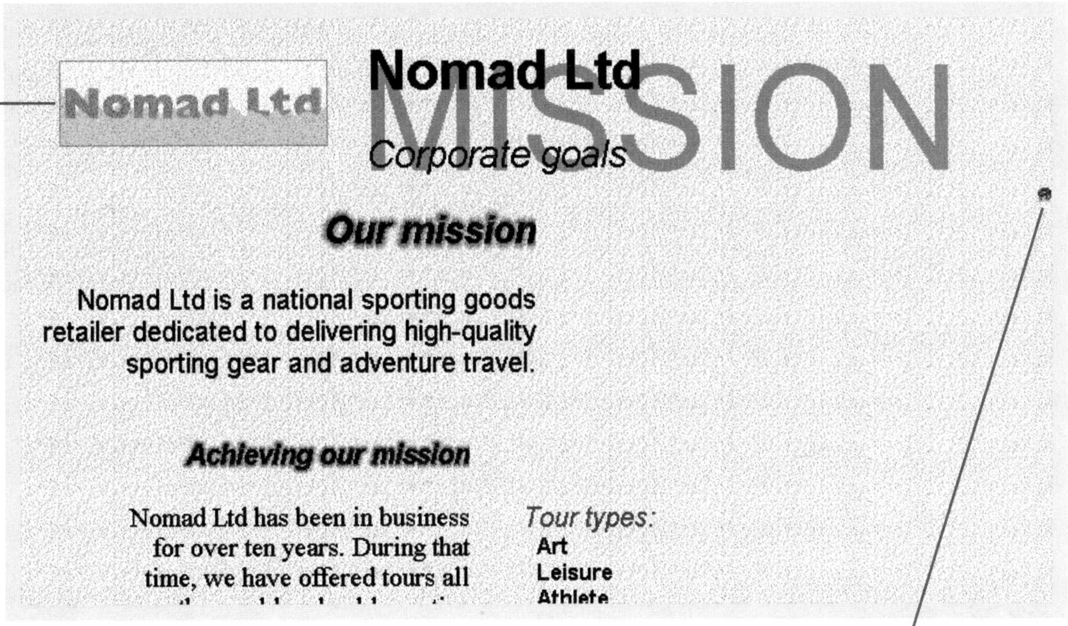

Graphic appearing gradually using "blend" transition

Nomad Ltd

Nomad Ltd
MISSION
Corporate goals

Our mission

Nomad Ltd is a national sporting goods retailer dedicated to delivering high-quality sporting gear and adventure travel.

Achieving our mission

Nomad Ltd has been in business for over ten years. During that time, we have offered tours all

Tour types:
Art
Leisure
Athlete

Earth graphic as it appears at start of load

HTML

HTML

Filtering Content

DHTML includes several tools that let you change the basic appearance of text and graphics by varying the size, color, and other characteristics of selected elements. In addition, Internet Explorer supports an extended set of properties, known as **filters**, that allow you to modify element appearance in complex ways. Table M-1 lists and describes the filters available in Internet Explorer 4. ✎ Lydia wants to call attention to headings in her presentation page without adding more colored text to the page, so she decides to try filtering the headings instead.

Steps

1. Start your text-editor program, open **HTML M-1.htm**, then save it as a text document with the filename **Presentation filter.htm**

2. Select the text **[replace with misshead filter code]** in the embedded style sheet, then press **[Delete]**

3. Type **{height: 14pt; filter: glow(color=#B8860B)}**
   To apply a filter using a DIV or SPAN tag, the text must be absolutely positioned or have a defined height or width. In order to meet this requirement without affecting her layout, Lydia sets the height to 14pt, which is the same height as the heading text.

4. Select the text **[replace with second filter code]** in the #achieve style definition, then press **[Delete]**

5. Type **height: 12pt; filter: glow(color=#B8860B, strength=3)**
   Because the font size in the second heading is smaller than in the first, Lydia decides to lower the intensity of the glow by assigning a strength value. This keeps the glow effect proportional to the text dimensions. Figure M-3 shows the completed code for the glow filters in the embedded style sheet.

6. Scroll down until the **<H2>** heading "Our mission" appears in the document window
   Lydia wants to apply the filter to the text within the H2 tags. However, filters are incompatible with all heading tags, so she has to embed the H2 tags within DIV tags and then call the filter from the opening DIV tag instead.

7. Type **<DIV ID="misshead">** before **<H2>** Our mission **</H2>**, then position the insertion point after the closing H2 tag and type **</DIV>**

8. Check your document for errors, make changes as necessary, then save **Presentation filter.htm** as a text document

9. Open **Presentation filter.htm** in your Web browser
   See Figure M-4, which shows the presentation Web page containing the filtered text. If you are using Internet Explorer 4, the filter adds a halo of color around each letter.

Combining filters

In addition to the unique effect that each filter can create on a Web page, you can increase the possibilities by combining filters, a process known as **chaining**. You can add as many filters as you desire to an element by simply listing them in the element's tag or style sheet description. You must separate the code for each filter by a space. For example, you can chain a drop shadow and a glow to a graphic by calling both of these filters in the picture's style sheet description as follows: **#image: {position: absolute; top: 150px; filter: dropshadow(color=#483D8B, OffX=3, OffY=3) glow(color=#9933CC, strength=5)}.** This code would add both drop shadow and glow effects to the graphic.

FIGURE M-3: Web document containing filter code

```
#heading {position: relative; left: 250px}
#mission {width: 375px; font-family: arial}
#misshead {height: 14pt; filter: glow(color=#B8860B) }
#main {position: absolute; left: 60px; width: 275px}
#earth {float: right; position: relative; top: -20px}
.norm {font-weight: normal}
#head1 {font-style: italic; color: #8E236B}
#head2 {font-style: italic; color: #6B8E23}
#head3 {font-style: italic; color: #7093DB}
#head4 {font-style: italic; color: #9400D3}
#achieve {height: 12pt; filter: glow(color=#B8860B, strength=3) }
.font12 {font-size: 12pt}
.bot {color: #3232CD}
.space {line-height: 6pt; position: relative}
.item {position: relative; left: 10px; font-size: 10pt; font-weight: bold}
UL {position: relative; left: -20px; top: -20px; font-size: 10pt; font-
weight: bold}
.sidebar {float: right; position: absolute; left: 375px; font-family: arial;
width: 200px}
</STYLE>

</HEAD>

<BODY BACKGROUND="Egg shell.jpg">

<DIV ID="logo">
```

Style code to add
filter effect to text

FIGURE M-4: Web page displaying filtered text

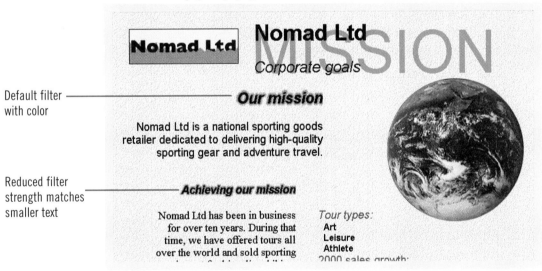

Default filter
with color

Reduced filter
strength matches
smaller text

TABLE M-1: Internet Explorer 4 filter effects

filter effect	description	filter effect	description
Alpha	Sets a transparency level	Grayscale	Drops color information from the image
Blur	Creates the impression of moving at high speed	Invert	Reverses the hue, saturation, and brightness values
Chroma	Makes a specific color transparent	Light	Projects light sources onto an object
Drop Shadow	Creates an offset solid silhouette	Mask	Creates a transparent mask from an object
FlipH	Creates a horizontal mirror image	Shadow	Creates a solid silhouette of the object
FlipV	Creates a vertical mirror image	Wave	Creates a sine wave distortion along the x- and y-axes
Glow	Adds radiance around the outside edges of the object	XRay	Shows just the edges of the object

Scaling Content

One drawback of using basic DHTML positioning is a layout's reliance on a particular window size. For example, an image may fit well in a layout at a certain indentation in a maximized browser window on an SVGA screen. However, on a lower-resolution monitor or on a non-maximized browser window, the element may appear much closer to the right edge of the screen, thus changing the original layout design. Using basic scripts to complement CSS-P, however, you can automatically adjust the position of your Web page elements based on the browser window size. Because Navigator does not recognize changes in style properties (including element dimensions) after the page has loaded, this feature works only in Internet Explorer. Lydia has laid out her page in a maximized browser window set at a resolution of 800 × 600. However, she wants her layout to remain as consistent as possible in smaller windows and at lower resolutions.

Steps

1. Open **HTML M-2.htm** in your text editor, then save it as a text document with the filename **Presentation scale.htm**

2. Scroll down to the script tags in the page's head section, select the text **[replace with scale script]**, then press **[Delete]**

   Lydia has already inserted a browser-detection script, along with a line of code to suppress errors in Navigator.

3. Type the following script, pressing **[Enter]** at the end of each line:

```
function change() {
    if (document.body.clientWidth < 640) {
        bgword.style.fontSize="48pt"
        earth.style.width="25%"
    }
    else {
        bgword.style.fontSize="64pt"
        earth.style.width="35%"
    }
}

window.onresize=change
window.onload=change
```

   (handwritten annotations: "width of web page", "small", "big")

   Instead of trying to adjust every screen element to fit on a smaller screen, Lydia focuses on the elements along the right edge of the screen: the heading background text and the earth graphic. Her script adjusts both elements to a size that fits into a maximized browser window set at a 640 × 480 resolution. Figure M-5 shows the Web page document code containing the script.

4. Check your document for errors, make changes as necessary, then save **Presentation scale.htm** as a text document

5. Open **Presentation scale.htm** in your Web browser, then make sure your browser window is maximized

6. If you are using Internet Explorer and your display mode is 800 × 600 or greater, click the **Restore Window button** 🗗 at the top right of the browser window to decrease the size of the document window a fixed amount

   If your display is in 640 × 480 mode, note that the large background text and the earth graphic fit on the screen without requiring you to scroll right. Figure M-6 shows the presentation Web page in a reduced window. The scale script you inserted reduced the background text size and the graphic size to fit better in a limited display area.

FIGURE M-5: Web page document code containing scaling script

```
<SCRIPT LANGUAGE="javascript">
<!--
Nav4 = (document.layers) ? 1:0;
IE4 = (document.all) ? 1:0;

if(!IE4) {window.onerror=null}

function change() {
        if (document.body.clientWidth < 640) {
                bgword.style.fontSize="48pt"
                earth.style.width="25%"
        }
        else {
                bgword.style.fontSize="64pt"
                earth.style.width="35%"
        }
}

window.onresize=change
window.onload=change
//-->
</SCRIPT>

</HEAD>

<BODY BACKGROUND="Egg shell.jpg">
```

Script to resize elements based on window size

FIGURE M-6: Scaled objects in reduced browser window

Browser window size reduced from maximized view

Reduced text and graphic sizes fit in window

Scaling by percent

Specifying element dimensions in percentages, rather than pixels or points, has many applications in DHTML design. Usually, you can simply specify the height, width, or font size in percent. Because percentage measurements reflect a percentage of the parent element dimension, a percentage-sized element automatically resizes when the window size changes. To make sure the element remains proportionally scaled when specifying element dimensions, be sure to specify only height or width, but not both. Sometimes, screen elements need to change position depending on the screen size or when an element such as a graphic would look distorted if it became too big or too small. In these cases, you need a scaling script to resize your pages.

Animating Element Position

By creating simple scripts to interact with position and layer information, you can add impressive features to your Web pages without requiring extensive system resources on a user's computer. To create basic animation, for example, you can script an element's position coordinates to increase or decrease slowly when the user first opens the page, until the element reaches its final, absolute coordinates. Lydia decides to animate the Nomad Ltd logo to move into place when a user first opens the page.

Steps 1 2 3 4

1. Open the file **HTML M-3.htm** in your text editor, then save it as a text document with the filename **Presentation position animate.htm**

2. Scroll down to the **function slide()** in the head section and examine the script
   The function slide() positions the logo graphic out of screen range on the right side of the page and then incrementally reduces its left coordinate until it reaches the final position of 30. Lydia also has changed the left coordinate for the #logo style to -1000, a value that triggers the slide() function.

3. Scroll down to the opening BODY tag, select the text **[replace with event handler]**, then press **[Delete]**

4. Type **onLoad="slide()"**
   The onLoad event handler triggers the "slide" script every time the browser loads the BODY section. Figure M-7 shows the code for the event handler to call the slide() function.

5. Check your document for errors, make any necessary changes, then save **Presentation position animate.htm** as a text file

6. Open **Presentation position animate.htm** in your Web browser
   As Figure M-8 shows, the graphic slides into position from the right edge of the window after you open the page. Because Navigator can't change a page's style information after loading, it does not display the logo in its final location.

FIGURE M-7: Web document showing code to call slide() function

Slide function in page head

Event handler triggers slide script when page opens

```
window.onresize=change
window.onload=change

function slide() {
       var pic = document.all.logo;
       if (-1000 == pic.style.pixelLeft) {
              pic.style.pixelLeft = document.body.offsetWidth +
document.body.scrollLeft;
       }
       if (50 <= pic.style.pixelLeft) {
              pic.style.pixelLeft -= 20;
              setTimeout("slide();", 50);
       }
       else {pic.style.pixelLeft =30;}
}
//-->
</SCRIPT>

</HEAD>

<BODY BACKGROUND="Egg shell.jpg" onLoad="slide()">

<DIV ID="logo">
<IMG SRC="nomad.jpg">
</DIV>
```

change to zero

FIGURE M-8: Nomad Ltd logo sliding into position

Nomad Ltd logo sliding right to left into final position

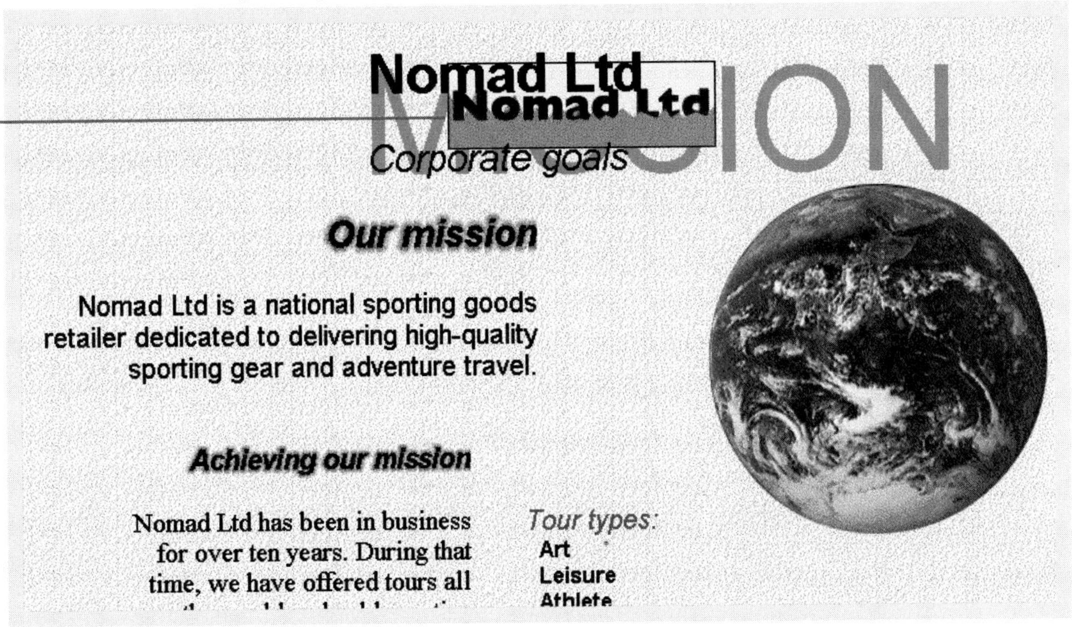
Nomad Ltd
Nomad Ltd
MISSION
Corporate goals
Our mission
Nomad Ltd is a national sporting goods retailer dedicated to delivering high-quality sporting gear and adventure travel.
Achieving our mission
Nomad Ltd has been in business for over ten years. During that time, we have offered tours all
Tour types:
Art
Leisure
Athlete

HTML

Creating 3D Animation

You can easily create simple animation on your Web pages with a script that slowly adjusts an element's top or left attribute over a period of time. By incorporating changes in element size, using the width and height properties, you also can create the illusion of 3D movement. Although animation in standard multimedia formats can require special software or browser extensions and significant computer memory, DHTML animation creates the effect of movement using just one image and a small script running on the user's browser. A lot of animation could distract users from the rest of your Web page, but a short animation, or animation of a small element, can make a page interesting and distinctive. ▶ Lydia decides that instead of having the Nomad Ltd logo graphic move into position sideways, she would like the earth graphic to appear to approach the user. She creates this effect with 3D animation.

Steps

1. Open the file **HTML M-4.htm** in your text editor, save it as a text document with the filename **Presentation 3D animate.htm**

QuickTip
You can use a semicolon to mark the end of a line of code in JavaScript. The semicolon is not required at the end of a line, and it is often used only after short commands in a script.

2. Scroll down and select the text **[replace with 3D animation script]** in the page's head section, press **[Delete]**, then type the following script, pressing **[Enter]** at the end of each line:

```
function grow() {
    if (earthpic.width<250) {
        x=window.setTimeout('grow()', 100)
        earthpic.width=earthpic.width + 10
    }
}

window.onload = grow;
```

Figure M-9 shows the Web page code containing the script. The script uses the graphic's HTML width property, rather than the CSS width, because HTML width is easier to work with in this situation. Lydia has deleted the logo animation script.

3. Scroll down to the IMG tag for the earth graphic, and replace the text **[replace with width property]** with **WIDTH=0**

The script you entered increases the width value by 10 pixels at a time and pauses for a fraction of a second between each increase, which creates the illusion of animation.

4. Check your document for errors, make any necessary changes, then save **Presentation 3D animate.htm** as a text document

5. Open **Presentation 3D animate.htm** in your Web browser

Figure M-10 shows the page as it is loading. As the page loads, the earth graphic appears and slowly grows as it seems to move toward you.

FIGURE M-9: Web document containing grow script

3D animation script
for earth graphic

```
window.onload=change

function grow() {
        if (earthpic.width<250) {
                x=window.setTimeout('grow()', 100)
                earthpic.width=earthpic.width + 10
        }
}

window.onload = grow;
//-->
</SCRIPT>

</HEAD>

<BODY BACKGROUND="Egg shell.jpg">

<DIV ID="logo">
<IMG SRC="nomad.jpg">
</DIV>

<DIV ID="bgword">
MISSION
</DIV>

<DIV ID="heading">
```

FIGURE M-10: 3D animation of earth graphic

Gradual size
increase on load
creates illusion of
earth approaching

Animated GIFs

Another popular way to create animation in Web pages is to create **animated GIFs**. A GIF is a graphic file in a specific format. Although most GIFs are static, showing just one image, the GIF format also supports animation. To create an animated GIF, you use special software to combine two or more static graphics and to specify the delay between the display of each frame. You can create a movie-like movement effect with animated GIFs, but one of their most widespread uses on the Web today is in banner advertisements on Web pages. These static GIFs often alternate between two different frames of information, such as an advertising motto and the company logo. Although DHTML animation is easier and cheaper to create, animated GIFs are not limited to fourth-generation browsers and are thus accessible by a wider Web audience.

HTML

Unit M
HTML

Transitioning Elements

Beyond simply hiding and showing an element, or applying filters to an element's display, you can affect the way an element becomes visible or hidden by using filter effects known as **transitions**. For example, one popular transition effect is to make an element appear or disappear gradually in a checkerboard pattern. Because Navigator does not recognize transitions, this feature works only with Internet Explorer. Internet Explorer 4 comes with two transition filters: **blend**, which creates a simple fade-in or fade-out effect, and **reveal**, which allows the more complex filtering effects. These effects, which can be applied to text as well as graphics, can keep a user's interest and distinguish your pages from others on the Web. ✎ Lydia decides to use the blend transition on the Nomad Ltd logo when the page opens.

Steps

1. Open the file **HTML M-5.htm** in your text editor, then save it as a text document with the filename **Presentation transition element.htm**

2. Select and replace the text **[replace with style information]** which is in the **#logo** style specification in the page's embedded style sheet with **visibility: hidden; filter: blendTrans(duration=7)**

   The blend transition can switch from hidden to visible or vice versa. Lydia specifies that she wants the graphic to start out hidden and then become visible using the blendTrans filter. The duration variable details the length of time in seconds of the transition from beginning to end.

3. Scroll down to the end of the page's head section, then replace the text **[replace with transition function]** with the following script, pressing **[Enter]** at the end of each line:

   ```
   function doTrans() {
       logo.filters.blendTrans.Apply();
       logo.style.visibility="visible";
       logo.filters.blendTrans.Play();
   }
   ```

   Unlike standard filters, transition filters require scripts to define what happens when they run. The first line of the doTrans() function calls the transition's Apply method, which creates the final state defined in the next line, which is "visible." Finally, the Play method starts the transition filter itself to create the smooth change from hidden to visible. Figure M-11 shows the Web document code containing the function.

4. Scroll to the bottom of the document just before the closing page tags, delete the text **[replace with function call]**, insert opening and closing script tags, and type **doTrans()** as the body of the script

   This script, shown in Figure M-12, calls the doTrans() function when the page finishes loading in the browser window.

5. Check your document for errors and make any necessary changes, then save **Presentation transition element.htm** as a text document

6. Open **Presentation transition element.htm** in your Web browser

   As Figure M-13 shows, the Nomad Ltd logo slowly fades into view as the page opens.

Trouble?

If the logo does not appear gradually, your video card or monitor is probably not compatible with transitions.

FIGURE M-11: **Document code containing function**

Function controlling transition effect

```
window.onload = grow;

function doTrans() {
      logo.filters.blendTrans.Apply();
      logo.style.visibility="visible";
      logo.filters.blendTrans.Play();
}
//-->
</SCRIPT>

</HEAD>
```

FIGURE M-12: **Document code containing script to call function**

Script triggers doTrans() function after page loads

```
<DIV>For more information on Nomad Ltd, please email our <A
HREF="MAILTO:relations@nomadltd.com">community relations
department</A>.</DIV>

</DIV>

<SCRIPT LANGUAGE="javascript">
<!--
doTrans()
//-->
</SCRIPT>

</BODY>
</HTML>
```

FIGURE M-13: **Nomad Ltd logo showing blend transition**

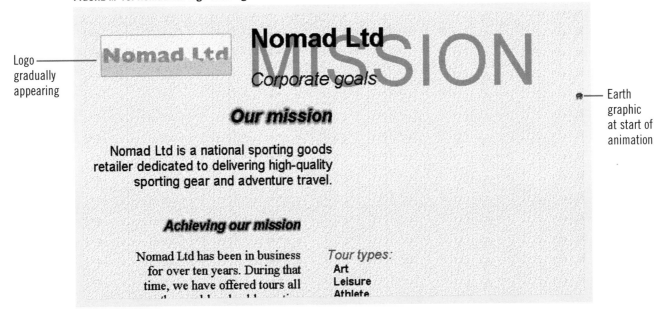

Logo gradually appearing

Earth graphic at start of animation

HTML

Creating a Slideshow

Presentation software, such as Microsoft PowerPoint, allows you to move through a related set of pages, or **slides**, by clicking a mouse button. It is easy to add this effect to Web pages with scripting. Although standard HTML hyperlinks can create a similar effect, DHTML features enable your users to advance by clicking anywhere on the page, rather than scrolling to locate and click a hyperlink. Also, by eliminating navigation-specific elements, you can keep your pages focused on the presentation topic and create a more unified design. ◀━━━ Lydia has created the second page for her Web presentation. She wants to script the first page to open the second in response to a mouse click, which will allow Internet Explorer users to click anywhere on the Web page to advance to the second Web page.

Steps

1. Open the file **HTML M-6.htm** in your text editor, then save it as a text document with the filename **Presentation slideshow.htm**

2. Scroll down to the opening BODY tag, select and replace the text **[replace with event handler]** with **onClick="window.location.href='Presentation page 2.htm'"**
   This event handler changes the window's HREF, or page address, to "Presentation page 2.htm," the second page that Lydia prepared.

3. Scroll down below the text "Corporate goals," then select and replace the text **[replace with instruction text]** with the following script, pressing **[Enter]** at the end of each line:
   <DIV ID="instr">
   Click anywhere to advance to next slide.
   </DIV>
   This text tells users how to navigate through the presentation. Figure M-14 shows the Web page code containing the event handler and the instruction text. Lydia has already added an embedded style for the instructions and has edited the scaling code to reposition the text in smaller window sizes.

4. Check your document for errors, make any necessary changes, then save **Presentation slideshow.htm** as a text document

5. Open **Presentation slideshow.htm** in your Web browser, then click anywhere on the page
   The second presentation page opens, as shown in Figure M-15. By simply adding the event handler to all presentation pages except for the last one, Lydia can enable users to easily page through the presentation online.

FIGURE M-14: Web page code containing event handler and instruction text

Event handler
allows easy
navigation to
second page

```
</HEAD>

<BODY BACKGROUND="Egg shell.jpg" onClick="window.location.href='Presentation
page 2.htm'">

<DIV ID="logo">
<IMG SRC="nomad.jpg">
</DIV>

<DIV ID="bgword">
MISSION
</DIV>

<DIV ID="heading">
<H1>Nomad Ltd</H1>
<H2 CLASS="norm">Corporate goals</H2>
</DIV>

<DIV ID="instr">
Click anywhere to advance to next slide.
</DIV>

<DIV ID="earth">
<IMG SRC="earth.jpg" ID="earthpic" WIDTH=0>
</DIV>
```

Navigation
instructions

FIGURE M-15: Second presentation page

Nomad Ltd

Nomad Ltd HISTORY
Corporate beginnings

Where we came from

Jasper Barber started Nomad Ltd in 1987 as a single store in Boulder, Colorado, a popular area for many types of outdoor recreation. Jasper set out to create a store offering affordable, high-quality outdoor supplies. After opening two more stores in Colorado, Jasper began to expand Nomad Ltd nationally. In 1991 we introduced the Nomad line of outdoor equipment, and 1993 saw

HTML

Transitioning Between Pages

In addition to creating transition effects for specific elements on a Web page, you can apply transitions when opening or closing a page. In this situation, transitions can grab and hold a viewer's attention, and can help your page to stand out among pages a user has recently seen. Each Web page can trigger transitions upon opening and exiting, independent of the preceding or following page. ⬛ As a final touch, Lydia decides she wants Internet Explorer 4 users to see a closing transition to each of the pages in her Web presentation. She starts by adding a closing transition that appears when the first page closes.

Steps

1. Open the file **HTML M-7.htm** in your text editor, then save it as a text document with the filename **Presentation page transition.htm**

2. Scroll down below the embedded style sheet in the page's head section and replace the text **[replace with META tag]** with **<META http-equiv="Page-Exit" CONTENT="RevealTrans(Duration=5,Transition=3)">**

   Figure M-16 shows the Web page code containing the META tag. Creating an interpage transition requires no scripting. Instead, you insert an HTML META tag in the page's head section, calling the transition and defining its properties. You can set the http-equiv property, which tells when the transition takes effect, to "Page-Enter" or "Page-Exit." You use the CONTENT property to specify the transition filter name and parameters, just as you do with the STYLE property for element transitions. Lydia uses the reveal transition's "Circle out" pattern, indicated by the Transition number 3. Table M-2 lists other reveal transitions and their number codes.

3. Check your document for errors, make any necessary changes, then save **Presentation page transition.htm** as a text document

Trouble?

Depending on your computer speed, you may see a small white circle in the center of the screen just before the transition starts.

4. Open **Presentation page transition.htm** in your Web browser, then click anywhere on the page

   The second presentation page opens in a circle spreading outward from the center of the browser window, as shown in Figure M-17. You can apply other transition patterns, as listed in Table M-2, to open or close pages.

5. Make and save changes in your text-editor program as needed, check changes in your Web browser program, close your Web browser program, then close your text editor program

FIGURE M-16: Web page code containing META tag

META tag inserted to control interpage transition

```
.sidebar {float: right; position: absolute; left: 375px; font-family: arial;
width: 200px}
</STYLE>

<META http-equiv="Page-Exit" CONTENT="RevealTrans(Duration=5,Transition=3)">

<SCRIPT LANGUAGE="javascript">
<!--
Nav4 = (document.layers) ? 1:0;
IE4 = (document.all) ? 1:0;

if(!IE4) {window.onerror=null}

function change() {
        if (document.body.clientWidth < 640) {
                bgword.style.fontSize="48pt"
                earth.style.width="25%"
        }
        else {
                bgword.style.fontSize="64pt"
                earth.style.width="35%"
        }
}

window.onresize=change
window.onload=change
```

FIGURE M-17: Web page closing with "Circle out" reveal transition

First presentation page

Second presentation page opening outward in circle

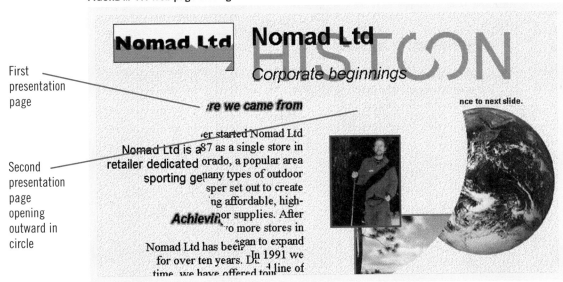

TABLE M-2: Reveal transition effects

reveal transition name	value	reveal transition name	value	reveal transition name	value
Box in	0	Vertical blinds	8	Split horizontal out	16
Box out	1	Horizontal blinds	9	Strips left down	17
Circle in	2	Checkerboard across	10	Strips left up	18
Circle out	3	Checkerboard down	11	Strips right down	19
Wipe up	4	Random dissolve	12	Strips right up	20
Wipe down	5	Split vertical in	13	Random bars horizontal	21
Wipe right	6	Split vertical out	14	Random bars vertical	22
Wipe left	7	Split horizontal in	15	Random	23

Practice

► Concepts Review

Label the advanced DHTML effects indicated on Lydia's Web page in Figure M-18.

FIGURE M-18

Element transition 1

Glow 2

3D Animation 3

Match each term with its description.

4. Filter *e*
5. Position animation *c*
6. 3D animation *a*
7. Transition *b*
8. Scaling *d*

a. Gradually changes element size, using the width and height properties
b. Gradually changes element appearance, becoming visible or hidden
c. Gradually changes element position, using top and left style properties
d. Fits page elements to lower screen resolution or smaller window size
e. Property that modifies element appearance in complex ways

Select the best answer from the list of choices.

9. You can continually create new advanced DHTML features by combining basic features with
   a. CSS.   *but can be all*
   b. Dynamic style.
   c. Dynamic content.
   d. Scripts.

10. Which of the following is *not* a filter?
    a. Shadow
    b. Blur
    c. Animation
    d. Blend transition

11. What is the advantage of using DHTML animation rather than other animation methods on the Web?
    a. DHTML animation doesn't require scripts.
    b. DHTML animation uses few system resources.
    c. DHTML animation uses special software.
    d. DHTML animation uses no system resources.

12. Which method will *not* change an element's appearance over a period of time?
    a. Position animation
    b. 3D animation
    c. Glow filter
    d. Blend transition filter

13. Which HTML tag do you use to implement an interpage transition?
    a. <LINK>
    b. <META>
    c. <A>
    d. <SCRIPT>

14. Which is an advantage of using animated GIFs rather than DHTML animation?
    a. Animated GIFs use no system resources.
    b. Animated GIF display is not limited to fourth-generation browsers.
    c. Creating animated GIFs requires no special software.
    d. Animated GIFs can show 3D animation.

▶ Skills Review

1. Filter content.
    a. Open HTML M-8.htm in your Web browser and explore the page.
    b. Open HTML M-8.htm in your text editor and save a copy as Tours filter.htm.
    c. In the embedded style sheet, select the text [replace with histhead filter code], then press [Delete].
    d. Type height: 14pt; filter: glow(color=#6B8E23)
    e. Select the text [replace with second filter code] in the #tourshead style definition, then press [Delete].
    f. Type height: 12pt; filter: glow(color=#6B8E23, strength=3)
    g. Check your document for errors, make changes as necessary, then save Tours filter.htm.
    h. Open Tours filter.htm in your Web browser.

2. Scale content.
    a. Open HTML M-9.htm in your text editor, then save a copy as Tours scale.htm.
    b. Select the text [replace with scale script], then press [Delete].
    c. Enter the opening tags for a JavaScript script, then type the following script, pressing [Enter] at the end of each line:

```
function change() {
        if (document.body.clientWidth < 640) {
                bgword.style.fontSize="48pt"
        }
        else {
                bgword.style.fontSize="64pt"
        }
}


window.onresize=change
window.onload=change
```

    d. Enter the closing script tags, check your document for errors, make changes as necessary, then save Tours scale.htm.
    e. Open Tours scale.htm in your Web browser, then click the Restore Window button to decrease the size of the document window a fixed amount and note the changes to the background text in the heading. If necessary, drag the right edge of the window to the left to decrease the screen width until the change takes place.
    f. Click the browser maximize button.

3. Animate element position.
    a. Open the file HTML M-10.htm in your text editor, then save it as a text document with the filename Tours position animate.htm.
    b. Scroll down to the opening BODY tag, select the text [replace with event handler], then press [Delete].
    c. Type onLoad="slide()"
    d. Check your document for errors, make any necessary changes, then save as Tours position animate.htm.
    e. Open Tours position animate.htm in your Web browser.

4. Create 3D animation.

a. Open the file HTML M-11.htm in your text editor, then save it as a text document with the filename Tours 3D animate.htm.

b. Select the text [replace with 3D animation script] in the page's head section, press [Delete], then type the following script, pressing [Enter] at the end of each line:

```
function grow() {
        if (mtnpic.width<180) {
                x=window.setTimeout('grow()', 100)
                mtnpic.width=mtnpic.width + 10
        }
}
```

c. In the BODY tag, delete the text [replace with event handler], and type onLoad="grow()"

d. Scroll down to the IMG tag for the mountain graphic and replace the text [replace with width setting] with WIDTH=0

e. Check your document for errors, make any necessary changes, then save as Tours 3D animate.htm.

f. Open Tours 3D animate.htm in your Web browser.

5. Use transition elements.

a. Open the file HTML M-12.htm in your text editor, then save a copy as Tours transition element.htm.

b. In the #logo style specification in the page's embedded style sheet, replace the text [replace with style information] with visibility: hidden; filter: revealTrans(Transition=12, Duration=5)

c. Scroll down to the end of the page's head section and replace the text [replace with transition function] with the following, pressing [Enter] at the end of each line:

```
function doTrans() {
        logo.filters.revealTrans.Apply();
        logo.style.visibility="visible";
        logo.filters.revealTrans.Play();
}
```

d. Scroll to the bottom of the document just before the closing page tags, delete the text [replace with function call], insert opening and closing script tags, and type doTrans() as the body of the script.

e. Check your document for errors, make any necessary changes, then save as Tours transition element.htm.

f. Open Tours transition element.htm in your Web browser.

6. Create a slideshow.

a. Open the file HTML M-13.htm in your text editor, then save it as a text document with the filename Tours slideshow.htm.

b. Scroll down to the opening BODY tag and replace the text [replace with event handler] with onClick="window.location.href='Tours page 2.htm'"

c. Scroll down below the text "Tours division", select and replace the text [replace with instruction text] with the following script, pressing [Enter] at the end of each line:

```
<DIV ID="instr">
Click anywhere to advance to next slide.
</DIV>
```

d. Check your document for errors, make any necessary changes, then save Tours slideshow.htm.

e. Open Tours slideshow.htm in your Web browser, then click anywhere on the page.

7. Transition between pages.

   a. Open the file HTML M-14.htm in your text editor, then save a copy as Tours page transition.htm.

   b. Scroll down below the embedded style sheet in the page's head section and replace the text [replace with META tag] with the following: <META http-equiv="Page-Exit" CONTENT="RevealTrans(Duration=5,Transition=10)">

   c. Check your document for errors, make any necessary changes, then save as Tours page transition.htm.

   d. Open Tours page transition.htm in your Web browser, then click anywhere on the page.

▶ Independent Challenges

1. The owners of the Green House plant store have seen transition filters in use on other Web pages and think this effect would make their pages more interesting. You decide to add the "random dissolve" reveal transition to the secondary heading on the "Popular supplies" page.

  To complete this independent challenge:

   a. Open the file HTML M-15.htm in your text editor, then save it as a text document with the filename Green House transition.htm.

   b. Add the following style to the embedded style sheet in the page's head section:
#subhead {visibility: hidden; height: 16pt; filter: revealTrans(Transition=12, Duration=5)}.

   c. Scroll down to the end of the page's head section and replace the text [replace with transition function] with the following script, pressing [Enter] at the end of each line. Be sure to include opening and closing script tags.
function doTrans() {
       subhead.filters.revealTrans.Apply();
       subhead.style.visibility="visible";
       subhead.filters.revealTrans.Play();
}

   d. In the opening BODY tag, replace the text [replace with function call] with onLoad="doTrans()".

   e. Check your document for errors, make any necessary changes, then save Green House transition.htm.

   f. Open Green House transition.htm in your Web browser and verify that the subhead text appears slowly, in a random dissolve pattern.

2. You've long wanted to add an animated bus graphic to the home page you created for Sandhills Regional Public Transit (SRPT). Now that you know how to animate the position of Web page objects, you want to script this feature at the top of each SRPT Web page.

  To complete this independent challenge:

   a. Open the file HTML M-16.htm in your text editor, then save it as a text document with the filename SRPT animated.htm.

   b. To create space at the top of the page and to avoid overlapping elements, change the "top" values in the embedded style sheet for the following styles to the values indicated:
#bus: 75px
#head1: 60px
#head2: 300px
#instr: 75px

   c. Add the following entry to the embedded style sheet for the moving graphic:
#move {position: absolute; left: -1000px}

   d. You have already inserted the slide() function for this task. Look at the script in the page's HEAD section, noting the differences from the one you used in this unit. Try to predict how this script will behave differently, if at all.

e. Add the following event handler to the opening BODY tag:
onLoad="slide()"

f. Add the following IMG tag for the moving bus graphic immediately after the page's opening BODY tag:
<IMG SRC="busmove.jpg" ID="move">

g. Check your document for errors, then save SRPT animated.htm.

h. Open SRPT animated.htm in your Web browser and verify that the new bus graphic moves across the page without overlapping other elements.

3. The public-relations coordinator of Community Public School Volunteers wants to make sure the organization's Web page has an appealing layout, regardless of the computer's screen resolution or window size. Rather than using a scaling script, however, you decide to specify element dimensions in percentages to ensure uniform appearance.

To complete this independent challenge:

a. Open the file HTML M-17.htm in your text editor, then save it as a text document with the filename CPSV scale.htm.

b. In the #logo definition in the page's embedded style sheet, set the width value to 90%.

c. In the #box definition, change the width value to 75% and the left value to 12.5% (these settings ensure that the box is centered at any window size).

d. In the #instr definition, change the left value to 5% and the width value to 90% (these settings ensure that the text is centered in the box).

e. Check your changes, then save as CPSV scale.htm.

f. Preview CPSV scale.htm in your Web browser, then use your text editor to make any necessary changes, as well as any positioning and sizing changes that you think would improve the page's layout.

4. In addition to the filters and transitions that you've used in this unit, Internet Explorer 4 and 5 offer large selections of each of these features. To complete this independent challenge, connect to the Internet and locate a Web page that explains specific filters and transitions in detail. You can find this information on the Microsoft Web site, as well as on other DHTML sites. Find and print information on one standard filter and one Reveal transition filter that you have not used before. Make sure the information you print includes the name of the filter, the syntax for using it in your style specifications, and an explanation of any special parameters that it allows you to set. Then create a simple Web page named Unit M IC 4.htm, which contains one element. Apply the standard filter to the element and apply the Reveal transition filter to the page exit. Submit the printouts from your research and your file containing the filter and transition to your instructor.

▶ Visual Workshop

The owner of Touchstone Booksellers would like users to see an interesting effect when they first view his page. You decide to try an interpage transition that takes effect when the page opens. Save a copy of the file HTML M-18.htm as Touchstone transition.htm. Insert the necessary code to add the "Random bars vertical" transition, shown in Figure M-19. Use Table M-2 to look up the Transition value for this effect. The http-equiv value for this transition should be "Page-Enter" for the transition to occur as the page first loads. To test your changes, save your file, then open the file "Touchstone open.htm" in your Web browser, and click the link "Touchstone home page" to open the page you created.

FIGURE M-19

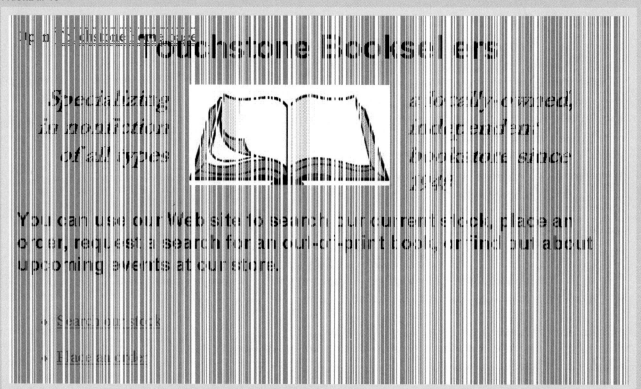

Structuring
Data with XML

Objectives

► **Understand eXtensible Markup Language (XML)**
► **Define XML elements and structure**
► **Enter XML data**
► **Bind XML data to HTML**
► **Format XML data with HTML**
► **Display XML data with HTML**
► **Modify an XML document**
► **Alter XML data view with HTML**

HTML has evolved from a way of structuring information into a language for controlling the format, or display, of Web content. With the vast growth of data on the Web, and the creation of many new applications, it has become critical to have a standard but expandable means to define, structure, and exchange the data on the Web. The **eXtensible Markup Language (XML)** is designed to ensure a **universal data structure** that can be read by any XML-compliant browser yet still allow Web designers the freedom to create **custom data definitions** for an endless variety of applications (e.g., a book or movie database). Lydia would like to create a "Recommended Backpacking Books" page for backpacking enthusiasts on the Nomad Web site. The HTML page will display book data she stores using XML and custom data definitions.

Understanding eXtensible Markup Language (XML)

XML (eXtensible Markup Language) is a text-based syntax especially designed to describe, deliver, and exchange structured data. XML documents use the file extension .xml and, like HTML files, can be created with a simple text editor. XML is not meant as a replacement for HTML but, rather, as a means to vastly extend its descriptive and structural power. XML uses a syntax that is similar to HTML, with four basic differences. These rules guarantee that a document is well-formed. A **well-formed** document requires that data be uniformly structured by tagsets so it can be read correctly by any XML-compliant program. Lydia is new to using XML, so she researches the language before starting to create the backpacking book list. To understand how the syntax of XML differs from HTML, Lydia examines each XML syntax rule carefully.

All elements must have start and end tags

An **element** consists of the start tag and corresponding end tag along with the content between the tagset. Unlike HTML, where you can mark up a document without using some closing tags (e.g., </P>), XML requires that both opening and closing tags be present. For example, the first line in Figure N-1 shows the correct way to code XML with both the start and end paragraph tags necessary to create a well-formed XML document. The same line in Figure N-2 lacks the required closing "</P>" tag, and thus violates the first rule of XML syntax.

All elements must be nested correctly

Just as in HTML, when writing XML, you should close first whatever tagset you opened last. However, you cannot overlap elements in XML. The second line of code in Figure N-1 shows the heading tagset "<H2></H2>" correctly nested inside of the paragraph tagset "<P></P>." The same line in Figure N-2 breaks this rule by placing the closing "</H2>" tag after the end paragraph tag "</P>." Although this code would display properly in HTML, it is not well-formed and would not display in XML because of the inherent stricter rule enforcement.

All attribute values must appear with quotation marks

HTML requires that only certain attribute values, such as URLs and strings, be in quotes. Values such as image and font size may be used without quotes. In XML, attributes must appear in quotes. The third line of code in Figure N-1 illustrates the proper way to code by quoting the font size attribute value "16," whereas the same line in Figure N-2 shows the font attribute value without quotes and, thus, wrongly marked up for XML.

All empty elements must be self-identifying by ending with "/>"

An **empty element** is one that doesn't have a closing tag (e.g., <BR>, <HR>, and <IMG> in HTML). The last tag on the fourth line of code in Figure N-1 demonstrates the proper way to identify an empty element in XML by ending it with "/>." This forward slash at the end of the tag indicates that the element, or container, is not broken (i.e., missing a closing tag) but simply empty. The same tag in Figure N-2 does not contain the necessary ending slash and, hence, would prevent an XML document from being well-formed.

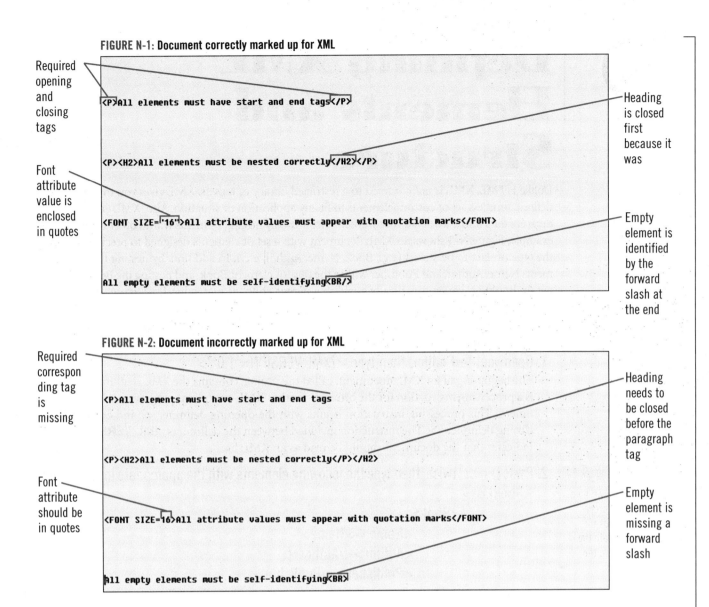

FIGURE N-1: Document correctly marked up for XML

Required opening and closing tags

`<P>All elements must have start and end tags</P>`

Heading is closed first because it was

`<P><H2>All elements must be nested correctly</H2></P>`

Font attribute value is enclosed in quotes

`<FONT SIZE="16">All attribute values must appear with quotation marks</FONT>`

Empty element is identified by the forward slash at the end

`All empty elements must be self-identifying<BR/>`

FIGURE N-2: Document incorrectly marked up for XML

Required corresponding tag is missing

`<P>All elements must have start and end tags`

Heading needs to be closed before the paragraph tag

`<P><H2>All elements must be nested correctly</P></H2>`

Font attribute should be in quotes

`<FONT SIZE=16>All attribute values must appear with quotation marks</FONT>`

Empty element is missing a forward slash

`All empty elements must be self-identifying<BR>`

CLUES TO USE

Benefits of XML

With XML, it is possible to identify data in meaningful ways, much like a database lets you identify and organize data with unique fieldnames and records. XML allows custom "vocabularies," or element sets, to be defined for particular types of data, such as books, movies, auto parts, legal cases, and medical information. In other words, these custom vocabularies act like the fieldnames in a conventional database to clearly identify and segment data. If these highly descriptive elements come into widespread use on the Web, XML has the potential to organize the Web into a coherent body of knowledge. For instance, this new level of semantics should improve the ability of now-overburdened search engines to rapidly find relevant information—in the same way queries can quickly locate relevant data in a database. Additionally, XML offers the means to exchange and process data from otherwise-incompatible information repositories on the Internet. XML and DHTML also enable a significant portion of the processing load to be shifted from Web servers to Web browsers (clients). Consequently, applications that require high-level compatibility and performance, such as those in electronic commerce, will greatly benefit from the implementation of XML. Finally, intelligent Web applications that seek out choice bits of information on the Web to match the preferences of individual users also should realize equally significant gains in accuracy as a result of clearly labeled XML data.

HTML

Defining XML Elements and Structure

Unlike HTML, XML is not confined to a restricted library of tagsets. XML gives you the freedom to define a limitless set of custom elements to fit any application or situation. Also, XML enables you to organize data into a tree-like hierarchical structure by nesting elements within other elements. For example, Figure N-3 shows an XML document with a set of elements designed to precisely describe the type of data to be stored (e.g., Book, Name, Author, etc.). In addition, by nesting the child elements Name, Author, and Publisher within the parent element Book, and nesting the Book elements within BookList, you automatically establish a parent-child, or hierarchical, structure similar to the one illustrated in Figure N-4. After completing her basic research on XML, Lydia decides to define the XML elements and structure necessary to store the data in the backpacking book list.

Steps

1. Open your text editor, then type <?XML VERSION='1.0'?>

The beginning of an XML document, called the prolog, contains the XML declaration, which is a processing instruction for the browser or other XML-compliant program reading the document. This processing instruction begins with the opening delimiter <? and ends with the closing delimiter ?>. The instruction included between the delimiters, XML VERSION='1.0', indicates that the document should be read as an XML file.

QuickTip

The indentation shown here is unnecessary for proper processing but helps to more clearly delineate the relationship between the document elements.

2. Press [Enter] twice, then type the following elements with the appropriate indentations:

```
<BookList>
        <Book>
                <Name></Name>
                <Author></Author>
                <Publisher></Publisher>
        </Book>
</BookList>
```

The elements in an XML document are ranked from the outermost set to the innermost elements. The highest ranked element forms the "root" of a tree-like structure, while the lower ranked elements make up the successive "branches" of the tree, as shown in Figure N-4. Thus, the rank of an element determines how much of the tree it controls.

3. To create two more instances of the Book elements, begin by selecting the highlighted area shown in Figure N-5

4. Press [Ctrl][c] to copy the highlighted area

QuickTip

The prefix "XML" is reserved for XML syntax, so you can't use it as a prefix for tag name (e.g., XMLbook).

5. Place the insertion point at the end of the Book element </Book>, then press [Enter] twice

6. Press [Ctrl][v] to paste a second Book record

A second instance of the Book elements appears in your document.

QuickTip

XML is case-sensitive. For example, the element <Author></Author> is not equivalent to the element <AUTHOR></AUTHOR>.

7. Press [Enter] once, paste another instance of the Book elements, then press [Delete]

Your document should now look like the one shown in Figure N-3.

8. Save the file as a text document with the filename books.xml

You are now ready to enter the data into your XML document.

FIGURE N-3: Elements and structure of book list XML document

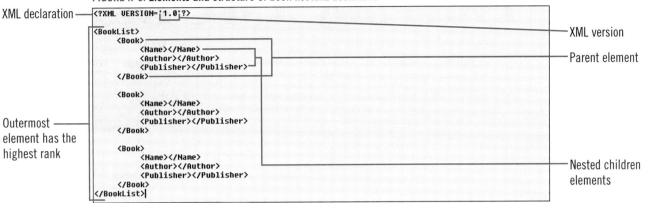

XML declaration ⎯
XML version
Parent element
Outermost element has the highest rank
Nested children elements

FIGURE N-4: Tree-like hierarchical structure of XML document

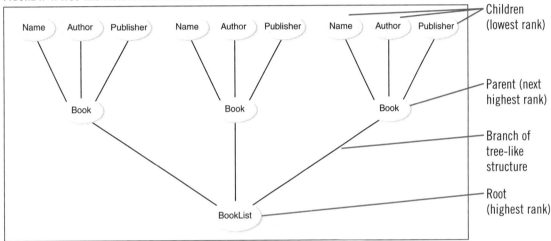

Children (lowest rank)
Parent (next highest rank)
Branch of tree-like structure
Root (highest rank)

FIGURE N-5: Highlighted book elements to copy

```
<?XML VERSION='1.0'?>

<BookList>
    <Book>
        <Name></Name>
        <Author></Author>
        <Publisher></Publisher>
    </Book>
</BookList>
```

Area to copy ⎯

Document Type Definition (DTD) and XML schemas

A **Document Type Definition (DTD)** is the formal specification of the rules of an XML document—namely, which elements are allowed and in what combinations. A Web page designer would create a DTD to ensure that any XML document using the DTD will be **valid** (i.e., comply with the formal specification). For example, a DTD could be set up to ensure that all XML files dealing with drug prescriptions include certain data elements (e.g., the prescribing doctor's name, expiration date, and refill information). Although a DTD can be called from an XML file, it uses a different syntax from XML. An

XML schema combines the concepts of a DTD, relational databases, and object-oriented designs to create a richer and more powerful way to formally define the elements and structure of an XML document. In addition, XML schemas use the same syntax as XML, so they will be able to appear in the same document. However, support for XML schemas are not supported in Internet Explorer 4 and DTDs only enjoy limited support. To learn more about DTDs and XML schemas, visit http://www.microsoft.com/xml/, or search the http://www.microsoft.com for information on XML.

HTML

Entering XML Data

You enter data into an XML document the same way you do an HTML page—either manually with an editor or automated with a sophisticated HTML form. Lydia wants to enter data about three backpacking handbooks in the XML file to test her knowledge of how this new technology works. She decides to use a text editor to enter the data.

Steps

1. Make sure that **books.xml** is open in your text editor

2. Position the insertion point between the first set of **<Name></Name>** tagsets, as shown in Figure N-6

QuickTip

All the content of an XML element is treated as data, including white space. Make sure not to include unwanted blank space in between any opening and closing tagsets.

3. Type **The Backpacker's Field Manual**

4. Place the insertion point between the **<Author></Author>** tagset directly below, then type **Rick Curtis**

5. Move the insertion point between the **<Publisher></Publisher>** tagset directly below, then type **Crown Publishers Inc.**

   The text editor should match the contents of Figure N-7.

6. Type the following data in the appropriate tagsets for the next two instances of the Book elements:

   The Modern Backpacker's Handbook   **The Backpacker's Handbook**

   Glenn Randall   **Chris Townsend**

   Lyons and Burford Publishers   **Ragged Mountain Press**

   The text editor window should look like the one shown in Figure N-8.

7. Save, then close the file

FIGURE N-6: Insertion point position

```
<?XML VERSION='1.0'?>

<BookList>
     <Book>
          <Name>|</Name>
          <Author></Author>
          <Publisher></Publisher>
     </Book>

     <Book>
          <Name></Name>
          <Author></Author>
          <Publisher></Publisher>
     </Book>

     <Book>
          <Name></Name>
          <Author></Author>
          <Publisher></Publisher>
     </Book>
</BookList>
```

Correct insertion
point position

FIGURE N-7: XML document with first data record

```
<?XML VERSION='1.0'?>

<BookList>
     <Book>
          <Name>The Backpacker's Field Manual</Name>
          <Author>Rick Curtis</Author>
          <Publisher>Crown Publishers Inc.</Publisher>
     </Book>

     <Book>
          <Name></Name>
          <Author></Author>
          <Publisher></Publisher>
     </Book>

     <Book>
          <Name></Name>
          <Author></Author>
          <Publisher></Publisher>
     </Book>
</BookList>
```

Data record

FIGURE N-8: XML document with all data entered

```
<?XML VERSION='1.0'?>

<BookList>
     <Book>
          <Name>The Backpacker's Field Manual</Name>
          <Author>Rick Curtis</Author>
          <Publisher>Crown Publishers Inc.</Publisher>
     </Book>

     <Book>
          <Name>The Modern Backpacker's Handbook</Name>
          <Author>Glenn Randall</Author>
          <Publisher>Lyons and Burford Publishers</Publisher>
     </Book>

     <Book>
          <Name>The Backpacker's Handbook</Name>
          <Author>Chris Townsend</Author>
          <Publisher>Ragged Mountain Press</Publisher>
     </Book>
</BookList>
```

Data
record 1

Data
record 2

Data
record 3

Binding XML Data to HTML

XML-compliant browsers such as Internet Explorer 4 support XML by including an XML parser and an XML Data Source Object (XML DSO). An **XML parser** dissects and interprets XML elements, whereas the **XML DSO** enables binding of the XML data to the HTML document using the DHTMLObject Model. Thus, the parser and DSO cooperate to allow the display, or **rendering**, of XML data in HTML. Lydia wants to display the data in the books.xml file in an HTML document that will become part of Nomad Ltd's Web site. Before she can format the data, Lydia must first create the HTML document and bind the XML data to it.

Steps

1. Open your text editor, then type
   ```
   <HTML>
   <HEAD>
           <TITLE>Backpacking Book List</TITLE>
   </HEAD>
   <BODY>
   <H2>Recommended Backpacking Books</H2>
   ```
   The text editor screen now should look like the one shown in Figure N-9. Lydia is ready to enter the XML DSO Java applet necessary to bind the XML data you created in the last lesson. A **Java applet** is a small program written in the Java programming language that is summoned using the <applet></applet> tagset.

2. Press [Enter] twice, then type
   ```
   <APPLET CODE="com.ms.xml.dso.XMLDSO.class" WIDTH="100%" HEIGHT="25"
   ID="xmldso" MAYSCRIPT="true">
       <PARAM NAME="url" VALUE="books.xml">
   </APPLET>
   ```
   The document should appear as shown in Figure N-10. Notice that the opening applet tag causes the browser to call the XML DSO Java applet. The parameter tag "<PARAM NAME="url" VALUE="books.xml">" specifies a URL with the name of the XML file to bind to this HTML document.

3. Press [Enter], then type:
   ```
   </BODY>
   </HTML>
   ```
   With these closing HTML tags entered, the text editor screen should now match Figure N-11.

4. Save the file as a text document with the filename books.htm
   Now Lydia has created an HTML document to which the XML data entered in the previous lesson is bound. The next step is to construct a table to format and display the bound data in your HTML document.

FIGURE N-9: **Beginning HTML markup**

```
<HTML>
<HEAD>
     <TITLE>Backpacking Book List</TITLE>
</HEAD>
<BODY>
<H2>Recommended Backpacking Books</H2>
```

FIGURE N-10: **Applet to call the XML DSO**

```
<HTML>
<HEAD>
     <TITLE>Backpacking Book List</TITLE>
</HEAD>
<BODY>
<H2>Recommended Backpacking Books</H2>

<APPLET CODE="com.ms.xml.dso.XMLDSO.class" WIDTH="100%"
HEIGHT="25" ID="xmldso" MAYSCRIPT="true">
     <PARAM NAME="url" VALUE="books.xml">
</APPLET>
```

Parameter name
that specifies
source as a URL

Value that specifies
XML document
filename

Applet to bind XML
document to this
HTML page

FIGURE N-11: **HTML document with data-binding code**

```
<HTML>
<HEAD>
     <TITLE>Backpacking Book List</TITLE>
</HEAD>
<BODY>
<H2>Recommended Backpacking Books</H2>

<APPLET CODE="com.ms.xml.dso.XMLDSO.class" WIDTH="100%"
HEIGHT="25" ID="xmldso" MAYSCRIPT="true">
     <PARAM NAME="url" VALUE="books.xml">
</APPLET>
</BODY>
</HTML>
```

Formatting XML Data with HTML

Once the data in an XML document has been bound to an HTML page, you can use all of the available formatting capabilities in HTML (plus CSS) to control its presentation in a browser. Because XML data often consists of a list, or database, the table feature in HTML is an ideal vehicle for displaying this tabular data. In addition to the conventional table attributes, several new HTML attributes enable Web page designers to control the binding of XML data to their documents. Table N-1 describes these new attributes. ➤➤➤ Lydia decides to use a table to format and display her book-list data in the XML file.

Steps

1. Make sure the file books.htm is open in your text editor
2. Place the insertion point below the </APPLET> tag, then press [Enter]
   Lydia wants to use a table to display the data in the books.xml file.

QuickTip

You can use all the power and flexibility of DHTML to manipulate XML data once it appears in an HTML document.

3. Carefully type the following:

```
<TABLE ID="table" BORDER="2" WIDTH="100%" DATASRC="#xmldso"
CELLPADDING="5">
<THEAD>
<FONT FACE="Arial" SIZE="2">
    <TR>
        <TH>TITLE</TH>
        <TH>AUTHOR</TH>
        <TH>PUBLISHER</TH>
    </TR>
</FONT>
</THEAD>
<FONT FACE="Times New Roman" SIZE="2">
    <TR>
        <TD VALIGN="top"><DIV DATAFLD="NAME"
        DATAFORMATAS="HTML"></DIV></TD>
        <TD VALIGN="top"><DIV DATAFLD="AUTHOR"
        DATAFORMATAS="HTML"></DIV></TD>
        <TD VALIGN="top"><DIV DATAFLD="PUBLISHER"
        DATAFORMATAS="HTML"></DIV></TD>
    </TR>
</FONT>
</TABLE>
```

The text editor screen should match Figure N-12. This code creates a table that uses an Arial font style, with a size of 2, to display the headings TITLE, AUTHOR, and PUBLISHER across the top row. The DATAFLD attributes in this code specify the element from the XML document to be bound to each column. The DATAFORMATAS attributes indicate that the XML-based data should be displayed in HTML format. In other words, the DATAFORMATAS attributes tell your browser to interpret and format the imported XML data as HTML content. This code will create as many rows as necessary to display all the data (records) in your XML file.

4. Check your work to make sure your typing was completely accurate
5. Save, then close the file

FIGURE N-12: Table code to format and bind XML data

```
<HTML>
<HEAD>
     <TITLE>Backpacking Book List</TITLE>
</HEAD>
<BODY>
<H2>Recommended Backpacking Books</H2>

<APPLET CODE="com.ms.xml.dso.XMLDSO.class" WIDTH="100%"
HEIGHT="25" ID="xmldso" MAYSCRIPT="true">
     <PARAM NAME="url" VALUE="books.xml">
</APPLET>

<TABLE ID="table" BORDER="2" WIDTH="100%"
DATASRC="#xmldso" CELLPADDING="5">
<THEAD>
<FONT FACE="Arial" SIZE="2">
     <TR>
          <TH>TITLE</TH>
          <TH>AUTHOR</TH>
          <TH>PUBLISHER</TH>
     </TR>
</FONT>
</THEAD>
<FONT FACE="Times New Roman" SIZE="2">
     <TR>
          <TD VALIGN="top"><DIV DATAFLD="NAME"
          DATAFORMATAS="HTML"></DIV></TD>
          <TD VALIGN="top"><DIV DATAFLD="AUTHOR"
          DATAFORMATAS="HTML"></DIV></TD>
          <TD VALIGN="top"><DIV DATAFLD="PUBLISHER"
          DATAFORMATAS="HTML"></DIV></TD>
     </TR>
</FONT>
</TABLE>
```

Font settings for table headings

Font settings for table rows

DATAFORMATAS attribute indicates the bound data should be displayed as HTML

DATAFLD attribute specifies the AUTHOR element be bound to this column

Table column heading for XML data

TABLE N-1: New table data-binding HTML attributes

attribute	description
DATASRC	Identifies the XML DSO applet used to bind the data.
DATAFLD	Specifies the particular column to bind the element to.
DATAFORMATAS	Indicates how the bound data should be rendered in the specified column (e.g., in HTML).
DATAPAGESIZE	Controls how many records are displayed in a table at once.

Formatting XML data with the Extensible Style Language (XSL)

In addition to formatting XML data with HTML and CSS, you also can use an XSL (Extensible Style Language) stylesheet. An **XSL stylesheet** is a set of programming rules that determine how XML data is displayed in an HTML document. Because XSL is designed to work with XML, it has the same flexibility and syntax as XML. However, native support for XSL is not built into Internet Explorer 4 or other browsers. To apply an XSL stylesheet to an XML document using Internet Explorer 4, first you must download and install the **Microsoft XSL ActiveX control**. This control is based on Microsoft's object-oriented ActiveX technology and is freely distributed. In fact, you can embed a script in your HTML document to automate the downloading and installation process. For more information on XSL and the XSL ActiveX control, see http://www.microsoft.com/xml/.

HTML

Displaying XML Data with HTML

Once you have created an HTML document to bind and format your XML-based data, you simply need to start your browser and open the HTML page to view the results. The XML document storing the data and the HTML page presenting it can reside on your local computer, network, or a remote Web server on the Internet. Lydia wants to see the XML data displayed in her HTML document.

Steps

QuickTip
Use Internet Explorer 4 to display XML data with HTML. Netscape Navigator 4 doesn't support XML, Navigator 5 will.

▶ **1.** Start your browser, then open the **books.htm** file

The document shown in Figure N-13 should appear, complete with the formatted data read from your books.xml file. Notice the colored line above the table indicating that the XML was successfully loaded: "file:/A:/books.xml." If the load was unsuccessful, this line indicates an error in parsing the XML file.

Trouble?
If no error appears, yet the table fails to display correctly, then your installation of Internet Explorer may be missing the Java VM (Virtual Machine). The Java VM is available from the Internet Explorer downloads section at the Microsoft Web site. See your instructor or technical support person for assistance.

▶ **2.** If your HTML document displays an error when attempting to load the books.xml file like the one shown in Figure N-14, you need to edit your XML document, recheck your typing, and fix any syntax mistakes

Unlike HTML, an XML document won't load correctly unless you obey all the rules of a well-formed document.

▶ **3.** After successfully viewing the book list in the HTML table, close your browser

FIGURE N-13: **HTML document displaying formatted XML data in a table**

Column headings

Rows of XML data

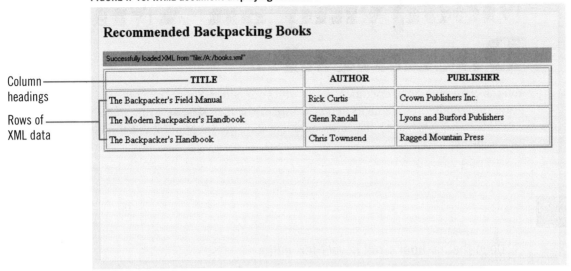

Recommended Backpacking Books

Successfully loaded XML from "file:/A:/books.xml"

TITLE	AUTHOR	PUBLISHER
The Backpacker's Field Manual	Rick Curtis	Crown Publishers Inc.
The Modern Backpacker's Handbook	Glenn Randall	Lyons and Burford Publishers
The Backpacker's Handbook	Chris Townsend	Ragged Mountain Press

FIGURE N-14: **HTML document displaying a parsing error**

Highlighted line indicates nature of the problem

Recommended Backpacking Books

Error loading XML document 'books.xml'.   com.ms.xml.parser.ParseException: Close tag BOOK does not match start tag PUBLISHER

TITLE	AUTHOR	PUBLISHER
The Backpacker's Field Manual	Rick Curtis	Crown Publishers Inc.

CLUES TO USE

Multiple views of data

Once data has been moved into your browser, it can be displayed in many different ways. A Web page designer might build several different views of the same data depending on the audience. For example, in the case of a movie database, the average user might just want to see the title, actors, and general plot of films, whereas some devoted fans will want to view all the particulars like the date the movie was released, who directed it, and so forth. Because XML only describes data, not its appearance, a Web page designer is free to use HTML/CSS to create unique views of the data for different classes of users. In addition, with use of DHTML, the view of XML data can be manipulated easily by the end user to suit his or her needs and tastes.

Modifying an XML Document

You can change an XML document easily with your editor. Simply open the file and use the edit features to modify the elements and structure of the file. ➤ Lydia wants to add two new elements to her XML book file. She would like store the ISBN number and publication date of each book.

Steps

1. Open the file **books.xml** in your text editor

2. Position the insertion point at the end of the **first Publisher element**, as shown in Figure N-15

3. Press **[Enter]** to insert a blank line, use tabs to align the insertion point directly beneath the beginning of the tag above, then type

   <ISBN>0517887835</ISBN>

4. Press **[Enter]** again, align the insertion point, and type

   <Date>March 1998</Date>

   The text in the editor should now match Figure N-16. All that remains is to enter the new elements for the other two book records.

5. Insert the following elements in the two remaining book records:

   <ISBN>1558212485</ISBN>   **<ISBN>0070653151</ISBN>**

   <Date>February 1994</Date>   **<Date>October 1996</Date>**

   The XML document should now contain the text shown in Figure N-17.

6. Save, then close the file

FIGURE N-15: Correct position for insertion point

```
<?XML VERSION='1.0'?>

<BookList>
     <Book>
          <Name>The Backpacker's Field Manual</Name>
          <Author>Rick Curtis</Author>
          <Publisher>Crown Publishers Inc.</Publisher>|
     </Book>

     <Book>
          <Name>The Modern Backpacker's Handbook</Name>
          <Author>Glenn Randall</Author>
          <Publisher>Lyons and Burford Publishers</Publisher>
     </Book>

     <Book>
          <Name>The Backpacker's Handbook</Name>
          <Author>Chris Townsend</Author>
          <Publisher>Ragged Mountain Press</Publisher>
     </Book>
</BookList>
```

— Insertion point at the end of the first Publisher element

FIGURE N-16: XML with two new elements

```
<?XML VERSION='1.0'?>

<BookList>
     <Book>
          <Name>The Backpacker's Field Manual</Name>
          <Author>Rick Curtis</Author>
          <Publisher>Crown Publishers Inc.</Publisher>
          <ISBN>0517887835</ISBN>
          <Date>March 1998</Date>
     </Book>

     <Book>
          <Name>The Modern Backpacker's Handbook</Name>
          <Author>Glenn Randall</Author>
          <Publisher>Lyons and Burford Publishers</Publisher>
     </Book>

     <Book>
          <Name>The Backpacker's Handbook</Name>
          <Author>Chris Townsend</Author>
          <Publisher>Ragged Mountain Press</Publisher>
     </Book>
</BookList>
```

— ISBN element

— Date element

FIGURE N-17: XML file modifications complete

```
<?XML VERSION='1.0'?>

<BookList>
     <Book>
          <Name>The Backpacker's Field Manual</Name>
          <Author>Rick Curtis</Author>
          <Publisher>Crown Publishers Inc.</Publisher>
          <ISBN>0517887835</ISBN>
          <Date>March 1998</Date>
     </Book>

     <Book>
          <Name>The Modern Backpacker's Handbook</Name>
          <Author>Glenn Randall</Author>
          <Publisher>Lyons and Burford Publishers</Publisher>
          <ISBN>1558212485</ISBN>
          <Date>February 1994</Date>
     </Book>

     <Book>
          <Name>The Backpacker's Handbook</Name>
          <Author>Chris Townsend</Author>
          <Publisher>Ragged Mountain Press</Publisher>
          <ISBN>0070653151</ISBN>
          <Date>October 1996</Date>
     </Book>
</BookList>
```

— All records include new ISBN and Date elements

Altering XML Data View with HTML

When you add elements to an XML document, you must make corresponding changes to the HTML document you are using to view the data; otherwise, the new data will not be displayed. Fortunately, it is easy to bring the HTML document into alignment with the new XML elements. Simply insert the code necessary to display the new elements in the format you desire. ✐ Lydia decides to display the ISBN and publication date in the same table with the rest of her book-list data.

Steps 1234

1. Open the file books.htm in your text editor

2. Change the font face for the Table header from Arial to Arial Black in the opening Table tag

3. Place the insertion point at the end of <TH>PUBLISHER</TH>

4. Press [Enter] to insert a blank line, tab over to align up directly beneath the tag above, then type <TH>ISBN</TH>

5. Press [Enter] to insert a blank line, align with the tag above, then type

   <TH>DATE</TH>

   These tags will create two new column headings—ISBN and DATE—for the data table.

6. Place the insertion point at the end of the last row in the table, as shown in Figure N-18

7. Press [Enter], align the insertion point directly under the beginning of the first tag above, then type

   <TD VALIGN="top"><DIV DATAFLD="ISBN"
   DATAFORMATAS="HTML"></DIV></TD>

8. Press [Enter], align the insertion point, then type

   <TD VALIGN="top"><DIV DATAFLD="DATE"
   DATAFORMATAS="HTML"></DIV></TD>

   The text in the editor should match Figure N-19. Check it carefully to make sure there are no typos.

9. Save the file, then close the document and text editor

10. Start your browser, then open the books.htm file to view the changes made to the table
    The HTML document appears with the two new column headings and corresponding data, as shown in Figure N-20.

Trouble?

If your HTML document displays a parsing error, use your text editor to find the syntax mistake in the books.xml file, then refresh your browser screen.

FIGURE N-18: Position insertion point to enter column data tags

```
<HTML>
<HEAD>
        <TITLE>Backpacking Book List</TITLE>
</HEAD>
<BODY>
<H2>Recommended Backpacking Books</H2>

<APPLET CODE="com.ms.xml.dso.XMLDSO.class" WIDTH="100%"
HEIGHT="25" ID="xmldso" MAYSCRIPT="true">
        <PARAM NAME="url" VALUE="books.xml">
</APPLET>

<TABLE ID="table" BORDER="2" WIDTH="100%"
DATASRC="#xmldso" CELLPADDING="5">
<THEAD>
<FONT FACE="Arial Black" SIZE="2">
        <TR>
                <TH>TITLE</TH>
                <TH>AUTHOR</TH>
                <TH>PUBLISHER</TH>
                <TH>ISBN</TH>
                <TH>DATE</TH>
        </TR>
</FONT>
</THEAD>
<FONT FACE="Times New Roman" SIZE="2">
        <TR>
                <TD VALIGN="top"><DIV DATAFLD="NAME"
                DATAFORMATAS="HTML"></DIV></TD>
                <TD VALIGN="top"><DIV DATAFLD="AUTHOR"
                DATAFORMATAS="HTML"></DIV></TD>
                <TD VALIGN="top"><DIV DATAFLD="PUBLISHER"
                DATAFORMATAS="HTML"></DIV></TD>
        </TR>
```

Insertion point at the end of the line

FIGURE N-19: HTML altered to display new XML data

```
<H2>Recommended Backpacking Books</H2>

<APPLET CODE="com.ms.xml.dso.XMLDSO.class" WIDTH="100%"
HEIGHT="25" ID="xmldso" MAYSCRIPT="true">
        <PARAM NAME="url" VALUE="books.xml">
</APPLET>

<TABLE ID="table" BORDER="2" WIDTH="100%"
DATASRC="#xmldso" CELLPADDING="5">
<THEAD>
<FONT FACE="Arial Black" SIZE="2">
        <TR>
                <TH>TITLE</TH>
                <TH>AUTHOR</TH>
                <TH>PUBLISHER</TH>
                <TH>ISBN</TH>
                <TH>DATE</TH>
        </TR>
</FONT>
</THEAD>
<FONT FACE="Times New Roman" SIZE="2">
        <TR>
                <TD VALIGN="top"><DIV DATAFLD="NAME"
                DATAFORMATAS="HTML"></DIV></TD>
                <TD VALIGN="top"><DIV DATAFLD="AUTHOR"
                DATAFORMATAS="HTML"></DIV></TD>
                <TD VALIGN="top"><DIV DATAFLD="PUBLISHER"
                DATAFORMATAS="HTML"></DIV></TD>
                <TD VALIGN="top"><DIV DATAFLD="ISBN"
                DATAFORMATAS="HTML"></DIV></TD>
                <TD VALIGN="top"><DIV DATAFLD="DATE"
                DATAFORMATAS="HTML"></DIV></TD>
        </TR>
</FONT>
```

Font face for table headings changed to Arial Black

Inserted column headings

New attributes to bind data to columns

FIGURE N-20: Five-column table with new data

New table headings

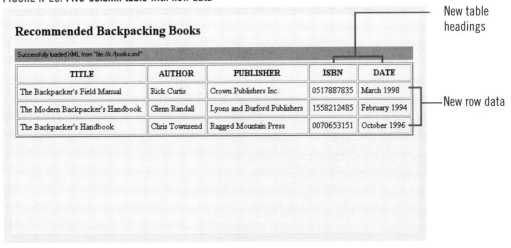

New row data

Practice

► Concepts Review

Label each item marked in Figure N-21.

FIGURE N-21

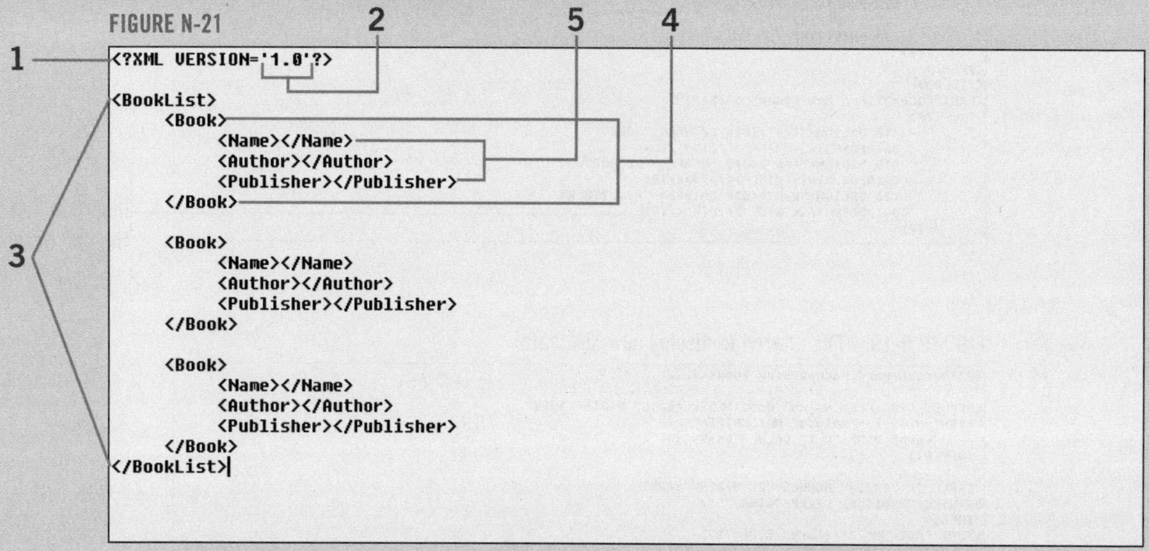

```
<?XML VERSION='1.0'?>

<BookList>
    <Book>
        <Name></Name>
        <Author></Author>
        <Publisher></Publisher>
    </Book>

    <Book>
        <Name></Name>
        <Author></Author>
        <Publisher></Publisher>
    </Book>

    <Book>
        <Name></Name>
        <Author></Author>
        <Publisher></Publisher>
    </Book>
</BookList>
```

Match each term with its description.

6. Element
7. Parser
8. XML
9. Correctly nested
10. Empty element

a. An element that doesn't have a closing tag
b. A text-based format that lets you describe, deliver, and exchange structured data
c. No overlapping elements
d. Dissects and interprets XML
e. The start and corresponding end tags, plus the contents in between the tagset

Select the best answer from the list of choices.

11. The XML declaration, in the prolog of an XML document, indicates that the document should be
    a. Encoded with XSL.
    b. Processed as an XML file.
    c. Rendered using HTML.
    d. Displayed as HTML.

12. Which is *not* an XML syntax rule?
    a. All elements must have start and end tags.
    b. All elements must be nested properly.
    c. All attribute values must appear within quotation marks.
    d. All empty elements must be terminated with "//>".

13. **Which statement is False?**

    a. Blank space appearing in the content of an element is read as data.

    b. XML is organized in a tree-like structure.

    c. The elements <Wine>red</Wine> and <wine>red</wine> are equivalent in XML.

    d. XML brings structure and customization to the Web.

14. **Which is *not* a new table data binding attribute for HTML?**

    a. DATASRC

    b. DATAFLD

    c. DATAFORMAT

    d. DATAPAGESIZE

15. **Which one of the following is *not* required to display XML data in a browser?**

    a. parser

    b. Cascading Style Sheet (CSS)

    c. data-binding applet

    d. data-binding attributes

 # Skills Review

1. **Define XML elements and structure.**

    a. Open your text editor, then type <?XML VERSION='1.0'?>

    b. Two lines down, enter the following elements, using the appropriate indentation to signify the structure of the document:

```
<Catalog>
        <Product>
                <Model></Model>
                <Price></Price>
                <Description></Description>
        </Product>

        <Product>
                <Model></Model>
                <Price></Price>
                <Description></Description>
        </Product>

        <Product>
                <Model></Model>
                <Price></Price>
                <Description></Description>
        </Product>
</Catalog>
```

    c. Verify your typing and correct any typos.

    d. Save the file as a text document with the filename products.xml.

2. Enter XML data.

    a. Make sure products.xml is open in your text editor.

    b. Position the insertion point between the first instance of the <Model></Model> element and type "Cleaner 100".

    c. Type "$495" between the Price tags directly below the first Name element.

    d. Type "Domestic robot to vacuum and dust your home." between the Description tags.

    e. Enter the following content for the next two Product records:
    Whacker 300
    $1,195
    Yard robot that mows and trims the edges of your lawn.

    Nursemaid 400
    $4,995
    Personal robot to care for purchasers of Cleaner 100 and Whacker 200 robot models.

    f. Save and close the document.

3. Bind XML data to HTML.

    a. Start your text editor, then in a new document, type the following code with indicated alignments:
```
<HTML>
<HEAD>
<TITLE>Robot Product Catalog</TITLE>
</HEAD>
<BODY>
<H2>Robot Product Catalog</H2>
```

    b. Create two blank lines at the bottom the document, then bind the products.xml file to this HTML document by entering the following code:
```
<APPLET CODE="com.ms.xml.dso.XMLDSO.class" WIDTH="100%" HEIGHT="25"
ID="xmldso" MAYSCRIPT="true">
        <PARAM NAME="url" VALUE="products.xml">
</APPLET>
```

    c. Type the following HTML closing tags:
```
</BODY>
</HTML>
```

    d. Check the document for errors, making changes as necessary.

    e. Save the file as a text document with the filename products.htm.

4. Format XML data with HTML.

    a. Make sure products.htm is open in your text editor.

    b. To create a table to bind, format, and display the data in the products.xml file, type the following HTML code just below the closing applet tag:
```
<TABLE ID="table" BORDER="2" WIDTH="100%" DATASRC="#xmldso" CELLPADDING="5">
<THEAD>
<FONT FACE="Arial" SIZE="2">
<TR>
        <TH>MODEL</TH>
        <TH>PRICE</TH>
        <TH>DESCRIPTION</TH>
```

```
        </TR>
            </FONT>
        </THEAD>
        <FONT FACE="Times New Roman" SIZE="2">
            <TR>
                    <TD VALIGN="top"><DIV DATAFLD="MODEL" DATAFORMATAS="HTML"></DIV></TD>
                    <TD VALIGN="top"><DIV DATAFLD="PRICE" DATAFORMATAS="HTML"></DIV></TD>
                    <TD VALIGN="top"><DIV DATAFLD="DESCRIPTION" DATAFORMATAS="HTML"></DIV></TD>
            </TR>
        </FONT>
        </TABLE>
```

   c. Check the document for errors, making changes as necessary, then save and close the file.

5. Display XML data with HTML.
   a. Start your browser, then open the file products.htm.
   b. If you receive a parsing error, use your text editor to find and fix typos in either the products.htm or products.xml documents, then open the products.htm file again with your browser.
   c. When you are done examining the table of data, print the page, then close your browser.

6. Modifying an XML document.
   a. Open the file products.xml in your text editor.
   b. In the first Product element, insert the following new elements just below the Description element:
     `<Options>Turbo jet engine</Options>`
     `<Delivery>2-4 weeks</Delivery>`
   c. Enter the following elements for the last two records in your XML file:
     `<Options>Leaf collector</Options>`
     `<Delivery>2-4 weeks</Delivery>`

     `<Options>Medicine tray</Options>`
     `<Delivery>4-6 months</Delivery>`
   d. Check the document for errors, making changes as necessary, then save the file.

7. Alter XML data view with HTML.
   a. Open the file products.htm in your text editor.
   b. Insert the following HTML aligned below <TH>DESCRIPTION</TH>:
     `<TH>OPTIONS</TH>`
     `<TH>DELIVERY</TH>`
   c. Type
     `<TD VALIGN="top"><DIV DATAFLD="OPTIONS" DATAFORMATAS="HTML"></DIV></TD>`
     `<TD VALIGN="top"><DIV DATAFLD="DELIVERY" DATAFORMATAS="HTML"></DIV></TD>`
   d. Check the file for errors, making changes as necessary, then save the file and close your text editor.
   e. Open the products.htm file in your browser, and view the newly expanded table.
   f. If you receive a parsing error, use your text editor to find and fix the typing mistakes in either the products.htm or products.xml documents, then open the products.htm file once more with your browser.
   g. Print the document, then close your browser.

► Independent Challenges

1. You have just started buying music CDs and you would like to keep a list of them on your computer as your collection grows. You decide to use an XML file to store the name, song titles, and type of music for each music CD. At this point, you just want to create the custom elements and hierarchical structure of the XML document.

To complete this independent challenge:

a. Open your text editor.

b. Enter the prolog for an XML document, use the [Enter] key to create a couple of blank lines in the document, then type "<CDlist>".

c. On the next line, press [Tab] once, then type "<CD>".

d. On the next line down, press [Tab] twice, then type "<Name></Name>".

e. On the next line down, press [Tab] three times, then type "<Song1></Song1>".

f. Repeat Step 5 until you have entered tagsets for 10 songs (i.e., <Song2></Song2>...<Song10><Song10>).

g. Below the last Song tagset, type "<Category></Category>".

k. On the next line, press [Tab] once, then type "</CD>".

i. Copy the <CD> element, and all its children elements, three times.

j. At the bottom of the document, at the beginning of a new line, type </CDlist>, then save the file as music list.xml.

k. Print a copy of the document, then close your text editor.

2. Your best friend collects and sells comic books for a living. She asks you to help her create a computerized list of her collection that she can display on her personal Web site. You decide to use XML and HTML as the means of storing and displaying information about her comics. You use five records to test the design.

To complete this independent challenge:

a. Open your text editor, then create an XML file with the root element <ComicList>.

b. Add the parent element <ComicBook> and the children elements <Name></Name>, <Issue></Issue>, <Publisher></Publisher>, and <Value></Value>.

c. Copy the ComicBook element and its children elements four times.

d. At the bottom of the document, on a blank line, type "</ComicList>".

e. Save the XML file as comics.xml.

f. Enter the data from the table below into each ComicBook element in your XML document:

g. Save the document, print it, then open a new document.

h. Create an HTML document to display your XML data. Use the following code to bind the XML data to a table in your HTML file:

```
<APPLET CODE="com.ms.xml.dso.XMLDSO.class"
WIDTH="100%"
HEIGHT="25" ID="xmldso" MAYSCRIPT="true">
<PARAM NAME="url" VALUE="comics.xml">
</APPLET>
<TABLE ID="table" BORDER="2" WIDTH="100%" DATASRC="#xmldso" CELLPADDING="5">
<THEAD>
  <TR>
    <TH>TITLE</TH>
```

name	issue	publisher	value
Bombastic Five	4	Cool Comics	$22,000
Radioactive Dog	12	Cool Comics	$640
Sludge Man	34	Night Owl	$26
Bombastic Five	7	Cool Comics	$18,500
Sludge Man	19	Night Owl	$35

```
        <TH>ISSUE #</TH>
        <TH>PUBLISHER</TH>
        <TH>VALUE</TH>
    </TR>
</THEAD>
    <TR>
        <TD VALIGN="top"><DIV DATAFLD="NAME" DATAFORMATAS="HTML"></DIV></TD>
        <TD VALIGN="top"><DIV DATAFLD="ISSUE" DATAFORMATAS="HTML"></DIV></TD>
        <TD VALIGN="top"><DIV DATAFLD="PUBLISHER" DATAFORMATAS="HTML"></DIV></TD>
        <TD VALIGN="top"><DIV DATAFLD="VALUE"  DATAFORMATAS=""HTML"></DIV></TD>
    </TR>
</FONT>
</TABLE>
```

i. Format the table using the font style Arial with point size of 2.

j. Save the file as a text document called comics.htm, then close your text editor.

k. Open comics.htm in your browser to view your XML data. If the data fails to display, use your text editor to check your typing in comics.xml and comics.htm, and correct any typos.

l. Print a copy of comics.htm from your browser.

3. You have been asked to inventory all the computers in your building at work and make the results available for viewing on your company's Intranet. Management would like to know the make, model, year, and location of each machine.

To complete this independent challenge:

a. Create an XML file called computers.xml with the root element <Computers></Computers>.

b. Add the parent element <Make></Make>, with the children elements <Model></Model>, <Year></Year>, and <Location></Location>. Copy the <Make></Make> element and its children elements five times.

c. Populate the Model elements with data from the table below:

d. Create an HTML file called computers.htm that will display the XML data in a table; use Arial as the font face.

e. Open the HTML file in your browser.

f. Print a copy of the document from your browser.

make	model	year	location
Mega Bite	T-Rex	1998	Office 101
Mega Bite	T-Rex	1998	Office 102
Mega Bite	Raptor	1998	Office 103
Tera Gig	Condor	1997	Office 104
Mega Bite	Raptor	1998	Reception Area

4. You have decided to use XML and HTML to store and display a list of your favorite movies. Be sure to include custom elements (e.g., <MovieTitle></MovieTitle>) to store important information such as the name of the movie, your favorite actor, the plot, and other interesting data. Use the Internet to search for movie data if your information is not complete. In an XML file called movies.xml, structure the movie data so that each movie record is a child element of the parent element <MovieList></MovieList>. Display the data in a table with headings in an HTML file called movies.htm. Open the movies.htm file in your browser, then print the document.

Visual Workshop

Create a Web application using XML and HTML to display the table of formatted data shown in Figure N-22. Print the document from your browser.

FIGURE N-22

XML Products

Successfully loaded XML from "file:/A:/products.xml"

PRODUCT	COMPANY	DESCRIPTION
HoTMetaL Application Server	SoftQuad	Automates the database-to-XML and XML-to-HTML conversion process.
iNet Developer 4.0	Pictorius	Includes tools for parsing Document Type Definitions (DTD's) and converting HTML documents to XML.
XML Pro	Vervet Logic	A program that allows users to create and edit XML documents.

Appendix A: JavaScript

JavaScript Object Reference

The following are some of the more important JavaScript objects, properties, methods, and event handlers.

TABLE AP-1: **JavaScript objects, properties, methods, and event handlers**

JavaScript	descriptions and examples
button	**A push button in an HTML form. Buttons can be referred to using their button names. For example, to emulate the action of clicking a button named "RUN," use the following expression: RUN.click();**
Properties	
name	The name of the button element
value	The value of the button element
Methods	
click()	Emulates the action of clicking the button
Event Handlers	
onClick	Used to run JavaScript code when the button is clicked
checkbox	**A check box in an HTML form. Check boxes can be referred to using their field names. For example, to emulate the action of clicking a check box named "SUBSCRIBE," use the following expression: SUBSCRIBE.click();**
Properties	
checked	A Boolean value that indicates whether or not the check box is checked
defaultChecked	A Boolean value that indicates whether or not the check box is selected by default
name	The name of the check box element
value	The value of the check box element
Methods	
click()	Emulates the action of clicking the check box
Event Handlers	
onClick	Used to run JavaScript code when the check box is clicked
date	**An object containing information about a specific date or the current date. You can assign a date object to a variable using standard date and time formatting, for example: SomeDay = new Date("June, 15, 2000, 14:35:00").You can also assign the values for each date and time component, such as day or seconds, individually; using this method, the same date object would read: SomeDay = new Date(2000, 5, 15, 14, 35, 0). The values in parentheses are year, month, day, hour, minute, second.**
	You can create a variable containing the current date and time by removing the date and time values. For example: Today = new Date();
Methods	
getDate()	Returns the day of the month from 1 to 31
getDay()	Returns the day of the week from 0 to 6 (Sunday = 0, Monday = 1, ...)
getHours()	Returns the hour in military time from 0 to 23
getMinutes()	Returns the minute from 0 to 59
getMonth()	Returns the value of the month from 0 to 11 (January = 0, February = 1, ...)
getSeconds()	Returns the seconds
getTime()	Returns the date as an integer representing the number of milliseconds since January 1st, 1970 at 00:00:00
getTimesoneOffset()	Returns the difference between the local time and Greenwich Mean Time in minutes
getYear()	Returns the number of years since 1900 (in other words, 1996 is represented by "96.") This value method is inconsistently applied past the year 1999.

JavaScript	descriptions and examples
setDate(*date*)	Sets the day of the month to the value specified in *date*
setHours(*hour*)	Sets the hour to the value specified in *hour*
setMinutes(*minutes*)	Sets the minute to the value specified in *minutes*
setMonth(*month*)	Sets the month to the value specified in *month*
setSeconds(*seconds*)	Sets the second to the value specified in *seconds*
setTime(*time*)	Sets the time using the value specified in *time*, where *time* is a variable containing the number of milliseconds since January 1st, 1970 at 00:00:00
setYear(*year*)	Sets the year to the value specified in *year*
toGMTString()	Converts the date to a text string in Greenwich Mean Time
toLocaleString()	Converts a date object's date to a text string, using the date format that the Web browser is set up to use
UTC()	Returns the date in the form of the number of milliseconds since January 1st, 1970, 00:00:00
document	**An HTML document**
Properties	
alinkColor	The color of active hyperlinks in the document
anchors	An array of anchors within the document. Use anchors[0] to refer to the first anchor, anchors[1] to refer to the second anchor, and so forth.
bgColor	The background color used in the document
cookie	A text string containing the document's cookie values
fgColor	The text color used in the document
form	A form within the document (the form itself is also an object)
forms	An array of forms within the document. Use forms[0] to refer to the first form, forms[1] to refer to the second form, and so forth.
lastModified	The date the document was last modified
linkColor	The color of hyperlinks in the document
links	An array of links within the document. Use links[0] to refer to the first hyperlink, links[1] to refer to the second hyperlink, and so forth.
location	The URL of the document
referrer	The URL of the document containing the link that the user accessed to get to the current document
title	The title of the document
vlinkColor	The color of followed hyperlinks
Methods	
clear()	Clears the contents of the document window
close() ·	Closes the document stream
open	Opens the document stream
write()	Writes to the document window
writeln()	Writes to the document window on a single line (used only with preformatted text)
elements	**Elements within an HTML form**
Properties	
length	The number of elements within the form
form	**An HTML form within a document. You can refer to a specific form using that form's name. For example, for a form named "REG," you can apply the submit method with the following expression: REG.submit();**
Properties	
action	The location of the CGI script that receives the form values
elements	An array of elements within the form (including input boxes, check boxes, buttons, and other fields). Use elements[0] to refer to the first element, elements[1] to refer to the second element, and so forth. Use the field name of the element to work with a specific element.

JavaScript	descriptions and examples
encoding	The type of encoding used in the form
method	The type of method used when submitting the form
target	The name of the window into which CGI output should be directed
Methods	
submit()	Submits the form to the CGI script
Event Handlers	
onSubmit	Used to run JavaScript code when the form is submitted by the browser
frame	**A frame window within the Web browser**
Properties	
frames	An array of frames within the frame window. Use frames[0] to refer to the first frame, frames[1] to refer to the second frame and so forth.
parent	The name of the window that contains the frame
self	The name of the current frame window
top	The name of the topmost window in the hierarchy of frame windows
window	The name of the current frame window
Methods	
alert(*message*)	Displays the text contained in *message* in a dialog box
clearTimeout(*name*)	Cancels the time out whose value is *name*
close()	Closes the window
confirm(*message*)	Displays the text contained in *message* in a dialog box along with OK and Cancel buttons
prompt(*message*, *default_text*)	Displays the text contained in *message* in a dialog box with a text entry box into which the user can enter a value or text string. The default value or text is specified by the value of *default_text*.
setTimeout(*expression, time*)	Evaluates the value of *expression* after the number of milliseconds specified in the value of *time* has passed
hidden	**A hidden field on an HTML form. Hidden fields can be referred to using their field names. For example, to change the value of the hidden field "PWORD" to "newpassword," use the expression: PWORD.value = "newpassword"**
Properties	
name	The name of the hidden field
value	The value of the hidden field
history	**An object containing information about the Web browser's history list**
Properties	
length	The number of items in the history list
Methods	
back()	Goes back to the previous item in the history list
forward()	Goes forward to the next item in the history list
go(*location*)	Goes to the item in the history list specified by the value of *location*. The *location* variable can be either an integer or the name of the Web page.
image	**An embedded image within the document (available only in Netscape Navigator 3.0 or higher)**
Properties	
border	The value of the BORDER property of the <IMG> tag
complete	A Boolean value that indicates whether or not the image has been completely loaded by the browser
height	The height of the image in pixels
hspace	The horizontal space around the image in pixels
lowsrc	The value of the LOWSRC property of the <IMG> tag
src	The source of the inline image

JavaScript	descriptions and examples
vspace	The vertical space around the image in pixels
width	The width of the image in pixels
link	**A link within an HTML document**
Properties	
target	The target window of the hyperlinks
location	**An object that contains information about the location of a Web document**
Properties	
hash	The location's anchor name
host	The location's hostname and port number
href	The location's URL
pathname	The path portion of the location's URL
port	The port number of the location's URL
protocol	The protocol used with the location's URL
math	**A JavaScript object used for advanced mathematical calculations. For example, to calculate the square root of 27 and store this value in the variable "SQ27," use the following JavaScript expression: var SQ27 = math.sqrt(27);**
Properties	
E	The value of the base of natural logarithms (2.7182...)
LN10	The value of the natural logarithm of 10
LN2	The value of the natural logarithm of 2
PI	The value of pi (3.1416...)
Methods	
abs(*number*)	Returns the absolute value of *number*
acos(*number*)	Returns the arc cosine of *number* in radians
asin(*number*)	Returns the arc sine of *number* in radians
atan(*number*)	Returns the arc tangent of *number* in radians
ceil(*number*)	Rounds *number* up to the next highest integer
cos(*number*)	Returns the cosine of *number*, where *number* is an angle expressed in radians
exp(*number*)	Raises the value of E (2.7182...) to the value of *number*
floor(*number*)	Rounds *number* down to the next lowest integer
log(*number*)	Returns the natural logarithm of *number*
max(*number1, number2*)	Returns the greater of *number1* and *number2*
min(*number1, number2*)	Returns the lesser of *number1* and *number2*
pow(*number1, number2*)	Returns the value of *number1* raised to the power of *number2*
random()	Returns a random number between 0 and 1
round(*number*)	Rounds *number* to the closest integer
sin(*number*)	Returns the sine of *number*, where *number* is an angle expressed in radians
tan(number)	Returns the tangent of *number*, where *number* is an angle expressed in radians
navigator	**An object representing the Web browser currently in use**
Properties	
appCodeName	The code name of the Web browser
appName	The name of the Web browser
appVersion	The version of the Web browser
userAgent	The user-agent text string sent from the client to the Web server

option	**An option from a selection list**
Properties	
defaultSelected	A Boolean value indicating whether or not the option is selected by default
index	The index value of the option
selected	A Boolean value indicating whether or not the option is currently selected
text	The text of the option as displayed on the Web page
value	The value of the option
password	**A password field in an HTML form. You can refer to a specific password field using the field name. For example, for a password field named "PWORD," you can apply the focus() method with the following expression: PWORD.submit();**
Properties	
defaultValue	The default value of the password
name	The name of the password field
value	The value of the password field
Methods	
blur()	Emulates the action of leaving the text area box
focus()	Emulates the action of moving into the text area box
select()	Emulates the action of selecting the text in a text area box
radio	**An array of radio buttons on an HTML form . Use the name of the radio button set to refer to individual buttons. For example if the name of the radio button set is "Products," use Products[0] to refer to the first radio button, Products[1] to refer to the second radio button, and so forth.**
Properties	
checked	A Boolean value indicating whether or not a specific radio button has been checked
defaultChecked	A Boolean value indicating whether or not a specific radio button is checked by default
length	The number of radio buttons in the set
name	The name of a set of radio buttons
value	The value of a specific radio button
Methods	
click()	Emulates the action of clicking the radio button
Event Handlers	
onClick	Used to run JavaScript code when the radio button is clicked
reset	**A Reset button in an HTML form. You can refer to a specific Reset button using the button's name. For a Reset button named "RELOAD," you can apply the click() method with the following expression: RELOAD.click();**
Properties	
name	The name of the Reset button
value	The value of the Reset button
Methods	
click()	Emulates the action of clicking the Reset button
Event Handlers	
onClick	Used to run JavaScript code when the Reset button is clicked
select	**A selection list in an HTML form. You can refer to a specific selection list using the selection list's name. For example, to determine the number of options in a selection list named "PRODUCT," use the following expression: PRODUCT.length;**
Properties	
length	The number of options in the selection list
name	The name of the selection list

HTML

JavaScript	descriptions and examples
options	An array of options within the selection list. Use options[0] to refer to the first option, options[1] to refer to the second option, and so forth. See the options object for more information on working with individual selection list options.
selectedIndex	The index value of the selected option from the selection list
Event Handlers	
onBlur	Used to run JavaScript code when the user leaves the selection list
onChange	Used to run JavaScript code when the user changes the selected option in the selection list
onFocus	Used to run JavaScript code when the user enters the selection list
string	**An object representing a text string or string of characters. For example, to italicize the text string "Order Today!", use the following expression: "Order Today!".italics();**
Properties	
length	The number of characters in the string
Methods	
anchor(*name*)	Turns the text string into a hyperlink anchor with a name value set to *name*
big()	Modifies the text string to display big characters (similar to the effect of applying the <BIG> tag)
blink()	Modifies the text string to display blinking characters (similar to the effect of applying the <BLINK> tag)
bold()	Modifies the text string to display characters in bold (similar to the effect of applying the <B> tag)
charAt(*index*)	Returns the character in the text string at the location specified by *index*
fixed()	Modifies the text string to display fixed-width characters (similar to the effect of applying the <FIXED> tag)
fontColor(*color*)	Modifies the text string to display text in a color specified by *color* (similar to applying the <FONT> tag to the text along with the COLOR property)
fontSize(*value*)	Modifies the text string to display text in the font size specified by the *value* parameter (similar to applying the <FONT> tag to the text along with the SIZE property)
indexOf(*string, start*)	Searches the text string and returns the index value of the first occurrence of the text string *string*. The search starts at the character indicated by the value of *start*.
italics()	Modifies the text string to display characters in italics (similar to the effect of applying the <I> tag)
lastIndexOf(*string, start*)	Searches the text string and locates the index value of the last occurrence of the text string *string*. The search starts at the character indicated by the value of *start*.
link(*href*)	Turns the text string into a hyperlink pointing to the URL contained in *href*
small()	Modifies the text string to display small characters (similar to the effect of applying the <SMALL> tag)
strike()	Applies the strikeout character to the text string (similar to the effect of applying the <STRIKE> tag)
sub()	Modifies the text string to display subscript characters (similar to the effect of applying the <SUB> tag)
substring(*first, last*)	Returns a substring of characters from the text string, starting with the character at the index number *first* and ending with the character at the index number *last*
sup()	Modifies the text string to display superscript characters (similar to the effect of applying the <SUP> tag)
toLowerCase()	Changes all of the characters in the text string to lowercase
toUpperCase()	Changes all of the characters in the text string to uppercase
submit	**A Submit button in an HTML form. You can refer to a specific Submit button using the button's name. For a Submit button named "SAVE," you can apply the click() method with the following expression: SAVE.click();**
Properties	
name	The name of the Submit button
value	The value of the Submit button
Methods	
click()	Emulates the action of clicking the Submit button
Event Handlers	
onClick	Used to run JavaScript code when the user clicks the Submit button

text

An input box from an HTML form. You can refer to an input box using the box's name. For example, to move the cursor to an input box named "ADDRESS," use the following expression: ADDRESS.focus();

Properties

defaultValue	The default value of the input box
name	The name of the input box
value	The value of the input box

Methods

blur()	Emulates the action of leaving the input box
focus()	Emulates the action of moving into the input box
select()	Emulates the action of selecting the text in an input box

Event Handlers

onBlur	Used to run JavaScript code when the user leaves the input box
onChange	Used to run JavaScript code when the user changes the value of the input box
onFocus	Used to run JavaScript code when the user enters the input box
onSelect	Used to run JavaScript code when the user selects some or all of the text in the input box

textarea

A text area box in an HTML form. You can refer to a specific text area box using the box's name. For example, to move the cursor out of a text area box named "COMMENTS," use the expression: COMMENTS.blur();

Properties

defaultValue	The default value of the text area box
name	The name of the text area box
value	The value of the text area box

Methods

blur()	Emulates the action of leaving the text area box
focus()	Emulates the action of moving into the text area box
select()	Emulates the action of selecting the text in a text area box

Event Handlers

onBlur	Used to run JavaScript code when the user leaves the text area box
onChange	Used to run JavaScript code when the user changes the value of the text area box
onFocus	Used to run JavaScript code when the user enters the text area box
onSelect	Used to run JavaScript code when the user selects some or all of the text in the text area box

window

The document window contained within the Web browser

Properties

defaultStatus	The default text string displayed in the window's status bar
frames	An array of frames within the window. Use frames[0] to refer to the first frame, frames[1] to refer to the second frame, and so forth. See the frames object for properties and methods that can be applied to individual frames.
length	The number of frames in the parent window
name	The name of the window
parent	The name of the window containing this particular window
self	The name of the current window
status	The text string displayed in the window's status bar
top	The name of the topmost window in a hierarchy of windows
window	The name of the current window

JavaScript	descriptions and examples
Methods	
alert(*message*)	Displays the text contained in *message* in a dialog box
clearTimeout(*name*)	Cancels the time out whose value is *name*
close()	Closes the window
confirm(*message*)	Displays the text contained in *message* in a dialog box along with OK and Cancel buttons
prompt(*message, default_text*)	Displays the text contained in *message* in a dialog box with a text entry box into which the user can enter a value or text string. The default value or text is specified by the value of *default_text*.
setTimeout(*expression, time*)	Evaluates the value of *expression* after the number of milliseconds specified in the value of *time* has passed
Event Handlers	
onLoad	Used to run JavaScript code when the window or frame finishes loading
onUnload	Used to run JavaScript code when the window or frame finishes unloading

JavaScript Operators

The following are some operators used in JavaScript expressions.

TABLE AP-2: **JavaScript operators**

operators	description
Assignment	**Assignment operators are used to assign values to variables.**
=	Assigns the value of the variable on the right to the variable on the left (x=y)
+=	Adds the two variables and assigns the result to the variable on the left (x+=y is equivalent to x=x+y)
–=	Subtracts the variable on the right from the variable on the left and assigns the result to the variable on the left (x–=y is equivalent to x=x–y)
*=	Multiplies the two variables together and assigns the result to the left variable (x*=y is equivalent to x=x*y)
/=	Divides the variable on the left by the variable on the right and assigns the result to the variable on the left (x/=y is equivalent to x=x/y)
%=	Divides the variable on the left by the variable on the right and assigns the remainder to the variable on the left (x%=y is equivalent to x=x%y)
Arithmetic	**Arithmetic operators are used for arithmetic functions.**
+	Adds two variables together (x+y)
–	Subtracts the variable on the right from the variable on the left (x–y)
*	Multiplies two variables together (x*y)
/	Divides the variable on the left by the variable on the right (x/y)
%	Calculates the remainder after dividing the variable on the left by the variable on the right (x%y)
++	Increases the value of a variable by 1 (x++ is equivalent to x=x+1)
--	Decreases the value of a variable by 1 (x-- is equivalent to x=x–1)
–	Changes the sign of a variable (–x)
Logical	**Logical operators are used for evaluating true and false expressions.**
&&	Returns true only if both expressions are true (also known as an AND operator)
||	Returns true when either expression is true (also known as an OR operator)
!	Returns true if the expression is false, and false if the expression is true (also known as a *negation* operator)
Comparison	**Comparison operators are used for comparing expressions.**
==	Returns true when the two expressions are equal (x==y)
!=	Returns true when the two expressions are not equal (x!=y)
>	Returns true when the expression on the left is greater than the expression on the right (x > y)
<	Returns true when the expression on the left is less than the expression on the right (x < y)
>=	Returns true when the expression on the left is greater than or equal to the expression on the right (x >= y)
<=	Returns true when the expression on the left is less than or equal to the expression on the right (x <= y)
Conditional (shorthand)	**Conditional operators determine values based on conditions that are either true or false.**
(*condition*) ? *value1* : *value2*	If *condition* is true, then this expression equals *value1*, otherwise it equals *value2*.

Appendix B: Cascading Style Sheets

The following are CSS1 fourth-generation browser supported styles.

TABLE AP-3: CSS1 fourth-generation browser supported styles

property	explanation/syntax	example
Font Properties		
font-style	• *normal* • *oblique* (similar to italic, but created manually rather than using italic typeface) • *italic*	{font-style: italic}
font-variant	• *normal* (default) • *small-caps*	{font-variant: small-caps}
font-weight	• *extra-light* • *bold* • *demi-light* • *demi-bold* • *light* • *extra-bold* • *medium*	{font-weight: extra-bold}
font-size	a number with a unit abbreviation {font-size: 16pt} • points (*pt*) • pixels (*px*) • inches (*in*) • centimeters (*cm*) • percentage of default point size (%) • multiple of width of "m" character in current font family (*em*)	
line-height	sets distance between baselines of two adjacent elements; specify multiplication factor for font size as a value (such as 1.2), percentage (120%), or measurement (1.2em)	{line-height: 1.2}
font-family	any combination of the following, in order of preference • specific typeface name (*times new roman*) • general type family (*times*) • font type (*sans-serif*)	{font-family: "times new roman", times, garamond, serif}
font	shorthand for setting all six font-related attributes at once; no commas, except between font-family settings; order: font-style, font-variant, font-weight, font-size, line-height, font-family	{font: italic small-caps extra-bold 16pt 0.75in "times new roman", times, garamond, serif}
text-decoration	• *none* • *italic* • *underline* • *line-through*	{text-decoration: italic}
Color and Background Properties		
color	hexadecimal or keyword color equivalent for element color	{color: #93DB70}
background-color	hexadecimal or keyword color equivalent for background color	{background-color: navy}
background-image	• none • *url*(url)	{background-image: url(me.jpg)}
background-repeat	specifies if and how background image is repeated • *repeat* (tiles over entire background) • *repeat-x* (repeats in single band horizontally) • *repeat-y* (repeats in single band vertically) • *no-repeat* (single image only)	{background-repeat: repeat-x}
background-attachment	• *scroll* (image scrolls with foreground) • *fixed* (image remains fixed as foreground scrolls)	{background-attachment: fixed}

property	explanation/syntax	example
background-position	specifies initial position of background image; coordinates (in percent) match point at those coordinates on image with those coordinates on background	{background-position: 100% 100%}
background	shorthand for setting all five background attributes at once; no commas; order: background-color, background-image, background-repeat, background-attachment, background-position	{background: navy url(me.jpg) repeat-x fixed 100% 100%

Text Properties

property	explanation/syntax	example
word-spacing	specifies additional width to insert between words (default=normal); may be negative	{word-spacing: 0.4em}
letter-spacing	specifies additional width to insert between words (default=normal); may be negative	{letter-spacing: 0.1em}
text-decoration	<ul><li>*underline*</li><li>*overline*</li><li>*line-through*</li><li>*blink*</li><li>*none* (default)</li></ul>	{text-decoration: underline}
vertical-align	<ul><li>*baseline*</li><li>*sub*</li><li>*super*</li><li>*top*</li><li>*text-top*</li><li>*middle*</li><li>*bottom*</li><li>*text-bottom*</li><li>percentage value, positive and negative numbers possible, specifies percentage of the element's line-height property in relation to the parent baseline</li></ul>	{vertical-align: super}
text-transform	<ul><li>*capitalize* capitalizes first character of each word</li><li>*uppercase* capitalizes all letters</li><li>*lowercase* makes all letters lowercase</li><li>*none*</li></ul>	{text-transform: capitalize}
text-align	<ul><li>*left*</li><li>*right*</li><li>*center*</li><li>*justify*</li></ul>	{text-align: center}
text-indent	positive and negative numbers possible, specifies indentation of first line, in an exact measurement, or a percentage of parent element width	{text-indent: 3em}
line-height	sets distance between baselines of two adjacent elements; specify multiplication factor for font size, as a value (such as 1.2), percentage (120%), or measurement (1.2em)	{line-height: 1.2}

Box Properties

property	explanation/syntax	example
margin-top	sets element's top margin as measurement or percentage of parent element width	{margin-top: 2%}
margin-right	sets element's right margin, as measurement or percentage of parent element width	{margin-right: 2em}
margin-bottom	sets element's bottom margin, as measurement or percentage of parent element width	{margin-bottom: 2%}
margin-left	sets element's left margin, as measurement or percentage of parent element width	{margin-right: 2em}
margin	shorthand property for specifying margin-top, margin-right, margin-bottom, and margin-left properties; order: top, right, bottom, left; if only one value given, applies to all four; if one or two values missing, missing value copied from opposite side	{margin 2% 2em}
padding-top	sets an element's top padding, as measurement or percentage of parent element width	{padding-top: 0.3em}
padding-right	sets an element's right padding, as measurement or percentage of parent element width	{padding-right: 20%}

property	explanation/syntax	example
padding-bottom	sets an element's bottom padding, as measurement or percentage of parent element width	{padding-bottom: 0.3em}
padding-left	sets an element's left padding, as measurement or percentage of parent element width	{padding-left: 20%}
padding	shorthand property for specifying padding-top, padding-right, padding-bottom, and padding-left properties; order: top, right, bottom, left; if only one value given, applies to all four; if one or two values missing, missing value copied from opposite side	{padding: 0.3em 20% 0.2em}
border-top-width; border-right-width; border-bottom-width; border-left-width;	• *thin* • *medium* • *thick* • measurement	{border-top-width: 2pt}
border-width	shorthand property for specifying all four border thicknesses; order: top, right, bottom, left; if only one value given, applies to all four; if one or two values missing, missing value copied from opposite side	{border-width: 3em}
border-style	can specify between one and four styles, with same organization as border-width above • *none* • *groove* • *dotted* • *ridge* • *dashed* • *inset* • *solid* • *outset* • *double*	{border-style: groove}
border-color	hexadecimal or keyword color equivalent for element color; can specify between one and four colors, with same organization as border-width above	{border-color: navy red red}
border-top border-right border-bottom border-left	shorthand properties for setting each border's width, style, and color	{border-bottom: thick solid red}
border	shorthand property for setting same width, color, and style on all four borders of an element	{border: thin inset green}
width	element width, as a length or percentage, negative values are allowed (default=auto)	{width: 200px}
height	element height, as a length or percentage, negative values are allowed (default=auto)	{height: 50%}
float	moves element to left or right, and wraps text on opposite side	{float: left}
clear	specifies if an element allows floating elements around it, or should be moved clear of them • *none* • *left* • *right* • *both*	{clear: both}

Classification Properties

property	explanation/syntax	example
display	• *block* • *inline* • *list-item* • *none*	{display: inline}
white-space	• *normal* white space collapsed • *pre* formatted like HTML PRE element • *nowrap* wrapping triggered only by elements	{white-space: nowrap}

property	explanation/syntax	example
list-style-type	specifies marker style for list items • *disc* • *upper-roman* • *circle* • *lower-alpha* • *square* • *upper-alpha* • *decimal* • *none* • *lower-roman*	{list-style-type: lower-alpha}
list-style-image	specifies an image to use as a list item marker	{list-style-image: url(reddot.jpg)}
list-style-position	• *inside* less space between marker and item • *outside* more space between marker and item (default)	{list-style-position: inside}
list-style	shorthand property for setting list-style-type, list-style-image, and list-style-position	{list-style: lower-alpha url(reddot.jpg) inside}

The following are CSS-P positioning properties.

TABLE AP-4: CSS-P positioning properties

property	value	description
position	static	normal position in page flow (default)
	absolute	outside normal page flow
	relative	relative to normal position in page flow
top, left	auto	(default)
	[length]	offset from default position in points, pixels, inches, or centimeters with respect to the element's top left corner
	[percent]	offset from default position in percentage of the parent element dimension
width, height	auto	(default)
	[length]	element dimension in points, pixels, inches, or centimeters
	[percent]	element dimension in percentage of parent element dimension
clip	auto	(default)
	rect(top right bottom left)	specifies rectangle coordinates that define document area available for displaying element
z-index	auto	(default)
	number	specifies element's position in the page's set of overlap layers; negative values possible
overflow	visible	entire contents displayed (default)
	hidden	contents that do not fit within the element are hidden
	auto	element contains scroll bar only when some contents do not fit within the element
	scroll	element always contains associated scroll bar
visibility	visible	element displays normally
	hidden	element takes up same space in page as it would normally, but is not visible

Appendix C: Filters and Transitions

The following are options available when creating filters and transitions for Microsoft Internet Explorer 4.

For all true/false parameters, false is represented by 0, and true is represented by 1.

TABLE AP-5: Filters for Microsoft Internet Explorer 4

filter effect	description	parameters	syntax
Filters	Change object or page appearance in complex ways		
Alpha	Sets a transparency level	• *opacity* Ranges from 0 (fully transparent) to 100 (fully opaque) • *finishopacity* (optional) Same values as *opacity*; allows opacity to change across object • *style* Shape of opacity gradient; 0 (uniform), 1(linear), 2 (radial), or 3 (rectangular) • *startX* X coordinate for start of opacity gradient • *startY* Y coordinate for start of opacity gradient • *finishX* X coordinate for end of opacity gradient • *finishY* Y coordinate for end of opacity gradient	{filter: alpha(opacity=*opacity*, finishopacity=*finishopacity*, style=*style*, startX=*startX*, startY=*startY*, finishX=*finishX*, finishY=*finishY*)}
Blur	Creates the impression of moving at high speed	• *add* True/false variable specifying whether original image should be added to motion-blurred image (true; default) or not (false) • *direction* Blur direction, in degrees (0-360) clockwise from vertical, rounded to 45-degree increments; default is 270 (left) • *strength* Number of pixels that blur extends (default=5)	{filter: blur(add=*add*, direction=*direction*, strength=*strength*)}
Chroma	Makes a specific color transparent	• *color* Color subject to transparency, expressed in hexadecimal format (#RRGGBB)	{filter: chroma(color=*color*)}
Drop Shadow	Creates an offset solid silhouette	• *color* Color for drop shadow effect, in hexadecimal format • *offX* X-axis offset of drop shadow, in pixels • *offY* Y-axis offset of drop shadow, in pixels • *positive* drop shadow of any nontransparent pixel (true; default), or drop shadow of any transparent pixel (false)	{filter: dropshadow(color=*color*, offX=*offX*, offY=*offY*, positive=*positive*)}
FlipH	Creates a horizontal mirror image	NONE	{filter: fliph}
FlipV	Creates a vertical mirror image	NONE	{filter: flipv}
Glow	Adds radiance around the outside edges of the object	• *color* Color of radiance around object, in hexadecimal format • *strength* Glow intensity (1-255)	{filter: glow(color=*color*, strength=*strength*)}
Grayscale	Drops color information from the image	NONE	{filter: gray}
Invert	Reverses the hue, saturation, and brightness values	NONE	{filter: invert}

filter effect	description	parameters	syntax
Light	Projects light sources onto an object	Methods: • *AddAmbient* Adds ambient light source • *AddCone* Adds cone light source • *AddPoint* Adds point light source • *ChangeColor* Changes light color • *ChangeStrength* Changes light strength • *Clear* Clears all lights • *MoveLight* Moves light source	{filter: light}
Mask	Creates a transparent mask from an object	• *color* Color painted on transparent regions, in hexadecimal format	{filter: mask(color=*color*)}
Shadow	Creates a solid silhouette of the object	• *color* Color of shadow effect, in hexadecimal format • *direction* Shadow offset direction, in degrees (0-360) clockwise from vertical, rounded to 45-degree increments; default is 225 (bottom-left)	{filter: shadow(color=color, direction=direction)}
Wave	Creates a sine wave distortion along the x-axis and y-axis	• *add* Adds original image to waved image (true; default) or does not add original image (false) • *freq* Number of waves appearing in distortion • *light* Strength of light on wave effect, in percent • *phase* Phase offset from start of sine wave effect, in percent (default=0) • *strength* Wave intensity	{filter: wave(add=*add*, freq=*freq*, lightstrength=*strength*, phase=*phase*, strength=*strength*)}
XRay	Shows just the edges of the object	NONE	{filter: xray}

TABLE AP-6 Transitions for Microsoft Internet Explorer 4

transition type	description	parameters	syntax
Transitions	Filters that vary over time		
blend	Creates simple fade-in or fade-out with specified duration	• *duration* Length of fade, in seconds	filter: blendTrans(duration=*duration*)
reveal	Allows choice of effects	• *duration* Length of effect, in seconds • *transition* Number corresponding to reveal transition effect, as listed in table that follows	filter: revealTrans(duration=*duration*, transition=*transition*)

HTML

TABLE AP-7: Reveal transition effects

reveal transition name	value
Box in	0
Box out	1
Circle in	2
Circle out	3
Wipe up	4
Wipe down	5
Wipe right	6
Wipe left	7
Vertical blinds	8
Horizontal blinds	9
Checkerboard across	10
Checkerboard down	11
Random dissolve	12
Split vertical in	13
Split vertical out	14
Split horizontal in	15
Split horizontal out	16
Strips left down	17
Strips left up	18
Strips right down	19
Strips right up	20
Random bars horizontal	21
Random bars vertical	22
Random	23

TABLE AP-8: Transition applications

transition application	description
interpage transition	Transition plays when containing page opens or exits Created with the META tag in the page head section; uses *http-equiv* parameter, specifying whether transition should play when page opens ("Page-Enter") or closes ("Page-Exit"), or site opens ("Site-Enter") or closes ("Site-Exit"). For example, the code to create the circle in transition when a page closes could read <META HTTP-EQUIV="Page-Exit" CONTENT="revealTrans(duration=7, transition=2)">
object transition	Requires three components: 1. **Transition filter reference** in style description for object to be filtered; for example, to filter an image with the horizontal blinds transition, the code could read <IMG ID="mypic" SRC="me.jpg" STYLE="filter: revealTrans(duration=5, transition=9)"> 2. **Script to manage filter** consisting of three lines at minimum: mypic.filters.revealTrans.apply() *creates the final transition state* mypic.src= "me2.jpg" *specifies new condition(s) of transitioned object* mypic.filters.revealTrans.play() *animates transition effect* 3. **Event handler** to trigger script

Glossary

Absolute positioning Positioning option that allows you to place an element at fixed coordinates in the browser window, relative to its parent object; removes positioned object from main page flow; *see also* **relative positioning**.

Animated GIFs A popular way to create animation in Web pages, using the GIF image format to display multiple images in a single area; compatible with browsers older than fourth-generation.

Arithmetic operators Symbols that allow you to program scripts to manipulate variables mathematically.

Blend A transition filter that creates a simple fade-in or fade-out effect.

Browser detection script A script that determines the user's browser brand and generation.

Bugs Errors in a script, causing it to return unexpected or undesired results.

Call To trigger or use a named object, such as a style or function, within your Web page code.

Cascading The system of precedence in CSS; embedded styles take precedence over external styles, and inline style takes precedence over both embedded and external style.

Cascading Style Sheets (CSS) A tool that allows you to specify attributes such as color and font size for all page elements marked by a specific tag, name, or ID.

Cascading Style Sheets - Positioning (CSS-P) An extension of cascading style sheets that allows precise positioning of page elements.

Case-sensitive Treats capital and lowercase versions of the same letter as different characters.

Chaining The process of combining filters to create complex effects.

Child element The element enclosed by another element, the parent.

Class An HTML property allowing you to assign a category name to multiple Web page elements; allows application of a named style to elements marked by different tags.

Client-side scripts Scripts that a browser interprets and runs; *see also* **server-side scripts**.

Clip Property that allows you to control how much of an element is visible on your Web page by acting as a layer above the element; *see also* **clip region**.

Clip region The hole you define with the clip property, through which the page contents are visible.

Conditional Programming decision point that allows your script to choose one of two paths, depending on a condition that you specify.

Cross-platform code DHTML code that works on both fourth-generation browsers.

CSS *See* **Cascading Style Sheets**.

CSS-P *See* **Cascading Style Sheets – Positioning**.

Custom data definitions In XML, tagsets that describe a specific type of data.

DHTML (dynamic HTML) A varied set of technologies that allow near-immediate response to user actions in a Web page without accessing the Internet server.

DHTML Object Models Extended DOM versions included in the browser code for Navigator 4 and Internet Explorer 4, which increase the range and versatility of DHTML.

DOM *See* **Document Object Model**.

Data-awareness A DHTML feature allowing a user to instantly view and manipulate a database in a Web page; *see also* **data binding**.

Data binding Linking a Web page to an external data file.

DATAFLD An HTML attribute that indicates the element from an XML document to be bound to a column.

DATAFORMATAS An HTML-based attribute that specifies how XML-based data should be displayed in HTML.

Debugging The process of systematically identifying and fixing a script's bugs.

Document Object Model (DOM) A Web browser's hierarchical system of organization that allows Web page developers to describe and work with the Web page elements in a browser window; categorizes and groups Web page elements into a tree-like structure.

Document Type Definition (DTD) The formal specification of the rules of an XML document, namely which elements are allowed and in what combination.

Dot syntax A method of referencing objects in an object hierarchy by beginning on the document level, and separating each level name with a period.

DTD *See* **Document Type Definition**.

Dynamic content A DHTML feature allowing a page to display different content based on a user's activities.

Dynamic HTML (DHTML) A varied set of technologies that allow near-immediate response to user actions in a Web page without accessing the Internet server; *see also* **static HTML**.

Dynamic style A DHTML feature that facilitates immediate style changes in response to user actions.

Element A start tag and corresponding end tag, plus the content between the tagset.

Embedded style CSS style formatting associated with HTML tags, class names, or IDs between the HEAD tags at the top of your Web page; *see also* **embedded style sheet**.

Embedded style sheet The set of code between a page's HEAD tags, consisting of a page's embedded styles.

Empty element An element that does not have a closing tag.

Event An action by a user.

Event handler A term that specifies a possible user action.

Expandable outline A Web page feature that hides the explanatory paragraphs in a bulleted list, displaying each only when the user clicks its corresponding bulleted item.

Extensible Markup Language *See* **XML**.

External style A style sheet contained in an external file and linked to a Web page; *also called* **linked style**; *see also* **external style sheet**.

External style sheet CSS style formatting contained in an external file and linked to a Web page; *see also* **external style**.

FAQ An acronym for Frequently Asked Questions, pronounced "fak".

Filters Predefined element formats in Internet Explorer 4 that affect element appearance in complex ways; *see also* **transition filters**.

Float Property to remove an element from the main text flow and display it to the side of the flow.

Fourth-generation browsers The 4.x versions of Navigator and Internet Explorer.

Function A set of script code that performs a certain task, grouped into a named unit.

Hang To stop functioning.

Inline style CSS style formatting specified in the opening tag surrounding an element.

InnerHTML A property that includes only an element's contents, but not the tags surrounding it; *see also* **outerHTML**.

Java applet A small program written in the Java programming language summoned using the <applet></applet> tagset.

JavaScript Scripting language adapted from Sun Microsystems' Java programming language; supported by both Internet Explorer 4 and Navigator 4.

JScript Microsoft's adaptation of Sun Microsystems' Java programming language for Web use; *see also* **JavaScript, VBScript**.

Layer A transparent virtual page that determines overlap order.

Linked style CSS style formatting contained in an external file and linked to a Web page; *also called* **external style**; *see also* **external style sheet**.

Method An action an object can carry out.

Microsoft XSL ActiveX control An object-oriented ActiveX program that applies XSL style sheets to format and display XML-based data in a document.

Null A value equal to zero or nothing.

Object An element in the browser window identified by JavaScript as a distinct unit; each object has a default name and set of descriptive features based on its location and function; *see also* **methods, properties, object hierarchy**.

Object hierarchy JavaScript's organization of objects; much like the system of folders used by Windows to keep track of disk contents.

OuterHTML A property that includes an element's contents and the tags surrounding it; *see also* **innerHTML**.

Overflow Property that allows you to create the equivalent of an independent frame, anywhere within your browser window.

Parent element The element enclosing another element, the child element.

Position A style sheet attribute used to specify absolute or relative positioning.

Positioning A DHTML feature allowing Web page designers to specify precisely the location of all page elements; *see also* **Cascading Style Sheets – Positioning**.

Presentation effects Web page effects in which elements appear in the browser window gradually and in a specific order.

Prolog The beginning of an XML document; contains the XML declaration. *See also* **XML declaration**.

Properties An object's qualities such as size, location, and type.

Proprietary features Features unique to just one of the two major Web browsers.

Relative positioning Positioning option that allows you to place an element at coordinates in the browser window based on the position of other screen elements; *see also* **absolute positioning**.

Reveal A transition filter that allows complex transitions.

Rollover A feature that changes the appearance of text when a user points at it.

Run time The period when a browser first interprets and displays a Web page and runs scripts.

Schema *See* **XML Schema**.

Script Program in a Web page that runs on the viewer's browser.

Scripting The process of writing scripts.

Scriptlet A script located in an external file that you can link to a Web page.

Server-side scripts Scripts stored and run on a Web server, rather than on a user's computer; *see also* **client-side scripts**.

Slide A single Web page that is part of a multi-page Web presentation.

Static HTML Coding style used to create simple Web documents whose interactivity is limited to hyperlinks; *see also* **dynamic HTML**.

Third-generation browsers The 3.x versions of Navigator and Internet Explorer.

Transition filters Predefined effects in Internet Explorer that cause elements to appear gradually and in specific patterns when a page opens or exits; *also called* **transitions**.

Transitions *See* **transition filters**.

Universal data structure Standardized structure for defining, describing, and exchanging data on the Web.

Values Pieces of information that you specify to JavaScript, often with instructions to perform functions on them.

Variable A nickname for a value, making repeated references easier and more efficient.

VBScript Microsoft's adaptation of its Visual Basic programming language for Web use.

W3C *See* **World Wide Web Consortium**.

Well-formed Adheres to the rules of structure necessary to be correctly parsed by an XML-compliant program.

World Wide Web Consortium (W3C) An international body whose mission is the creation of standards for WWW technologies.

XML (Extensible Markup Language) A text-based syntax especially designed to describe, deliver, and exchange structured data.

XML declaration A processing instruction for the browser or other XML-compliant program reading an XML document; appears in the prolog.

XML DSO Enables binding of XML data to an HTML document using the DHTML Object Model; included in XML-compliant browsers.

XML parser Dissects and interprets XML elements; included in XML-compliant browsers.

XML schema Combines the concepts of a DTD, relational databases, and object-oriented designs to create a way to formally define the elements and structure of an XML document.

XML VERSION Instruction that indicates to a browser or XML-compliant program in which version of XML the document should be read.

XSL stylesheet A set of programming rules that determine how XML data is formatted and displayed in an HTML document.

Z-index The property that determines a layer's position in a page's stack.

Index

Index

HTML tags. *See* tags
http-equiv property, HTML M-16
hyperlinks. *See* links
HyperText Markup Language. *See* HTML

▶I

ID property, HTML H-9
ID styles
  creating, HTML J-7
  global, HTML J-7
  names, HTML J-7
images. *See* graphic images
inline style
  example, HTML J-2–3
  uses of, HTML J-2
innerHTML property, HTML K-8, HTML K-10
Internet Explorer. *See* Microsoft Internet Explorer
Invert filter effect, HTML M-5

▶J

Java applets, HTML N-8
JavaScript. *See also* scripts
  browser-detection script, HTML J-8–9
  case-sensitivity of, HTML H-6
  creating scripts using, HTML H-4–5
  event handlers, HTML H-10–11
  methods in, HTML H-8–9
  object reference, HTML AP-1–8
  objects in, HTML H-8–9
  operators, HTML AP-9
  uses of, HTML H-3
Java VM (Virtual Machine), HTML N-12
JBScript, HTML H-3
JScript, HTML H-3

▶L

LANGUAGE attribute
  for <SCRIPT> tags, HTML H-4–5
layers
  defined, HTML L-10
  stacking screen elements with, HTML L-10–11
<LAYER> tags, HTML I-5
left property
  animation effects using, HTML M-10
  specifying element position with, HTML L-4–5
Light filter effect, HTML M-5
linked style, HTML J-2. *See also* external style
links
  to external scripts, HTML H-5
<LINK> tags
  in external style sheets, HTML J-16
lists
  collapsible, HTML I-14–15
  expanding, HTML J-10–11
location objects
  defined, HTML I-8
  methods, HTML H-9

▶M

Mask filter effect, HTML M-5
menus
  hierarchical, HTML I-12–13
messages
  displaying in status bar, with JavaScript event
    handlers, HTML H-10–11
META tags
  for interpage transitions, HTML M-16–17
methods, HTML H-8–9
Microsoft Internet Explorer. *See also* Web browsers
  browser detection, HTML J-8–9
  cycling text in, HTML K-10
  DHTML code and, HTML I-10
  displaying XML data in, HTML N-12–13
  Document Object Model (DOM), HTML I-8–9
  dynamic font size in, HTML J-12
  filters, HTML AP-14–15, HTML M-4–5
  floating windows in, HTML K-9
  positioning in, HTML L-4–5
  proprietary features, HTML I-5, HTML I-6
  scaling, HTML M-6–7
  scripting compatibilities, HTML H-3
  transitions between pages in, HTML M-16–17
  transitions in, HTML AP 39–41, HTML M-12–13
Microsoft VM for Java, HTML N-12
Microsoft XSL ActiveX control, HTML N-11
multiple conditions
  testing, HTML H-17

▶N

named styles, HTML J-6
names
  for objects, HTML H-9
navigator objects, HTML I-8
nested XML structure, HTML N-2, HTML N-4–5
Netscape Navigator
  browser detection, HTML J-8–9
  DHTML code and, HTML I-10
  Document Object Model (DOM), HTML I-8
  dynamic font size in, HTML J-12
  floating windows in, HTML K-9
  positioning in, HTML L-4–5
  proprietary features, HTML I-5
  scripting compatibilities, HTML H-3
  scrollbars in, HTML L-14
null value
  assigned by functions, HTML H-12
number sign (#)
  identifying ID style names with, HTML J-7

▶O

object hierarchy, HTML I-8–9
  dot syntax for, HTML H-8
  in JavaScript, HTML H-8
objects, HTML I-8
  defined, HTML H-8
  naming, HTML H-9

<OBJECT> tags, HTML K-14–15
onAbort event handler, HTML H-11
onBlur event handler, HTML H-11
onChange event handler, HTML H-11
onClick event handler, HTML H-11, HTML K-6, HTML K-8
onError event handler, HTML H-11
onFocus event handler, HTML H-11
onLoad event handler, HTML H-11, HTML M-8
onMouseOut event handler, HTML H-10–11, HTML K-12
onMouseOver event handler, HTML H-10–11,
  HTML J-12, HTML K-12
onSelect event handler, HTML H-11
onSubmit event handler, HTML H-11
onUnload event handler, HTML H-11
outerHTML property, HTML K-6
outlines
  expandable, HTML J-10–11
overflow property, HTML L-12–13
overlapping screen elements
  with positioning, HTML L-2

▶P

page elements. *See also* elements (XML); text
  adjusting to browser window size, HTML M-6–7
  animating position of, HTML M-8–9
  controlling visibility of, with clip property,
    HTML L-13
  customized, inserting dynamically, HTML K-4–5
  cycling through, HTML K-10–11
  modifying appearance of, with filters, HTML M-2,
    HTML M-4–5
  showing and hiding, HTML J-10–11
  sizing manually, HTML L-8–9
  sizing relative to parent window, HTML L-9
  stacking, HTML L-10–11
page layout. *See also* DHTML page design; Web page
  design
  with positioning, HTML L-2
PARAM attribute
  for <OBJECT> tags, HTML K-14
<PARAM> tags, HTML N-8–9
parent elements
  in CSS-P, HTML L-4–5
  in XML, HTML N-4–5
parentheses ( )
  in scripts, HTML H-6
percentage measurements
  positioning and sizing using, HTML L-9
  scaling by, HTML M-7
period (.)
  identifying style name with, HTML J-6
pixel measurements
  positioning using, HTML L-4
platforms
  cross-platform issues, HTML I-10
Play method
  for transition filters, HTML M-12
pointing
  changing elements in response to, HTML K-2
  changing graphics in response to, HTML K-12–13
  text changes in response to, HTML J-12
position attribute, HTML L-2

Index

data binding, HTML K-2
external, embedding, HTML I-5
sorting dynamically, HTML K-16—17
tags
XML syntax rules, HTML N-2—3
text. *See also* elements (XML); page elements
changing, when user moves pointer over, HTML J-12
draggable, HTML L-16—17
modifying appearance of, with filters, HTML M-4—5
positioning with float property, HTML L-14—15
width of, specifying manually, HTML L-8—9
third generation Web browsers, HTML I-10
3-D animation, HTML M-10—11
ToolTips, HTML K-9
top property
animation effects using, HTML M-10
specifying element position with, HTML L-4—5
transitions, HTML AP-15—16, HTML M-12—13.
See also filters
applications, HTML AP-16
defined, HTML M-2
between pages, HTML M-16—17
tree-like hierarchical structure
in XML, HTML N-4—5

►U

universal data structure, HTML N-1
user input
in forms, clearing with function, HTML H-12—13
incorporated into Web pages, using variables,
HTML H-14—15

►V

values
assigning to variables, HTML H-14—15
defined, HTML H-14
var command, HTML H-14
variables
assigning, HTML H-14—15
defined, HTML H-14
manipulating, HTML H-15

verify function, HTML H-16—17
Vertical blinds transition effect, HTML M-17
vocabularies
in XML, HTML N-3

►W

Wave filter effect, HTML M-5
W3C. *See* World Wide Web Consortium
Web browsers. *See also* Microsoft Internet Explorer;
Netscape Navigator
adjusting elements to window size, HTML M-6—7
detection of, HTML J-8—9
displaying XML data in, HTML N-12—13
error suppression for, HTML K-17
fourth generation, HTML I-10
hanging, HTML I-10
ignoring embedded style sheets, HTML J-4
interpretation of embedded style sheets, HTML J-4
proprietary features, HTML I-5
script-incompatible, hiding scripts from, HTML H-4
third generation, HTML I-10
variability of, HTML I-10—11
Web dialog boxes. *See* dialog boxes
Web page elements. *See* page elements
Web pages. *See also* HTML documents; Web sites
linking to external style sheet, HTML J-16—17
Web sites. *See* Web pages
well-formed documents
in XML, HTML N-2
width property
animation effects using, HTML M-10
in CSS-P, HTML L-8—9
window objects
methods, HTML H-9
Wipe down transition effect, HTML M-17
Wipe left transition effect, HTML M-17
Wipe right transition effect, HTML M-17
Wipe up transition effect, HTML M-17
World Wide Web Consortium (W3C), HTML I-10, HTML J-9
writeln() method, HTML H-9
write() method, HTML H-9

►X

XML, HTML N-1—17
benefits of, HTML N-3
binding XML data to HTML, HTML N-8—9
case-sensitivity of, HTML N-4
changing XML data view with HTML, HTML N-16—17
custom data definitions, HTML N-1
defined, HTML N-2
defining elements in, HTML N-4—5
defining structures in, HTML N-4—5
displaying XML data with HTML, HTML N-12—13
Document Type Definitions (DTD) for, HTML N-5
entering XML data, HTML N-6—7
formatting XML data with HTML, HTML N-10—11
HTML *vs.*, HTML N-2
modifying an XML document, HTML N-14—15
syntax rules for, HTML N-2—3, HTML N-12—13
universal data structure, HTML N-1
uses of, HTML N-2
well-formed documents in, HTML N-2
XML-compliant browsers
binding XML data to HTML documents, HTML N-8—9
XML data
binding to HTML, HTML N-8—9
displaying in different ways, HTML N-13
displaying with HTML, HTML N-12—13
entering, HTML N-6—7
formatting with HTML, HTML N-10—11
formatting with XSL, HTML N-11
XML declaration, HTML N-4—5
XML DSO, HTML N-8
.xml extension, HTML N-2
XML parsers, HTML N-8
XML prefix, HTML N-4
XML schemas, HTML N-5
XRay filter effect, HTML M-5
XSL
formatting XML data with, HTML N-11

►Z

z-index property, HTML L-10—11